125

ENDORSEMENTS

"I have enjoyed Mr. Youngblood's book immensely, as I know personally so many people of whom he writes. This is an excellent description of the duties—both personal and official—of the Secret Service, and I am a great admirer of their organization."

—Mamie Doud Eisenhower
(Original endorsement from first edition in 1973)

"This is an 'insider's book' simply because there is no one more inside the public and private personalities of top government executives than Rufus Youngblood. His matchless description of the senseless murder of President Kennedy in Dallas could be written only by someone like Youngblood. I was there in Dallas, but like so many others, I saw fragments. Rufus saw it all and lived every horrible minute. And his portrait of LBJ, strong leader, great heart, large warts, is history stuff. It's a simple book about complex men and absorbing events. Funny thing, I never knew Rufe could write this well, which shows the Secret Service is pretty good at keeping secrets about themselves as well as presidents."

—Jack Valenti, 1973
President, Motion Picture Association
Former Special Assistant to President Johnson
(Original endorsement from first edition in 1973)

———

"After all that happened in Dallas, our father trusted Rufus completely. They shared a special connection. No question, Daddy was a difficult taskmaster. Not wanting to be bridled, he often rushed into crowds not wanting to follow Secret Service requests. Rufus knew how to work with him. I never saw any breakdown in trust on either side. All of our family respected and loved Rufus."

—Lynda Johnson Robb

"Rufus was a patriot and a friend. He was an elegant gentleman who put his country first and did his duty always. We loved him dearly. His story is a noble one that deserves being shared."

—Luci Baines Johnson

"I began working in the U.S. Secret Service in 1955, during President Eisenhower's term, and I worked with 'Rufe.' Over the years, I saw his leadership help modernize the Secret Service. He was a great asset to the agency and a great man to work with."
—Herbert C. Dixon
Former SAIC of the Eisenhower Protective Detail

"During my career in the U.S. Secret Service, I worked very closely with and for Rufus Youngblood. During these years, I was always impressed with his work ethic and devotion to duty. I am proud to have worked with such a man and to have been his friend. He was truly an agent who lived up to the Secret Service code as 'Worthy of Trust and Confidence.'"
—Paul Rundle
Special Agent USSS 1958–1978

"I'm pleased to be asked to recall the friendship and contributions of Rufus Youngblood, whom I knew as an outstanding symbol of the United States Secret Service. I was a member of the White House Press Corps, so for a long time I had the pleasure of seeing or talking to Rufus and observing his dedication to duty. He was always pleasant, yet always a Secret Service agent fully occupied with the assignment at hand. Rufus's bravery during the tragic events in Dallas was not surprising. His trained reflexes took over at the sound of gunfire. He never lost his sense of duty to country nor worried about his own safety."
—Sid Davis
Former White House Correspondent

"It was my genuine honor to have known Rufus. When I arrived at the White House in 1965 as a very young (twenty-three-year-old) presidential aide, Rufus already had become somewhat of a legend because of the publicity surrounding his heroic actions in Dallas. We both had personal family roots in Macon, Georgia, and became good friends over the years. "I saw Rufus catch hell from President Johnson—at times when he did not deserve it. I also saw Rufus standing duty in rain, in snow, in storms—never asking more of the agents who worked under him than he did of himself. I saw him splattered with red paint from anti-war protestors in Australia. The life and times of a true American hero are captured magnificently within the pages of this book. "
—Tom Johnson
Former Special Assistant to the President
Publisher and CEO, *Los Angeles Times*
Chairman and CEO, Cable News Network
Chairman-emeritus, LBJ Presidential Foundation

20 YEARS
IN THE
SECRET SERVICE

20 YEARS
IN THE
SECRET SERVICE

My Life with Five Presidents

RUFUS W. YOUNGBLOOD

The authors have tried to recreate events, locations, and conversations from their memories of them. In some instances, in order to maintain their anonymity, the authors may have changed the names of individuals and places. The authors may also have changed some identifying characteristics and details such as physical attributes, occupations, and places of residence.

Copyright © 2018 by Rebecca Youngblood Vaughn
Second Edition
First Edition 1973, Second Edition 2018. First Edition written by Rufus W. Youngblood.

ISBN: 978-1-948638-99-9

10 9 8 7 6 5 4 3 2

0 1 0 4 1 8

Printed in the United States of America

Published by
Fideli Publishing, Inc.
www.FideliPublishing.com

www.rufusyoungblood.com

This book is dedicated to:

> *my wife and my children, Peggy, Joy, Mark, Candy, Rebecca;*
> *my sister, Ann;*
> *my former secretary, Mrs. Nancy Rocheleau;*
> *my friend and colleague Clarence Knetsch, who lost his life in a Texas flash*
>   *flood while helping others;*
> *and to my many associates in the Secret Service, those who never lost sight of*
>   *the mission...*

Contents

Foreword

by Clint Hill

I entered the U.S. Secret Service in Denver, Colorado, in 1958. During my first year of service I was required to spend a thirty-day temporary assignment on the White House Detail. President Eisenhower decided to go to the Augusta National Golf Course in Augusta, Georgia, and I, with the other members of the White House Detail, accompanied him. Augusta was in the Atlanta Secret Service office jurisdiction, so they sent an experienced agent to assist, working with local authorities and helping the detail as needed.

The agents on the detail had a habit of eating breakfast at a cafeteria near the hotel we used. I, a very junior agent, went along and stood in the cafeteria line to select my food. There was a white substance available, which I assumed was Cream of Wheat, a staple in North Dakota, my home state. I happened to say that out loud with a sense of joy, and the agent behind me said, "Son, that is not Cream of Wheat. Those are grits. You'll love 'em." That was my introduction to Rufus Youngblood, a Southerner through and through, and very proud of it.

While I was working on a White House Detail shift, traveling with President Eisenhower, Agent Youngblood's talents were being recognized by the assignments he received, including making advance arrangements for the president. He was highly regarded by the officials of the Secret Service and by the president and his staff as well. Agent Youngblood's attention to detail, making sure every "i" was dotted and every "t" was crossed, leaving no room for error or misunderstanding, was a lesson for all of us with less experience. We learned on the job, and the better the senior agent, the more you learned. Youngblood was considered one of the best.

On November 22, 1963, Youngblood's devotion to duty received the ultimate test. When the first sound of gunfire was heard as the president and vice president's motorcade was passing the Texas School Book Depository in Dallas, Texas, Agent Youngblood, without hesitation, threw himself over the vice president, protecting Johnson with his own body. He was willing to give his life to protect someone else's. It was an act of extreme heroism. He moved on to become the Special Agent in Charge (SAIC) of presidential protection, then to assistant director of protective forces and finally deputy director of the U.S. Secret Service. He was respected throughout the law enforcement community and especially by his fellow Secret Service agents.

In 1964, I returned to the White House Detail after spending the previous four years with Mrs. Jacqueline Kennedy. My first trip with President Johnson was to the LBJ Ranch in Texas. President Johnson identified me as the agent who had been with Mrs. Kennedy and had a close association with the Kennedys. He did not believe he could trust me. He called SAIC Youngblood and requested I be transferred off the detail. Mr. Youngblood informed the president that I was a professional, had also been with Eisenhower, and it would be in President Johnson's best interest if I remained on the White House Detail. The president said he would give it a try. A little over two years later, I was promoted to SAIC of presidential protection. President Johnson had accepted me because he trusted Youngblood's opinion.

Rufus Youngblood was always looking for improvement in whatever we did. He was the true professional. An agent's agent—"Worthy of Trust and Confidence." He was respected by me and my fellow agents, not because he demanded our respect, but because he earned our respect.

—Clint Hill
Assistant Director, U.S. Secret Service (Retired)
Author of *Five Presidents: My Extraordinary Journey with Eisenhower, Kennedy, Johnson, Nixon, and Ford*

Preface

Our father, Rufus Wayne Youngblood, truly valued his time in the U.S. Secret Service—so much so he wrote this memoir, *20 Years in the Secret Service: My Life with Five Presidents*, to record his experiences with this great organization. It was originally published in 1973 by Simon & Schuster.

Knowing how important those twenty years of his life were to him, my siblings and I weren't surprised to find a multitude of dusty boxes labeled "Secret Service" in our parents' Savannah, Georgia, home after his death in 1996. They were packed with neatly labeled files, news clippings, and other memorabilia—items beyond the many displayed portraits, photographs, and books (including over twenty volumes of the Warren Commission's findings). After our mother and his wife of fifty-three years, Peggy Denham Youngblood, died in 2007, we solemnly dispersed our parents' possessions and stored most of Dad's archives in my basement in Atlanta, Georgia. But life's fast pace precluded an in-depth study of their contents until a couple of years ago when I began researching my parents' lives to write their story.

The words "pack rat" came to mind when I opened the first box containing old campaign buttons, badges, invitations, and other items. Another box was loaded with chronologically labeled folders bearing meticulously written daily reports and travel expenses. There were boxes with yellowed newspaper clippings and onionskin papers bound with rusted paper clips. And then I found a handwritten letter from a thirteen-year-old boy from Baltimore, Maryland. It cited admiration for "Mr. Rufus Youngblood," whose example instilled in him a desire to one day become a Secret Service agent. This letter was filed next to one from Brigadier General Crumm, written on letterhead with a one-star flag, complimenting our father's actions on that dreadful day in Dallas, Texas. Yet another was from a boyhood friend in Atlanta, stating how proud he was, and not surprised, when he learned of Dad's "heroic actions." Some letters had news clippings attached describing how "Youngblood," immediately upon hearing shots being fired, pushed Lyndon B. Johnson (LBJ) to the floor of their limousine, shielding his body with his own on that tragic day when President John F. Kennedy was assassinated. There were hundreds of letters from across the country—across the world—from young and old, representing varied walks of life. Many had been neatly initialed "RWY" next to the word "answered" in Dad's writing.

Perhaps the press coverage and subsequent outpouring of letters arose because President Johnson honored our father with the Exceptional Service Award for his actions that day, or because a mourning country had sought something positive after the pain of losing a great president, or because Dad had been seen, though he had tried to be unseen, nearly everywhere LBJ was thereafter. Whatever the reason, Rufus W. Youngblood was a recognized name at one point in time.

Yet our father downplayed his "heroic actions," simply stating that he was "just doing his job," that his fellow agents would've done the same thing in his position. They were trained to "take the bullet" as the last line of defense to protect their principals. As was the case with Secret Service White House Police Officer Leslie Coffelt, who lost his life while protecting President Truman; Agent Clint Hill, who with near-Herculean reflexes bounded onto the president's limousine as shots were being fired so he could shield President and Mrs. Kennedy; Agent Larry Buendorf, who bravely grabbed the gun from Squeaky Fromme as she tried to shoot President Ford; as well as Agent Tim McCarthy, who stood, steadfast, and took the bullet that was intended for President Reagan.

That's what they do. They lay their lives on the line if need be.

It occurred to me that a unique relationship must exist between two people when one of the two is willing to sacrifice his or her life for the other. I suppose that no matter the circumstances, a bond is forged after this commitment is demonstrated. In my father's case, his commitment to protect LBJ, no matter the price, was demonstrated on that horrible day in Dallas, Texas. In turn, LBJ, who regarded loyalty as a great attribute, expressed his gratitude and placed his trust in our father thereafter. That trust, I have been told by numerous agents, was influential in LBJ's decision to preserve the duty of presidential protection within the Secret Service rather than transfer it to the FBI, as was proposed after the Kennedy assassination.

Beyond the professional aspect of being in the Secret Service, a personal association often evolves. Filed within another box, I discovered several letters from some of the presidents and first ladies our father protected—multiple typed, polite letters from the Trumans; two-page handwritten ones from "Mamie"; gracious notes from Lady Bird; and several typed, warm, letters on gold-embossed stationery from LBJ. One, written by Vice President Johnson in 1961, was addressed to our mother welcoming her new baby, who happened to be me. (He often liked to remind our mother that his mother was also named Rebecca.)

As deputy director of the Secret Service, our father maintained close contact with the former presidential detail. Thus, he frequently visited the former presidents and their families, as well as the agents watching over them. When former President Eisenhower, "the General," said, "Take good care of Mamie, Mr. Youngblood," Dad took his request very seriously. He maintained correspondence with her, never forgetting her birthday, and visited her regularly. My siblings and I sometimes drove with him to Gettysburg to "go see Mamie" and the Dixons (the agent in charge of the Eisenhower Detail and his family).

After studying our father's archives, I reread his book with new insight and a better appreciation of its relevance. This memoir is a firsthand account of some of our country's and our world's most defining moments—the Cold War, the Vietnam War, the Civil Rights Movement, and the tragic assassinations of President John F. Kennedy, Martin Luther King Jr., and Robert F. Kennedy—from the unique perspective of a Secret Service agent. Radical changes occurred in the country during our father's tenure reflected by changes in the Agency itself, some of which are exemplified in the five Inaugurations he participated in—from the outgoing President and Mrs. Truman leaving Washington,

D.C., bidding farewell to their agents from their train, presidential motorcades in open cars, and open ceremonial stands, to former-presidential protective details, armored car rides, and bulletproof enclosures. The complexities, constant tension, and risks of being in the Secret Service, along with the camaraderie within the Agency, is also described.

The last box I examined contained details of Dad's active book tour upon the initial publication of this book. With multiple endorsements in noteworthy journals, he appeared on numerous radio and television shows across the country, including *To Tell the Truth* ("Will the *real* Rufus Youngblood please stand up?") and *The Tonight Show* with Johnny Carson. I recall how disappointed Dad had been when his publisher declined to use photographs in the book and limited the release to hardback. Another influx of letters followed with inquiries of where to find the book. Later, in an interview for *Georgia Tech Alumni Magazine,* he jokingly stated that his book didn't stand a chance against the book *The Joy of Sex*, which was released around the same time.

Over the years, many people have encouraged us to republish our father's book. After reflecting upon the contents of all those boxes—I decided to do just that. In keeping with the times, this new publication is available in print, e-book, and audiobook. My siblings and I agree with our father that pictures do enhance this story and have added a photo gallery as well as audio inserts for the audiobook. It is our hope that readers find this memoir—written by a man who genuinely loved his country and his role in the U.S. Secret Service—insightful regarding a critical period of American history.

—Rebecca Youngblood Vaughn

CHAPTER 1

The Impossible Mission

The eyes of Texas were upon us for the second day, thousands of them, peering down from countless windows, from rooftops, staring excitedly from curbside and doorways, from wherever they could get a view over the heads of those in front. Fathers hoisted little children onto their shoulders, and as the line of cars approached, cameras were lifted, aimed, whirring and clicking as we passed, and then lowered when we were gone, their own private moment of history recorded. It was November 22, 1963, and President John F. Kennedy and Vice President Lyndon B. Johnson had come to Dallas with the express purpose of being seen by as many people as possible, hoping this would help change the opinion Dallas had shown at the polls in 1960 when the elections came around again the following year.

I was there, one of sixteen Secret Service agents in the motorcade for the protection of the president and the vice president. I was the agent in charge of the Vice Presidential Detail, and in this capacity I rode in the front seat of the Lincoln convertible that took Lyndon Johnson, Lady Bird, and Senator Ralph Yarborough through the crowded streets, two cars behind President and Mrs. Kennedy.

While the crowds watched the Kennedys and the Johnsons, the Secret Service watched the crowds. We were as unseen as the referee invariably is in a boxing arena.

This motorcade through Dallas, as planned, was virtually indistinguishable from three the previous day, in San Antonio, Houston, and Fort Worth. The streets through which a presidential motorcade moves may differ from city to city: the faces along the route are not the same, the worker sitting in an open window munching a sandwich on his lunch break is not the one you saw yesterday, yet there is a sameness about motorcades, whether they take place in New Delhi or New York, Dakar or Dallas—*if* they go according to plan. The Secret Service is there, in a sense, to maintain that sameness. It had been maintained in the other cities, but the Secret Service agent on protective duty lives on the brink of disaster. His job borders on the impossible.

It is a job of interception. When the eager young man with a camera in his hands breaks from the curb toward the cars, he must be intercepted and as unobtrusively as possible moved back into the crowd. The camera might not be a camera at all; it could be a bomb or a gun.

When the fellow standing in the front row half a block ahead, wearing a raincoat on a sunny day, pushes his hands into his pockets, an agent may drop almost casually off one of the cars and position himself between that man and the one he is assigned to protect.

As a Secret Service agent, you are constantly on the alert for the individual who somehow does not fit. You scan the crowd, the rooftops, the doorways, the windows, ready to take whatever action may be necessary should you observe something that could jeopardize your mission. You look into thousands of faces and you try to determine in each if he or she may be the one who came to do more than look. You seldom know whether some action on your part may have thwarted that individual—the young man with the camera or the man sweltering in the sun in the trench coat—because you have passed and he has melted back into the throng that dissolves in the wake of the motorcade. If he was the man, he may give it up altogether, or he may be at the corner of Fourth and Main in the next city when you get there, ready to try again.

He was there in Dallas, faceless, nameless so far, but he was there. He had a rifle powerful enough to bring down a grizzly bear, and he had a telescopic sight that extended its effectiveness. His training as a rifleman had been the best, the U.S. Marine Corps, and he had constructed a sniper's nest as perfect as a duck blind. He must have known the odds were in his favor; we—the Secret Service—knew it. The attack he planned was the one against which we were virtually defenseless at that time. We had long been concerned that when we had to move the president through the streets of a city in an open car, it was like moving him on the track of a shooting gallery and inviting one and all to step right up and take a shot.

The man in Dallas was not one of the faces at the windows, smiling and cheering. He hung back in the shadows, and as we moved directly toward him, we saw only a half-open empty window. The motorcade swung slowly into a tight curve directly beneath him, and one by one the big cars straightened, the Secret Service agents scanning the rooftops of the buildings and the windows where many of his coworkers sat and waved.

An agent in the lead car saw people standing on an overpass ahead, and he motioned for the Dallas policeman stationed there to move them away so that the cars would not have to pass below them.

The man, waiting patiently behind stacked cartons of schoolbooks in a dingy storeroom six floors up, saw the car bearing his quarry as it began to move down the incline toward the overpass. The car, moving straight away from him and slightly downward, presented him with a target that was, in effect, almost stationary. He lifted the rifle to his shoulder, his finger touched the trigger, and he positioned his eye against the scope. In the cross hairs, the open limousine must have seemed almost close enough to touch. The figures were clearly defined in the bright Texas sun, the young woman on the left, the man on the right, his head and shoulders plainly outlined above the seat back.

The rifle barrel inched out the window, across the ledge. The finger, with the steady, deliberate movement of the marksman, tightened on the trigger. Between the three quick blasts, the men on the floor below could hear the shell casings bouncing onto the floor above them. In a matter of seconds, it was all over.

The Secret Service had carried the mandate of presidential protection for sixty-one years, with the shadow of a failure of the first magnitude hanging over it twenty-four hours of every day. There had been some close ones, but the record of no losses had held.

That record ended a few seconds after 12:30 p.m., November 22, 1963, on Elm Street in Dallas, Texas.

CHAPTER 2

The U.S. Secret Service

I joined the Secret Service in 1951, not because of any burning desire to be a Secret Service agent—I had only a general idea of what the Service did—but because my chosen line of endeavor had fallen unexpectedly on hard times, and I had a family to support.

Like some sixteen million other Americans, I had put in my World War II time, some of it as a waist gunner aboard a B-17 bomber named *Jack the Ripper*. The GI Bill saw me through Georgia Tech, and I was well on my way with my industrial engineering degree.

At least that was my plan until an unaccustomed word—"recession"— began to crop up in everyday conversation. The recession hit the engineering profession, and I began looking elsewhere for work. The Georgia Tech Alumni Placement Office provided me with a lead: "*The United States Secret Service is seeking qualified applicants for Special Agent positions, starting salary $3,825 per year.*"

I was in the Atlanta Secret Service office almost before I finished reading the notice. I suppose most people can look back and find an individual who was instrumental in determining the direction of their life's work. With me, it was a man named Raymond Horton. Ray was the Special Agent in Charge (SAIC) of the Atlanta office who interviewed me for the job. In listening to him talk about the Secret Service, it came across as more than a mere job. I was sold, and on March 26, 1951, Ray Horton took me to the U.S. District Court in Atlanta, where I raised my right hand and, repeating the oath after Judge Frank A. Hooper, became Special Agent Youngblood of the U.S. Secret Service.

I was a special agent in name only as I began a cram, on-the-job course. I learned that the Service performed two basic functions: safeguarding the nation's currency and other Treasury obligations, and the protection of the President of the United States. The first included the investigation of such crimes as counterfeiting, forging and uttering (illegally circulating) government checks, and various other criminal activities involving Treasury obligations.

It was counterfeiting that brought the Secret Service into being, and it is not without a touch of irony that it was conceived in 1865 in the administration of Abraham Lincoln, the first president to die at the hands of an assassin. The original mandate of the Service did not include presidential protection; that was to come nearly four decades later. In 1865, counterfeiting was more than a full-time job. By some estimates, half the bills in circulation were bogus, and the first Secret Service chief, William P. Wood, was given the tremendous task of "restoring public confidence in the money of the country."

Wood and his operatives were not hampered by many of the restrictions under which law enforcement officers operate today. The times were rough, and it took rugged men to survive. As Wood himself put it, somewhat euphemistically: "It was my purpose to convince them [the counterfeiters] that it would no longer be healthy for them to ply their vocation without being handled roughly, a fact they soon discovered. I was threatened with every species of demolition, but I took my chances at capture or being captured in those lively undertakings."

The suppression of counterfeiting was still a major function of the Service, but the advent of the government check and the hundreds of federal programs that spewed out millions of the little negotiable punch cards daily had led to the bread-and-butter work of the field offices. For every counterfeiting case that turned up in our Atlanta office, there were a hundred check cases. And while the intrigue and glamour associated with the detection and smashing of a multimillion-dollar counterfeiting ring might make headlines, the business of apprehending an individual who plucked a Social Security check from a neighbor's mailbox, forged an endorsement, and cashed it was of equal or more importance because it happened thousands of times every day.

As a rookie field agent, my first job was working check cases. Our office of six agents covered the state of Georgia and included Special Agents Clayton Kober, Bob Hancock, Lane Bertram, Roy Letteer, Ray Horton, and myself. Bertram and Hancock were journeyman agents who spent most of their time traveling the state. Letteer had been in the Service for about a year, but he had had law enforcement experience with the Atlanta police force and was a great help to me in learning much of the fundamental work. Kober was a gun buff, and from him I learned the finer points of firing the service revolver agents were required to carry.

After a few months of working with these men, Horton began to assign cases to me. My assignments, which took me all over the state, did not include any protective duties until Vice President Alben Barkley paid a brief visit to Atlanta that summer. Letteer and I were to meet the vice president at the airport, escort him to the functions he was to attend, and get him safely back to the airport the following day. Secret Service protection had been extended to the vice president only recently, and Barkley arrived via Eastern Airlines with his one-man detail, Special Agent Bob Holmes.

The notion of assassinating Alben Barkley probably never crossed even the sickest mind, but on June 28, 1951, when he came down the ramp at Atlanta Airport, there was one green agent standing there watching everything that moved. As far as I was concerned, the place was crawling with potential assassins, and I was ready for them.

There was certainly nothing spectacular about Barkley's one-day stay in Atlanta. When he flew back to Washington, Roy and I went back to our routine work. It was not until the following spring, when I had completed my probationary period as a special agent, that I was assigned to protective duty again. This was a thirty-day training and orientation assignment in Washington, required of all agents.

I reported to the Washington Field Office in the Treasury Building on the morning of April 23, 1952. After three days of intensive training to augment what I had already been required to learn about protective work, Special Agent Jerry McCann showed me around the White House and familiarized me with the various posts and duties I would be performing. The extensive rebuilding of the mansion had been completed, and President Truman had recently moved back from Blair House. My first assignment was on the four-to-midnight shift, as a trainee, with Paul Usher as my supervisor.

From the original five men assigned to the protection of Theodore Roosevelt in 1902, the White House Detail had grown into a complex, tightly knit unit of well-trained and highly professional men whose job was as important as any in the world. I was impressed with the place, the job, and the people. Before coming to the White House as a Secret Service agent, I had never seen Harry Truman—or any other president. It was, to me, a rarefied atmosphere I worked in for the next few days, standing my assigned posts, learning my way around the White House, and moving with the president as part of the team.

Possibly, I was overimpressed. One morning, after I had been rotated to the eight-to-four shift, I saw what I considered a legendary figure moving through the White House to an early appointment with the president. I was on my way to report in, and as I reached the office, I stopped at shift leader John Campion's desk, where he was working on some papers.

"Guess who I just saw!" I said, pointing back toward the corridor.

Without looking up, he said seriously, "Not John Wilkes Booth, I hope."

The sarcasm missed me entirely for the moment. "No! General Omar Bradley, *that's* who!"

He looked up then, and, turning toward the clerk at the adjoining desk, he said, "Say, didja hear that? Youngblood just saw General Omar Bradley!" He looked around at me. "Say, Youngblood, with your luck, if you'd been around here about eighty years ago, you mighta seen General Grant. Yes sir, you sure might!"

"General ... Grant ..." I mumbled. I was learning more than protective work. In a nudist colony, you don't stare. At least not after the first couple of days.

That afternoon, just before the shift changed, I stood my post outside the president's Oval Office in the West Wing. The door opened, and Truman stepped out, his arms overflowing with papers. He glanced around, and, seeing no one in the immediate vicinity but a Secret Service agent, he said in his always polite tone, "Excuse me, sir, but I wonder if you would mind giving me a hand with these? I want to take them upstairs so I can read them this evening."

I was well aware that these were the first words spoken directly to me by the president. I was also aware that he was asking me to do something that normally I was not supposed to do, and that was to encumber myself in such a manner as to make it difficult to get to my revolver should the need arise.

Of course, President Truman was not intentionally asking me to violate my orders, and what could I do—let him stand there almost in a state of collapse while I explained why I was not supposed to do such things while on duty? We were inside the White House, completely surrounded by concentric circles of protection stretching as far out as the perimeter of the grounds.

"Why certainly, Mr. President," I said, and, with the divided load, we walked through the corridors to the elevator, where an aide relieved me. President Truman thanked me and went up to the living quarters with his homework.

Along with my training on this Washington assignment, I did some research on political assassinations, and how the Secret Service wound up with two basic jobs that seemed to have no logical connection with each other. For well over a century, our presidents were given protection only as the occasion seemed to demand, and by whatever resources were at hand. Before the assassination of Abraham Lincoln in 1865, if the question of a specially trained force for this particular purpose had come up at all, it could easily have been argued that whatever was being done was obviously sufficient.

Of the fifteen men who occupied the presidency before Lincoln, only one was the object of an overt assassination. On January 30, 1835, President Andrew Jackson was attending the funeral services of a South Carolina congressman in the Rotunda of the Capitol. As the casket and the procession of mourners moved slowly through the East Portico, a man by the name of Richard Lawrence suddenly stepped before the president, flung open his coat, and pulled two pistols from his pockets. He leveled one at Jackson and squeezed the trigger. The cap fired, but the powder failed to ignite.

Jackson, instead of attempting to throw himself out of harm's way, furiously rushed his assailant with the obvious intention of giving him a sound thrashing with his cane. Lawrence, meanwhile, raised the second pistol and, as the enraged president reached him, pressed the muzzle against Jackson's chest and squeezed that trigger.

Miraculously, the second pistol also failed to fire, thus saving Andrew Jackson's life. Lawrence, at his trial some months later, was adjudged not guilty by virtue of "having been under the influence of insanity at the time he committed the act."

Our presidents continued to move about freely and without serious incident for another quarter of a century. But in 1861, an operative of the famous Pinkerton Detective Agency founded by Allen Pinkerton got wind of a conspiracy involving a group of pro-Southern extremists who had selected eight of their number to assassinate President-elect Abraham Lincoln as he came through Baltimore on his way to Washington. By means of disguises and secret switching of railway cars, the plot was foiled, and Lincoln arrived safely in the capital.

But there was a bullet with Lincoln's name on it, for, as every student knows, he was shot while attending a play at Ford's Theater on the night of April 14, 1865. A Washington policeman had been assigned to accompany the president and his party and to stand watch outside the presidential box while the play was in progress. But the boredom of guard duty was apparently too much for the officer, and he meandered down the block to a tavern. By simply remaining at his post, he might have prevented the assassination, and he certainly would have lessened the ease with which John Wilkes Booth entered the box, barred the door behind him, and placed his derringer against Lincoln's head to fire the fatal shot.

But even the laxity of the guard was not the most incredible thing about the incident. Booth, who was an actor and, as such, had the run of Ford's Theater, had never made any secret about his view of presidential assassination as a road to immortality. This alone should have barred him from the theater while the president was there. It did not, however, and Booth even occupied himself during the afternoon prior to the evening performance by preparing the president's box for the assassination. He bored a peephole in the door, made certain the door could not be latched in the normal way from inside, and even constructed a device with which he could bolt the door himself after he had gained entry.

The most rudimentary protective measures would have discovered some or all of these elaborate preparations. There were no such measures, and the rest is history.

Even the death of Lincoln was not a sufficient catalyst to bring about substantial change in the way our presidents were protected, and this important function continued in the makeshift manner that had always characterized it. And again, for the next sixteen years, it seemed adequate as President Andrew Johnson, Ulysses S. Grant, and Rutherford B. Hayes served out their terms without any such incident.

James A. Garfield was less fortunate, for he scarcely had time to get settled in the White House before an assassin's bullet felled him. Sworn in on March 4, 1881, President Garfield was gunned down less than four months later as he was leaving the capital for a short trip to New England. At approximately nine o'clock on the morning of July 2, Garfield and Secretary of State James Blaine walked through the concourse of Washington's Baltimore and Potomac Railway Station to board the train. Absorbed in conversation, neither of them noticed a small man who strode quickly from behind a row of waiting-room benches and approached the president from the rear. The man, Charles J. Guiteau, leveled a .44-caliber British Bulldog pistol at Garfield's back and fired at point-blank range.

The president staggered forward under the impact of the bullet. "My God!" he cried. "What is this?" As he stumbled to his knees, Guiteau moved forward and fired a second shot. Although this bullet passed harmlessly through Garfield's sleeve, the first had done mortal damage, smashing his spine and some ribs, cutting a large artery, and lodging in his pancreas. The assassin, gazing down at his victim, calmly placed the pistol back in his pocket and surrendered without resistance to the police who came rushing at the sound of the shots.

Garfield lingered for more than two months. He died in Elberon, New Jersey, on September 19, 1881, and was succeeded by Vice President Chester A. Arthur, who served out the remainder of the term. The assassin, Guiteau, was hanged the following June.

As with John Wilkes Booth, Guiteau was a man whose activities and utterances would have guaranteed him a prominent place in even the crudest file of individuals to be kept under surveillance and away from the vicinity of the president.

The fact that the nation had lost its second president to an assassin in less than two decades caused some stir about the lack of protection for the chief executive. Perhaps if Garfield had been in office longer and had time to make his imprint upon the country, the problem would have been resolved at the time. For whatever reasons, nothing was done, and it was to take the assassination of still another president to tip the balance, and even then not entirely without reluctance. This unsought distinction fell to the twenty-fifth president, William McKinley. On September 6, 1901, McKinley was attending the Pan-American Exposition in Buffalo, New York. Unlike Lincoln and Garfield, his protection on that occasion seemed to be adequate, if only for the sheer number of guards assigned to him as he attended a reception on the Exposition grounds. Inside the Temple of Music, a huge gold-domed structure, McKinley was to receive the public. Reports of an anarchist plot to kill him had twice delayed the event, and each time it had been rescheduled by McKinley himself. His secretary, George Cortelyou, had tried in vain to persuade the president to call it off entirely, but McKinley had scoffed, "Why, George? No one would wish to hurt me."

There were no more postponements, and shortly after four o'clock on a hot and humid afternoon, the officers at the east entrance of the Temple of Music began admitting the people who had lined up to meet and shake hands with their president. The guard force was large by any standard. There were twelve uniformed policemen of the Exposition's own force on duty outside the entrance. Another eighteen policemen and eleven soldiers formed parallel lines inside the building. The people coming to meet McKinley had to pass slowly between these lines. In the immediate vicinity of the president, there were four Buffalo detectives and three Secret Service agents. However, Secret Service participation in this type of duty was no different from that of the other organizations represented. The Secret Service, being a federal agency with field offices scattered about the country, simply offered a source of manpower that could be tapped when the president was traveling outside the capital. The agents' training and expertise were strictly in the field of counterfeiting at that time.

Despite having to pass directly beneath the scrutiny of all these guards before reaching McKinley, twenty-eight-year-old Leon F. Czolgosz (pronounced Chol'-gosh), an avowed anarchist, was able to approach McKinley while carrying a pistol in his hand. As he moved slowly between the formation of soldiers and policemen, he stealthily took a .32-caliber Iver Johnson revolver from his pocket, covering it with a handkerchief. Purely by chance, a man just ahead of Czolgosz had a bandaged right hand, and when he reached the president he offered his left hand, which McKinley grasped.

The line shuffled on and now the assassin stood directly before his victim. McKinley, seeing the handkerchief and thinking it was a bandage, smiled and reached out to take Czolgosz's left hand. The revolver hidden beneath the cloth was aimed at the president's chest, cocked, and ready to fire. Czolgosz abruptly slapped the president's hand away, lunged forward, and with the pistol so close to McKinley that powder burns were later found on his vest, pulled the trigger twice before anyone could intervene.

The president, thrown back by the force of the bullets, stared incredulously at his assailant and then collapsed into the arms of the men nearest him. Others rushed Czolgosz and threw him to the floor. Fists pounded the assailant, and the soldiers began striking him with the butts of their rifles. McKinley, who had not lost consciousness, called out to them, "Be easy with him, boys."

Immediate surgery on McKinley failed to locate one of the bullets. However, for the next several days he seemed to be on the road to recovery. Vice President Theodore Roosevelt, who had rushed to Buffalo upon learning of the shooting, was so encouraged by the doctors' reports on the president's condition that four days later he joined friends on a mountain-climbing expedition in the Adirondacks.

The optimism proved to be premature. The president took a sudden turn for the worse, rallied briefly, then lapsed into a coma and died on September 14, 1901, eight days after being shot. Teddy Roosevelt was sworn in on the same day to become the twenty-sixth president—the third man to reach that pinnacle of power as a result of assassination. Czolgosz was indicted four days after the president died. The trial lasted less than two days and the jury deliberated scarcely half an hour before returning a verdict of guilty. Czolgosz, unrepent-ing to the end, died in the electric chair at Auburn State Prison on October 29, 1901.

Theodore Roosevelt himself was the victim of an assassination attempt eleven years later, after he had left office. He was in Milwaukee, Wisconsin, campaigning again for the presidency. His assailant, John Schrank, who had trailed Roosevelt through eight states waiting for the right moment, fired his revolver at the former president as Roosevelt was getting into a car at his hotel. The bullet struck him in the right side of the chest. The manuscript of the speech Roosevelt was preparing to deliver was credited with saving his life, as the bullet, fired from a distance of less than six feet, spent most of its force pene-trating the folded pages of the fifty-page manuscript before entering Roosevelt's chest. Teddy Roosevelt once more demonstrated his toughness by continuing his journey to the Milwaukee auditorium and delivering the speech before seek-ing medical aid.

The would-be assassin, Schrank, was found to be insane and was commit-ted to an institution for the remainder of his life.

The death of McKinley had raised a clamor across the country. Three of the last nine presidents had died violently at the hands of assassins. The presidency had become a surer route to the cemetery than Russian roulette. Something had to be done; a special force concerned only with the protection of the president had to be formed. At the time, the organizational structure of the Secret Service seemed to offer the best available source for such a unit. The nucleus of men permanently assigned to the president would be in a position to call on their fellow agents in the field offices for assistance when the president traveled about the country.

A few months after Teddy Roosevelt took office in the fall of 1901, Secre-tary of the Treasury Lyman Gage assigned a Secret Service detail to the White House. Under the leadership of Principal Operative Joe Murphy, the five-man detail thus began one of the most awesome jobs that could be laid at the door-step of any law enforcement agency.

Half a century later, when I reported to Washington for my thirty-day pro-tective indoctrination tour, the Secret Service could boast a record that showed no losses. Over the years, the scope of the job had been extended three times—in 1913 to include protection of the president-elect, four years later to the president's immediate family, and in 1951 to the vice president.

In this same span of time, there had been two overt assassination attempts. The first of these occurred on February 15, 1933. President-elect Franklin D. Roosevelt was to make a speech at Bayfront Park in Miami, Florida. In the crowd of some ten thousand people who had poured into the amphitheater to hear Roosevelt was one Giuseppe Zangara. Diverted from his original intention of killing President Herbert Hoover because of the cold weather in the north, Zangara had come south to sunny Florida to kill the president-elect.

Roosevelt had come into the amphitheater in an open car and had delivered a brief, humorous speech from the back seat. When he had finished his speech, he called out to Chicago Mayor Anton J. Cermak, who happened to be nearby, to come over to the car and talk to him.

Zangara, meanwhile, had met with resistance in his efforts to work his way down through the crowd toward the car. With the speech over, some of the people were beginning to leave, and Zangara, who was hindered in his view of his target by his five-foot height, suddenly climbed up onto a vacant chair, pointed his revolver in Roosevelt's direction, and, as rapidly as he could squeeze the trigger, fired off all five bullets in the gun.

The sprayed shots inevitably had to strike someone in the crowd. Five people were hit, four spectators and Mayor Cermak. Cermak's wound was fatal. Roosevelt was unscathed. As for Zangara, he died in the electric chair at Raiford Prison for the murder of Cermak. He was as unrepenting as Czolgosz had been, his only concern to the very end apparently being that he had failed to kill Roosevelt.

The second assassination attempt was on the life of Harry Truman, Roosevelt's successor in the presidency. During much of Truman's time in office, he lived at Blair House, as the White House was undergoing an almost total rebuilding that was to take several years to complete. Located diagonally across Pennsylvania Avenue from the White House, Blair House offered a more difficult situation from the protective point of view because of its smaller grounds and closer proximity to the street.

On November 1, 1950, two Puerto Ricans, Oscar Collazo and Griselio Torresola, arrived in Washington for the purpose of killing Harry Truman. Their plan was as suicidal as the flight of a kamikaze pilot. In fact, convinced that it was their last day, they dressed in their best suits. Torresola tucked a Luger under his belt, and Collazo a P-38 automatic under his, and they set out for a frontal assault on Blair House.

At about the same time, approximately two o'clock, Truman had finished his lunch and had stretched out in his upstairs bedroom to take a short nap prior to delivering a speech at a ceremony in Arlington National Cemetery.

Torresola and Collazo, meanwhile, strolled along the sidewalk in front of the temporary presidential residence, taking note of the west guard booth, manned by White House Police Officer Leslie Coffelt, and the east guard booth, inside which White House Police Officer Joseph O. Davidson was conferring with Secret Service Agent Floyd M. Boring, who was in charge of the eight-to-four shift. They also observed White House Police Officer Donald T. Birdzell, standing guard on the steps leading to the entrance of Blair House.

The two Puerto Ricans paused briefly at the corner, agreed on their plan of attack, and separated. Torresola was to approach from the west, Collazo from the east. As Collazo passed the front steps, he whipped out the P-38, aimed it at Birdzell, and pulled the trigger. There was a harmless click, and Birdzell spun around to find Collazo frantically banging the pistol with his hand in an effort to correct whatever had caused it to misfire. Before the officer could get his own revolver out of the holster, Collazo pulled the trigger again. This time it fired, striking Birdzell in the knee. Painfully wounded, Birdzell hobbled out into the street to draw Collazo's fire away from the building. Collazo now stood on the steps of Blair House, with Birdzell firing at him from the street and Davidson and Boring firing from the east guard booth, but the iron picket fence around the building hampered their accuracy.

At the moment Collazo opened fire on Officer Birdzell, Torresola had reached the west guard booth where he fired three quick shots at Officer Leslie Coffelt, then turned his gun on another White House policeman, Joseph H. Downs, who was entering a downstairs door into Blair House when the shooting erupted. Torresola's aim was deadly, dropping both officers. He then turned his attention to the aid of his confederate, Collazo, who was crouching on the steps reloading his pistol. Officer Coffelt, however, managed to drag himself outside the guard booth, and taking careful aim with his revolver, he sent one shot through Torresola's brain, killing him instantly. A bullet in the chest brought Collazo down, and the attack was over.

The Secret Service agents and White House police, at that moment, had no way of knowing whether there were others involved, and then an incredible thing happened. President Truman, awakened by the gunfire, appeared at his bedroom window and looked down to see what was happening. Had there been others involved in the attempt, he would have presented an easy target in the brief moment he stood framed in the open window.

One of the officers below saw him and yelled: "Get back! Get back!" The president got back, and stayed back.

Inside Blair House, Special Agent Stewart Stout demonstrated the results of good judgment and careful training. Presidential protection consists fundamentally of a series of concentric rings: the agent and the police engaged in the gun battle represented the outer ring, and Stout was part of the inner ring. The untrained observer might think that Stout should have rushed out to the aid of his fellow officers, guns blazing. Had he done this, the president would have been left completely vulnerable to any assailant who might have gained entry into the building. Instead, at the sound of the first shot, Sout readied a Thompson machine gun and took his position at the top of the stairs outside Truman's door.

The outer ring had held and neither of the assassins had succeeded in entering the building. The gunfire, however, had taken its toll. Officer Coffelt died while undergoing surgery for his wounds. Officer Birdzell was shot in both knees, and Officer Downs was critically wounded, although he did recover. Griselio Torresola lay dead in his neatly pressed suit beneath some shrubbery on the Blair House grounds. Collazo's wound was not serious, and he lived to stand trial for his crime. His death sentence was commuted to life imprisonment by the man he had intended murdering, Harry S. Truman.

By the time I completed my thirty-day tour of White House duty, I was convinced that this was what I wanted, and I applied for a permanent transfer to Washington. This was approved, and, in August, I was back in the capital, this time reporting to the supervisor of the Washington Field Office, SAIC Jim Beary. This field office performed the same functions as those in other parts of the country, but with a shift of emphasis. For example, one of the jobs of the Secret Service was to investigate applicants for jobs in various branches of the Treasury Department, and being in the nation's capital, the field office conducted an inordinate share of these investigations. It was also a reservoir of manpower for the protective forces, and again, its proximity to the White House called for more of this duty than in field offices in other localities.

The year 1952 was an election year, and although Harry Truman had declined to run for a second elective term—he had served more than three and a half years of the unexpired fourth term of Franklin Roosevelt and a four-year elective term of his own—he was far from inactive in the campaign that pitted Democrat Adlai Stevenson against Republican Dwight Eisenhower. Truman was a political campaigner of the old school. He was a whistle-stop man, and that fall the presidential railway car was kept busy going into the hinterlands, carrying Harry Truman and the message of the Democratic Party.

Truman was the last president to make extensive use of this mode of travel, which required far more elaborate protective measures than air travel. A jet aircraft is safe from outside attack while flying at thirty-five thousand feet. A train is vulnerable every foot of the way. When the president traveled by rail, a pilot train preceded his so that any bomb planted along the right-of-way would be set off before the president reached it. The entire route was carefully checked by railroad inspectors and Secret Service agents, with special attention to switches, underpasses, bridges, and tunnels.

All this resulted in a great drain on the White House Detail, and agents were pulled in from the Washington Field Office, usually to take over the routine White House chores while the regular detail was away.

During the fall of 1952, I was assigned almost exclusively to this type of duty, and the White House complex became almost as familiar to me as my own home. Even when the president was in residence, many of the White

House Detail personnel would be involved in advancing other trips for him, so I stayed on, and on many occasions, I was a part of the protective unit that accompanied Truman on his famous morning strolls. If there was one trait of Harry Truman's that had been a thorn for the Secret Service, it was the morning stroll. The Service knew very little about the man before he was so abruptly thrust into the presidency on April 12, 1945. This was before the Secret Service had been given any mandate at all regarding the vice president, and Harry Truman had been little more than an occasional visitor to the White House. With most presidents, the Service had the period of president-elect to adjust to his habits, but with Truman, it was strictly cold turkey.

His first morning as a resident of the White House, Truman caught the detail completely off guard. At six o'clock, the new president appeared downstairs in suit and hat and proceeded to leave the building and stride briskly up Pennsylvania Avenue. One startled agent tagged along, leaving a quick message with the officer stationed at the southeast gate sentry box and then trotting on with Mr. Truman up the avenue.

The two men were nearly half a mile from the White House, having turned the corner at Fifteenth Street, before reinforcements arrived at a gallop. Apparently unaware of the near panic he had caused by such an innocent activity as a morning walk, the president looked around at the agents who had appeared and smiled. "Well, now, it's very nice of you to join me." He took a deep breath of the crisp April air. "Beautiful day, isn't it!"

The incident, of course, was more embarrassing than dangerous, for if the Secret Service had not known about the walk before it had begun, a would-be assassin could hardly have been lying in wait along the route. But the continuation and regularity—and the publicity—created a condition that is a basic fear of security men, that is, predictability of movement. Secret Service Chief U. E. Baughman and SAIC Jim Rowley, supervisor of the White House Detail, agonized over this problem the entire time Truman was in office. In his memoirs, Chief Baughman told of his concern for the peripatetic president.

> The walks took place in exposed sections of a great city; they were usually over the same route; and they occurred at almost the same time every day.

Walking along a street, usually deserted at such an hour in the morning, made Mr. Truman a slow-moving target, the delight of a sharpshooter. A rifle with a telescopic sight slipped unobtrusively out of any of a thousand windows along the route, with plenty of time to aim carefully, and we would have been helpless to protect our charge. Or a fast-moving car coming suddenly out of a side street and swooping down on the President and his entourage was another possible method of attack; if such attackers carried a submachine gun and blazed away at us as they came abreast, we would have had little chance.

Chief Baughman's prophetic reference to a sharpshooter slipping a rifle with a telescopic sight out a window, of course, never came to pass with Harry Truman. And, fortunately, the two Puerto Rican assassins, Torresola and Collazo, apparently were not aware of, or did not see the possibilities inherent in, the president's habit, or their suicidal plan of attack might have been changed to one far simpler and with more reasonable chance of success.

The Harry Truman strolls of late 1952, well into his lame-duck term, were apparently less predictable than they had previously been. Perhaps the attack on Blair House had brought home the fact that there *were* people who were perfectly willing to give their own lives in even the most farfetched attempt to kill the President of the United States.

Harry Truman had two pastimes that served the purpose of breaking the constant tension inherent in the presidency, while at the same time presenting no problems for the Secret Service. He was an inveterate poker player, and a game of stud poker would frequently take place at the White House (or at Blair House while the Executive Mansion was being renovated) and often at the home of Clark Clifford or one of the other regulars. During these outings, the Secret Service would set up a protective perimeter around the house, assuring the president of a few pleasant and private hours with close friends.

He also had a genuine love for the piano, and while I am far from being a music critic, he did a pretty good job of tickling the ivories. Among the furnishings in the East Room was a grand piano, and it was a rare occasion for Harry Truman to pass in its vicinity without pausing to rip off a few bars, usually winding up with "The Missouri Waltz."

On November 4, 1952, Harry Truman slipped quietly from the news to the history books, as Dwight Eisenhower made a shambles of the Democratic efforts to hold on to the presidency. Following the Inauguration ceremony, on January 20, 1953, Bess and Harry Truman were escorted to Union Station by two Secret Service agents. As the train to Independence, Missouri, pulled out, Harry Truman saw his Secret Service escort, for the first time in more than seven years, standing on the platform waving goodbye as the train gathered speed and headed out of the capital.

CHAPTER 3

Ike

The Secret Service had grown accustomed to an early-rising president with Harry Truman. For all we knew, Ike would be an early starter too, but no one really expected to see him before midmorning on January 21, 1953. The Inauguration the previous day had, as always, been a tiring experience. As if the ceremony and the protracted parade that followed were not enough, there was the traditional Inaugural Ball in the evening. Actually, Inaugural Balls is a more accurate term, as the constantly expanding guest list made it impossible to squeeze everyone into one ballroom. Mamie and Ike, whose popularity was unbounded, had been up until the wee hours going from one ball to another.

My own daily report for Inauguration Day had included activities from 7:00 a.m. to 2:00 a.m., and when I reported to the White House to stand the eight-to-four shift, the last person I expected to see for at least a couple of hours was Dwight D. Eisenhower, President of the United States.

I had yet to learn that the unexpected is to be expected in the White House, for at five minutes after eight, the buzzer sounded. This was the signal the usher on the second floor gave when he boarded the elevator with the president, and moments later when the elevator doors slid open on the ground floors, I was standing my post at something approximating attention. Ike stepped out, as fresh and chipper as if he had had twelve hours' sleep.

"Would you show me where my office is?" he said to me. "I'd like to get an early start."

It struck me somehow as odd, after all the work he had done to get the job, that he wouldn't know where his office was. But the relationship between President Truman and President-elect Eisenhower had been, to put it mildly, strained. Truman, the lifelong Party man, had become cool toward the man who had seemingly vacillated between Democrat and Republican when being encouraged to run for the presidency. I recalled a Cabinet Room meeting between the two in the White House shortly after the election, a meeting that had concluded after only a few minutes, to the surprise of everyone. Apparently, Ike simply had never been shown where the president reported to work.

"Certainly, Mr. President," I answered, "just follow me."

We walked through the hallways and down the colonnade to the West Wing, where I ushered him into the Oval Office, overlooking the Rose Garden. He thanked me, and I took up my post outside the door.

A few moments later, the door opened, and Ike stepped out into the corridor, looking about curiously. He pointed toward the door of an adjoining room. "What's in there?"

"That's the Cabinet Room, sir."

"Hmmm ..." He nodded, perhaps recalling his brief meeting there with Truman. He shoved his glasses up on his nose. "What's that room across the hall?"

"The Fish Room, Mr. President." I was beginning to feel like a White House tour guide.

He walked over and opened the door. The room was full of women. Ike stared in for a moment, the women stared back at the familiar figure, then he stepped back and closed the door. "Who the devil are all those women?"

"That's your secretarial pool, sir. I doubt that they expected to see you this early."

He glanced at his watch and then at me. "I hope they don't consider eight fifteen early."

"Just today, sir. I meant that they probably didn't expect you to get started this early after yesterday and last night."

"Oh, that." He rubbed his jaw, looking up and down the hallway as if trying to decide on further exploration, then giving me a flash of his famous grin, he said, "Thank you," and disappeared back into the Oval Office to begin his first day on the job.

Ike had already given the Secret Service notice that it might have a tiger by the tail. During the campaign, he had made a promise that if he were elected he would personally visit Korea for a firsthand appraisal of the war situation. On November 29, 1952, West Point's most famous alumnus was absent from the annual Army–Navy football game, which I attended as part of President Truman's detail. President-elect Eisenhower was secretly carrying out his campaign promise. He was on his way to Korea.

Absolute secrecy was essential, for to publicize the president-elect's visit to the war zone would have been an open invitation to the North Koreans to try to do something about it. As president of Columbia University, Ike lived in the Morningside Heights section of New York City, and he continued to maintain this residence until moving to the White House. The press, quite naturally, kept a vigil at the house, and while the real professionals of the White House press corps had seldom failed to keep secrecy when it was in the national interest, it was far too risky under the particular circumstances to depend upon this.

It was decided that the entire movement would be carried out in absolute secrecy, and the problems presented by this were obvious. First, the absence of President-elect Eisenhower would have to be accounted for. This was done for the first three days by making it appear that he was still there. Various cabinet designees arrived at the house and ostensibly held lengthy meetings with Ike. Future Secretary of State John Foster Dulles was the first of these, arriving on the morning that Ike left for Korea. He stayed in the house for several hours, and when he came out, he accommodated reporters with a detailed account of the meeting.

Another problem was getting Ike's luggage out of the house without arousing suspicion. The bulk of it was hauled out under the noses of newsmen by a Secret Service agent dressed as a mailman and carrying Ike's gear in mailbags. The remainder was taken out by one of the maids who worked for the Eisenhowers, on the pretext that she was leaving for a vacation.

Getting the easily recognizable figure of Ike himself off the premises was accomplished simply by bringing a car to the front entrance at 5:45 a.m. on the morning the journey was to begin. The interior lights of the car had been disconnected and Ike simply walked out in the darkness, got into the car, and was driven off. Half an hour later, he boarded a plane at Mitchell Field and was winging his way westward.

Although the tight secrecy of the trip held, the time spent in Korea was a nightmare to his Secret Service detail. Ike insisted on visiting the front lines. Of course, front lines were nothing new to Ike, but on one occasion he stopped at a place where an American GI was killed by a sniper scarcely twenty-four hours later. More than once, the areas he visited were overrun and taken hours later by the enemy.

The Secret Service got Ike through the two-and-a-half-month period as president-elect, and now all that remained was to get him through the presidency. We knew of his fondness for golf, and it did not take long for Ike to begin exhibiting the symptoms that all presidents seem to show shortly after they move into the house they fought so hard to acquire. For its occupants, the White House seems to be a great place to visit for four to eight years, but a place in which they hate to live. Ike, in his eight-year tenancy, had several homes away from home. His favorite was Augusta National Golf Club in Augusta, Georgia. In fact, that was where he had flown immediately after the election returns had become conclusive, somewhat to the consternation of Secret Service Chief Baughman. Details had been assigned to both the Eisenhower camp in New York and the Stevenson headquarters in Chicago, ready to assume the duty of protecting the president-elect when one emerged as winner.

When it turned out to be Ike, and he announced his intention to fly to Augusta, the detail assigned to him had been able to wangle only two seats aboard the private plane that took the president-elect south. The two had, understandably, been less than was needed for the impromptu motorcade that developed in Augusta, even with the last-minute aid of additional agents who had reached Augusta from Washington. Members of the Eisenhower family had been separated from one another during the crush, and as Chief Baughman later said with regret, the Secret Service "had gotten off on the wrong foot with the Eisenhowers at the start."

We had another walking president, but one who disdained the salutary stroll down Pennsylvania Avenue for the pursuit of a golf ball over endless miles of roughs and fairways. At first glance, this would seem a Secret Service dream come true. What better protection than to have your man far from the madding crowd, in the fresh air and privacy of an exclusive golf club, spending hour after hour in such a healthful and harmless pursuit? After all, the only golfers you ever hear of getting killed are those who rush to the shelter of the nearest oak tree in a sudden thunderstorm.

But the president is exposed to a different sort of danger than the ordinary golfer. A golf course offers a route that is virtually as unalterable as a railroad track. The player—whether he be Joe Doakes playing his favorite municipal course or the president playing ultra-exclusive Augusta National—follows the ball from tee to green and hole to hole as methodically as the sun rises in the East and sets in the West.

The more exclusive the course, the more the tendency toward thickly wooded borders, which incidentally offer excellent cover for an assassin's ambush. As with the windows along Harry Truman's paths through the streets of Washington, a would-be killer had only to climb into a handy tree alongside the course, with a view of any hole, and his quarry would have to pass that way. Shooting fish in a barrel would have been difficult by comparison.

With this pessimistic outlook before them, Chief Baughman and Jim Rowley, head of the White House Detail, set about working out procedures to afford Ike maximum protection on the links. The basic plan came to include an operational radio base set up in the clubhouse, or in the case of Augusta, at Ike's residence alongside the course. From this base, agents were dispatched onto the course with the president. As a part of this detail, I trudged many a mile up and down the slopes of Augusta National and other courses, in golfer's attire, carrying a walkie-talkie and a golf bag from which protruded a dummy set of club heads and inside of which was cached a high-powered rifle or a submachine gun.

Road patrols of Secret Service agents and local law enforcement officers scoured the roads surrounding the course. Wooded areas and positions affording a clear view of the course were carefully searched and guarded. When Ike stepped up to the first tee, there would already be an agent on the green ahead, as well as agents flanking the fairway and bringing up the rear. One of his doctors always accompanied the entourage. On a relatively strange course, there might be a foursome of agents playing the hole ahead and another teeing off behind the president, providing a buffer fore and aft.

In effect, what appeared to be a simple golf game was in actuality a miniature military movement that began its advance on the first tee with its objective the eighteenth green. Of course, there was no outward evidence of this. Heavily armed agents appeared to be nothing more than fellow golfers, caddies, or a small gallery that had the peculiar habit of watching everything but the golfer.

Radio contact was constantly maintained with the base station, and the president's precise whereabouts on the course was known at all times.

Wherever Ike traveled, a set of golf clubs went along. He played hundreds of rounds during his eight years in office, on scores of golf courses, and if any would-be assassin considered trying his luck on the links, we did not learn of it. The deterrent effect of adequate protection is a factor that cannot be directly measured, for if nothing happens, you never really know how much your efforts had to do with the safe completion of the mission.

But if the efforts of the Secret Service were instrumental in keeping Ike safe while enjoying his hobby, the many miles of walking America's finest golf courses were not entirely without incident. Once, in Palm Springs, California, where, unlike the lush, natural foliage of Georgia, nature must be assisted in covering the terrain with greenery, Ike felt a call of nature while playing a hole that was particularly devoid of trees and shrubs. Improvisation protected the president from prying eyes as his Secret Service detail formed an inverted huddle while the presidential kidneys functioned, and then we were on our way again, pursuing the little white ball.

Golf carts were just coming into vogue in the early fifties, and Ike often enjoyed driving his own cart. One warm spring afternoon on Augusta National, Ike tooled his cart up to the edge of the green where his ball lay just off the putting surface. The moment he took his foot off the accelerator, it was apparent that something was wrong as the cart continued on under full power. Faced with a long downhill run to a creek, Ike made his decision and bailed out. But the driverless cart circled back sharply, and for a few tense moments, a strange procession moved across the lush fairway—the President of the United States in the lead, running for all he was worth, a rogue golf cart at his heels, and half a dozen Secret Service agents tearing along in pursuit. There was some shouted discussion as to whether the thing should be shot, just as three agents overtook it and, like a dogie at a rodeo, bulldogged it over onto its side.

There is a small movie theater in the White House just off the East Colonnade, and a selection of films is always available for the First Family. Ike was fond of Westerns and historical movies, especially of the Civil War era. If John Wayne or Randolph Scott was on, Ike would always stay till the end.

One evening when Mamie had picked out the movie, the First Family came down to the theater, and the projectionist rolled the film. The title flashed on the screen. It was a musical, *Gilbert and Sullivan*, and Ike immediately began to squirm. In less than ten minutes, he turned to Mamie and said, "You know, I'm meeting with the cabinet in the morning and I really should do a little reading tonight on some of the matters that will be discussed. You'll excuse me, won't you?" He rose and, patting her on the hand, smiled. "No, Mamie, you and the others stay and see the movie! Maybe I can see it some other time."

Another agent and I strolled out with President Eisenhower, and as we walked along the colonnade toward Ike's office, he looked around at us. "I'll just be damned if I can sit through another one of those blasted musicals!"

Dwight Eisenhower, by birth, was a Texan, but his life in the Army had never let him put down roots in one place for long. Despite the usual mother-in-law jokes, Ike—along with all the agents on his detail—was very fond of Mamie's mother, Mrs. John Doud, and we spent several weeks each year at Mrs. Doud's home in Denver, usually in late summer after the adjournment of Congress.

Nearby Lowry Field served as the working White House, while Mrs. Doud's home at 750 Lafayette Street became the White House residence. It was a comfortable two-story house in what is generally referred to as an upper-middle-class neighborhood, but it was quite a contrast security-wise to what the Secret Service was accustomed to in Washington.

When Ike was in residence, we had to take certain measures that inconvenienced Mrs. Doud's neighbors, such as closing off the block to through traffic. Those living on the block, of course, had access to their homes, but a stream of sightseers would have obstructed the street if we had not taken this action, and the neighbors were most understanding of our problem.

If we had had our preference, we would have vetoed Ike's long stays in Denver, simply because of the protective difficulties involved. But contrary to popular belief, the Secret Service does not tell the president what he can and cannot do, and so we handled the situation as best we could, posting agents around the house in such a manner that each man was always in line of sight with another, allowing no possible access to the house to go unobserved. One agent was posted in a radio car in front of the house, another maintained his vigil from the front porch, and others were stationed near the corners of the backyard. There was one fringe benefit to the neighborhood because of this miniature fortress in its midst: the burglary rate dropped to zero when Ike was in residence on Lafayette Street.

While in Denver, Ike often made side trips to Fraser, Colorado, to the rustic but comfortable mountain retreat of a friend, Aksel Nielsen. Nestled in the foothills of the Rockies, it was a place where Ike could indulge to his heart's content in three of his favorite pastimes—painting, fishing, and talking. Some of the most mouth-watering food I ever ate was on these trips, with Ike's fresh-caught trout as the main course, pan-fried with bacon.

One starlit night, I had the midnight shift, standing my post at the rear of the cabin with a view across a broad meadow where cattle grazed. Inside the cabin, Ike, Nielsen, and two more close friends, Cliff Roberts and George Allen, were talking. The conversation got around to the last days of World War II in Europe and Ike began to tell them why the decision was made to let the Russians reach Berlin ahead of the American armies.

"There were a number of reasons," he said. "War is costly, not only in money and material, but in men's lives, which are much dearer. We could have done it. Patton—bless his heart, I'll love him till I die—wanted to be the first in Berlin more than anything else. But the Russians wanted it for reasons of their own. Hitler had put them through hell and now it was their turn. My job as the Allied commander was to win the war, not just one battle. I knew it would be extremely costly in manpower for whoever took Berlin, and to me the decision was simple: if the mission could be accomplished, regardless of public opinion, then let the Russians have at it. I had some explaining to do to a lot of gung-ho Americans about this decision, and maybe the average American citizen never really understood it. But I'll damn well tell you every American mother who had a son over there, and every wife who had a husband over there, and perhaps some of the kids whose fathers were there—at least they understood. By letting the Russians do what they wanted to do, and at the same time accomplishing the mission, I slept a helluva lot better knowing I would not have to authorize the writing of thousands of letters to mothers and wives consoling them over the loss of their loved ones."

The conversation went on until Ike and his friends turned in after 2:00 a.m. I had always had a lot of respect for Ike, but I had even more after hearing what caused him to let himself in for so much criticism.

Ike suffered his first heart attack during one of the visits to Denver. On September 24, 1955, I was on the eight-to-four shift at the Doud residence. When we relieved the midnight shift that morning, they reported to us that President Eisenhower had not slept well, that lights had been going on and off upstairs throughout the night, and that Ike's personal physician had been called. First indications were that the president was having a severe attack of indigestion. Murray Snyder, an assistant to Press Secretary Jim Hagerty, informed the press that Ike was not feeling well and would not be going to his office at Lowry Field that day.

Shortly after this, Ike's doctors advised us that the president should be taken to Fitzsimons Army Hospital. We had the limousine brought to the front of the house, and Ike, with Jim Rowley supporting him on one side and Special

Agent Dick Flohr on the other, was assisted to the car, obviously in considerable pain.

We took him straight to Fitzsimons Army Hospital, where his condition was diagnosed as a coronary thrombosis, or in layman's terms, a heart attack. It was serious enough to keep President Eisenhower at Fitzsimons for more than a month and a half before he had sufficiently recovered to return to Washington and the White House.

One result of Ike's heart attack was a curtailment of the time he spent in Denver, due to the high altitude of the city. But the Eisenhowers, even before he became president, had begun to putter around Gettysburg, Pennsylvania, in search of a place to buy. Ike was a history buff, especially the history of wars, and one of his special fascinations was with the Civil War. So Gettysburg held a natural attraction for him. It had the additional advantage of being within easy driving distance of Washington. They found the place that suited them, and after a period of restoration, they began to call Gettysburg home.

Along with the remodeling of the old farmhouse, which was said to have been used by the Confederate forces as a hospital during the Battle of Gettysburg, the Secret Service put in some innovations of its own. We had the protective advantage of the house being well within the borders of the 190-acre farm, with open tilled fields in every direction. A guardhouse was constructed at the driveway entrance, and along the long drive itself, devices were built in so that if a vehicle rolled across them, a signal would be set off in the guardhouse. In the immediate vicinity of the farmhouse, electric-eye fences were set so that anyone crossing would break the light circuit and sound an alarm. Another device, relatively new at the time, was utilized to scan the grounds at night, and that was infrared light, with special binoculars so that the agents on duty could literally see in the dark.

Ike's grandchildren, the children of John and Barbara Eisenhower, were frequent visitors to the Gettysburg farm, and additional precautions were taken in securing their rooms. Specially constructed screens were installed in the windows so that an intruder who might get through the outer perimeter with the intent of kidnapping the children would set off a signal if the screens were tampered with.

The security measures taken satisfied Chief Baughman, with one exception. At various places around the Gettysburg area, observation towers had been constructed so that tour guides could point out the various areas of interest to visitors. One of these towers stood on Cemetery Ridge on Gettysburg Battlefield, and among the things that came under its direct view was the Eisenhower house and the grounds around it. We were confronted with the same haunting prospect of a rifleman, a vantage point, and patience.

One of the many oddities of providing for the president's safety is that those charged with the protective duty always feel there is something else that can be done to make that security just a bit tighter, while the one being protected seems to feel the opposite, that you are already overdoing it. This was the case with the Cemetery Ridge tower. Ike felt that the guardhouse, the electric eyes, the infrared light, the alarm systems, and the physical presence of agents and special officers were quite sufficient. He also expressed his feeling that, since the area was a National Military Park, the public had the right to access it.

Chief Baughman did not want to close the tower down entirely, but only while Ike was in residence at the farm. It seemed that we had all the makings of a stalemate—until Ike read a book that detailed the four unsuccessful and three successful assassination attempts on United States presidents. There was no question after that. The tower was closed to the public and was guarded against intruders whenever the Eisenhowers were in residence at the farm.

The jet age had not arrived when Ike took office, but having spent most of his life moving in and out of the country, he continued to be highly mobile after becoming president. The Korean trip as president-elect, of course, was the first. There was a short visit to Mexico, a couple of jaunts to Bermuda, and the first big overseas trip—the summit conference in Geneva in July 1955.

The conference brought together the leaders of the United States, Russia, England, and France, with the avowed purpose of lessening the tensions that had been steadily building between East and West in the ten years since the end of World War II. While President Eisenhower, Soviet Premier Nikolai Bulganin, British Prime Minister Anthony Eden, and French Premier Edgar Faure wrestled with problems of world peace at their conferences in the old League of

Nations Palace, and relaxed in their estates near the shores of Lake Geneva, the Secret Service wrestled with problems of Ike's security.

The Eisenhowers were housed in a palatial villa not far from the lake. One afternoon while Ike and the other world leaders were holding their summit meeting, Mamie lay down in her bedroom for a nap after lunch. Out of deference to the First Lady, everyone in the house moved about as quietly as possible. The villa was not to remain in this state of calm, however. A hard, steady rain had been pouring down since early morning, and down in the basement, rainwater had been seeping in. Because of a clogged drain, the water rose and, reaching a certain height, shorted an electrical circuit that set off a fire alarm in the local fire station.

The alert Swiss firemen, seeing that the supposed fire was at the villa of the President of the United States, turned out in force, and within minutes, a veritable motorcade of fire engines came roaring up the long, winding drive, their sirens splitting the lakeside serenity, the men shouting orders as they raced toward the house with their hoses ready. We met them outside, trying to explain that it was a false alarm. For several minutes, confusion reigned as we tried to overcome the language barrier. At last, they were convinced and drove away.

Mamie Eisenhower, whose years with Ike had obviously taught her to relax under any circumstances, slept through the whole slapstick affair.

Geneva in July of 1955 was probably the most secure place on the face of the earth. Scotland Yard was there with Eden. The French and the Russians had their security men in depth, and of course, Ike's Secret Service contingent was present. Backing it all up was the Swiss Army.

Foreign trips for the president, generally speaking, were less a security problem than trips around his own country. There were exceptions to this, and sometimes for reasons that could not be anticipated. During his last two years in office, as a lame-duck president, Ike toured the world in an effort to bring his country's message to people everywhere. In 1959, Ike ushered in the presidential jet age. Aboard the new Boeing 707, at half the speed of sound, there was no place on earth too far from Washington for a presidential visit. Ike's mission took him to India in December 1959, and directly into a situation that was without parallel before or since.

India had a shortage of almost everything but people, and when Ike landed at Palam Airport some twelve miles outside New Delhi and headed toward the city in the company of Prime Minister Nehru, the motorcade along Kitchener Road found itself penetrating a solid mass of humanity that seemed to stretch as far as the eye could see. I was back in Atlanta, and so was not on the detail that went with Ike on this memorable journey, but reports of it have become legend in the Secret Service.

Our training has always been to be alert for those intent on doing harm to the president. There was no evidence that so much as one individual among the countless thousands lining Kitchener Road felt anything but the utmost admiration for Ike. There were no rocks, bottles, or garbage thrown at the open limousine, but if everyone intent on tossing bouquets at the president had succeeded in doing so, we would have had the first president to die by floral suffocation.

The news that President Eisenhower was coming to New Delhi had spread across the countryside days in advance of his arrival. The result was an avalanche of people from as far away as time and mode of transportation would allow. The fear of most such state visits is that the turnout may be too sparse. This time, it was the opposite. As the cars of the motorcade plowed forward, bogging ever deeper into a quicksand of human bodies, the concern grew.

First, concern for the delay in the schedule; gradually into real concern for Ike, Nehru, and anyone who happened to be with them. Those thousands who had not managed to position themselves for a close view of Ike as he passed pressed forward to get closer. As there was no place for those in the front ranks to go, the crowds pressing in from either side of the road became a huge, writhing vise, with the motorcade between its jaws.

I learned from firsthand experience on later visits to India that the accepted method of crowd control on the part of the Indian police—whether the crowds be friendly or not—is the liberal use of the heavy wooden clubs they carry. They swing them with abandon, and those on the receiving end accept the blows in the same spirit they are given. But there is little to be gained by bludgeoning a man who is pressing forward under the relentless pressure of thousands behind him. They crammed in against the limousine, laughing, smiling, shouting greetings to Ike even as the clubs rained down on their heads.

At one point Nehru himself grabbed a club from a surprised officer and, shouting for the people to move back, took a few swings. At the moment when it seemed almost hopeless, the pressure began to lessen and the cars finally inched their way into the city.

I had gone back to the field by the time this trip came along. I had remained on the White House Detail through Ike's first term, and in the 1956 elections I had seen Adlai Stevenson go down to defeat by an even wider margin than the first time.

Late in 1957, as Ike rounded out his fifth year in the presidency, I began to reexamine my own career in the Secret Service. I had been in the Service almost seven years, and I decided that another tour of duty in the field would improve my chances for advancement. I requested and got a transfer back to Atlanta in January 1958.

CHAPTER 4

Back to the Field

Ray Horton had retired from the Service since I had left Atlanta, and the SAIC was now Barney Wentz, a veteran field-office man. It was good to be back in my hometown, but it did not take long for me to realize that something was wrong in the way the courts were handling lawbreakers. In some respects, it was almost as if I had been away six days, not six years. I was arresting the same people I had arrested six years ago. Some of them even seemed glad to see me, like an old friend who had been away.

There was one woman in particular who had never seemed to comprehend the criminality in stealing and cashing government checks. On my fourth day back in the Atlanta office, I found myself knocking on Duchess's door. She opened the door, took one look at me, and a smile spread across her face.

"Why, it's Inspector Bloodhound!" (Which was what she really thought my title and name were.) "When did you get back to Atlanta?"

I had to go along with the leniency of the courts on many check cases, and I could not help feeling sympathetic toward Duchess, but the law was the law—or I thought it should be. And to keep spending the taxpayers' money sending agents out to rearrest Duchess, only to have her out forging checks again within a month or so, always seemed a waste to me.

There was something else I noticed now that I was back in the field, and that was that certain items of equipment were not quite up to the standards that would have been used in Washington. I do not mean to infer that what we had was inadequate, or really inferior, but...well, take my automobile, for example. I was assigned a Chevy that had come to our field office through another Treasury agency, the Alcohol and Tobacco Tax Unit. It had been the property of a moonshiner whose luck had run out. The car, by law, was seized and eventually turned over to our office.

On an afternoon in early June, Barney dropped a file on my desk just as I was wrapping it up for the day. "I hate to ask you to work late, Rufus," he said, "but I think you'd better follow up on this one now. Tomorrow might be too late."

I leafed through the slim file. I'll call the suspect Jasper Jones, since that was not his name. He was old enough to be my grandfather, and his story had a sadly familiar ring. Jasper had been a resident of a cheap boardinghouse in Charlotte, North Carolina. One day, he had succumbed to the temptation of a fellow boarder's Social Security check lying among the day's mail. He had forged the boarder's name, cashed the check at an accommodating supermarket, and moved on with his slim but ill-gotten gains.

Check investigations began where the check was cashed, and the Charlotte office turned up information that Jasper Jones might be found at the Salvation Army dormitory on Atlanta's Marietta Street. My job was to check out the lead, and if it netted Jasper, to take him to Fulton Tower and jail him until he could get a hearing before the commissioner the following morning.

The lead was correct. He was there, using his own name, and when I identified myself and told him what he was charged with, he made no effort to deny it. In fact, he seemed relieved.

"That's right, Mr. Youngblood," he said. "I did take old Sam's check. I was broke, it's simple as that. Fact is, I haven't slept too good thinkin' about poor Sam."

I honestly felt sorry for the old man, but passing judgment was not my part of the job. I told him that he would have to stay in jail overnight, until he could have a hearing, and the two of us walked out and got into the Chevy. I put the key into the ignition and turned it. Nothing happened. I jiggled the key and tried again. Still nothing. There was no point in further jiggling; I knew what was wrong. The car had been slow to start earlier, and now the battery was stone dead.

Jasper looked over at me quizzically. There is nothing in the agent's manual dealing with dead batteries. It was a simple case of choosing from the available alternatives that would get Jasper to jail and me home.

There was no service station in the immediate area. However, if I could get the car rolling, put it in gear, and let the clutch out, it would probably start. That presented another problem. The car was on level ground, and that meant an outside power source would be required to get it rolling. The only handy sources of power were seated in the car—Jasper Jones and me. One look at Jasper narrowed that choice to me.

I flexed my hands on the wheel and sighed. "Jasper, we've got a problem. The damned car won't start. Now, I could phone my boss, but he's already gone home and he lives all the way across town."

"I see," he said, regarding me with concern.

I cut a glance at him. "Can you drive?"

He was obviously puzzled, but he nodded. "Yes sir. Fact is, I had one o' the first Model Ts back in—"

"Okay. I'm gonna get out and push this thing. You get over here at the wheel, and when I get up some speed, you put it in gear and let the clutch out. You know how to do that?"

"Oh, yes siree, Mr. Youngblood!" he replied, brightening for the first time since I had met him. "Done just that many a time!"

I got out and he slid over beneath the steering wheel. I stood there with the door open, wondering. He was working the accelerator and pushing the gearshift back and forth. I eased my coat back to let him get a glimpse of the .38 in the belt holster. "You know, Jasper, it wouldn't look good on my service record if I reported back to the office with my car and my prisoner gone."

He chuckled softly. "Oh, I can imagine it wouldn't."

"It would look better if the record showed I shot the prisoner while he was attempting to escape." Even as I said it, I knew Jasper didn't buy it. Secret Service agents do not shoot check forgers unless it is in self-defense.

He played along. "I'm sure it would. Just be doing your job, so to speak."

"So to speak," I echoed, and took one last look at him sitting there checking everything out. I wondered if beneath that thatch of gray, there might be burning the brain of some aging Barney Oldfield, if already in his thoughts he was roaring off down Marietta Street, chortling with delight.

I shut the door, moved back to get a grip, and leaned into it. The car began to roll. One shoe slipped, and I almost went down on my knee but got back up, and when I reached maximum thrust, I yelled, "Hit it!"

The car jerked, a black cloud snorted from the exhaust, the engine thundered like it must have done in bygone days getting set to bring another load of 'shine down the mountain, and then it seemed to coil itself and leap forward, tires blue-smoking against the concrete. I wasn't sure, but amidst all that racket, I thought I heard a faint "Wahoo!" from inside the car.

Barney Wentz will never believe this, I was already thinking as I watched the car roar off. Then, as suddenly as it had started, it slid to a stop. A gray head poked out the window, and grinning broadly, Jasper Jones hollered back, "We done it, Mr. Youngblood! First try, we done it!"

I felt good later when I learned that Jasper had been ordered to make restitution on the check and was given a probated sentence.

I was not back in Atlanta long before I realized that there was little to distinguish between the work I had been doing in Washington and what I was assigned to do in Georgia. Augusta, being in Georgia, was within our assigned territory. I had experience working with the White House Detail, and so when Ike planned to come to Augusta—which was increasingly often since "Mamie's Cabin" overlooking the eighteenth hole had been completed—somebody up there always remembered that Youngblood knew the layout, and Youngblood was down there in Georgia, so why not send him over to Augusta?

I had no objection to these assignments. In the Secret Service, there are agents whose talents and tendencies lean toward the investigative work that is the principal work of the field offices, and others whose preference is protective duty. I was discovering that my leanings were toward the latter, and with the president's frequent trips into our territory, I think Barney Wentz was pleased to have me there to take the assignment.

In addition to his regular visits to Augusta and an occasional quail-hunting trip in season to the Georgia estate of then Treasury Secretary George Humphrey, Ike also was putting mileage on his new presidential jet. I had done advance work for many domestic and several foreign trips during my White House duty, and during Ike's final year in office, I was called on to take part in advancing a trip he planned to South America. Special Agent H. Stuart Knight was to head up the Argentina advance team; my specific assignment was the Buenos Aires stop, with Special Agent Bill Cantrell to assist me.

The president's stay in Buenos Aires was to consist of a single day, but the security arrangements and the logistics problems with which Cantrell and I had to cope required that we go down a couple of weeks ahead of Ike's scheduled arrival.

Intelligence indicated immediately that there might be unpleasantness, or worse. Ousted dictator Juan Perón still had strong support in the country, and the anti-American Peronistas were not going to let the American president come to Argentina without their presence being made known, especially on his visit to the capital city.

Under such conditions, the Secret Service would prefer that such a stop simply be bypassed by the president. But it is extremely difficult for security to prevail over political considerations, or for a White House decision to be changed once it is committed, and *Air Force One* was on its way. By the time the big jet settled onto the runway at Ezeiza Airport outside Buenos Aires, Perón's name was smeared on practically every surface between the airport and the city.

We had, however, been given one concession. We strongly recommended cancellation of the planned motorcade into Buenos Aires due to a number of bombings that had taken place in the city, so Ike was flown by helicopter to U.S. Ambassador Beaulac's residence. The night before President Eisenhower's arrival, American flags had been torn down and burned along the route Ike and Argentina's President Arturo Frondizi were to take from the Embassy to Congress, where Ike was to deliver a speech.

We could not get that motorcade called off, and after lunch, it set out, winding through the crowded streets toward Government House. The first portion of the drive was marred principally by the mounted Grenadier Guards, who beat back the predominantly friendly crowds with the flats of their sabers while their horses lashed out behind, kicking and sitting on the fenders of the cars in the motorcade. Gangs of Peronistas chanted and shouted along the way, but we were spared any serious incident.

Between assignments with Ike, I continued to investigate check cases and chase counterfeiters in Georgia. I had been back in the field almost three years by the time John Kennedy and Lyndon Johnson edged out Richard Nixon and Henry Cabot Lodge by a scant two-tenths of 1 percent of the popular vote. It had been long enough to weigh my own preference between investigative and protective work. I requested another transfer, this time back to Washington.

CHAPTER 5

JFK and LBJ

Although he was elected to the job, John F. Kennedy very nearly never became president. During the period after the election and before the Inauguration, a seventy-three-year-old man by the name of Richard P. Pavlick arrived in Palm Beach, Florida, where President-elect Kennedy was staying at the family home. On Sunday morning, December 11, 1960, Pavlick eased his car to the curb outside the Kennedy home. In the car with him were seven sticks of dynamite that could be detonated by the simple closing of a knife switch. Ahead of this rolling bomb was the car that would shortly be used to take John Kennedy to Mass at a nearby Catholic church.

A Secret Service agent sat at the wheel of the car, another stood beside the rear door before ten o'clock, the front door of the house opened, and John Kennedy emerged. With him were other members of his Secret Service detail and, by the greatest of good fortune, his wife Jackie, daughter Caroline, and several nieces and nephews.

Although the members of his family were not attending Mass with him, they walked out to the car. Pavlick watched them. His target was Kennedy, not his wife and daughter. The plan Pavlick worked out in his disturbed mind was simple and deadly: the moment Kennedy entered the car, he would drive forward; ram the president-elect's car; close the knife switch; and blow himself, Kennedy, the Secret Service agents, and anyone else who happened to be there into eternity.

Kennedy got into the car, an agent closed the door, and Jackie and the children stood waiting for him to drive away. Pavlick made no move to carry out his plan. The sight of the wife and the children standing there apparently stirred something deep within him. When he later told of the incident, he explained his hesitation: "I did not wish to harm her or the children. I decided to get him at the church or someplace later."

Meanwhile, the Protective Research Section in Washington had received information from a postal inspector in Belmont, New Hampshire, that a local man, Richard P. Pavlick, had been overheard saying he intended to kill John Kennedy. In the routine follow-up of all such reports, Secret Service agents went to Belmont to talk to Pavlick, only to find that he had disappeared. The trail led to Palm Beach, and on Thursday, December 15, Secret Service agents placed Pavlick under arrest. He was still waiting for his opportune moment, and there can be little doubt that he would have soon found it.

He made no effort to deny his intention of killing President-elect Kennedy. Agents found in his possession pictures of the Kennedy home and the church John Kennedy attended, which Pavlick had been studying. Pavlick had not planned to leave an unsolved mystery behind. He had written a rambling, disjointed letter, which read in part:

> I believe that the Kennedys bought the Presidency and the White House and until he really became President it was my intention to remove him in the only way it was available to me; the Supreme Court wouldn't enter any motion of mine, if asked, to stop the oath of office. If death and destruction and injury to persons has resulted from my vicious action then I am truly sorry, but it won't help any. It is hoped that by my actions that a better country and a more attentive citizenry has resulted and corrected any abuses of ambitious moneyed persons or groups, then it will not have been in vain. It was unfortunate for the Kennedys that John was elected President because it was Jimmy Hoffa who was to have been my target of destruction because of his "Go to

hell the United States" attitude and because of the gutless cowards called the Congress of the United States who are afraid to clip his wings. ...

· Pavlick was adjudged insane and committed to a mental institution.

At the time this tragedy was averted in Florida, I was working with the president's detail in Augusta. Throughout December and up until the Inauguration, I continued on this assignment. On January 20, 1961, I had the pleasure of taking the last walk with Ike in the White House as he toured the offices of the West Wing, saying goodbye to people who had worked hard and faithfully with him for eight years.

At 11:30 a.m., President Eisenhower and President-elect Kennedy left the White House and drove down Pennsylvania Avenue to the Capitol, and shortly after noon, on a cold and snowy day, the country had a new president.

I did not remain long as a regular member of the White House Detail with Kennedy, although I had several assignments in connection with the new president, one of which was making security arrangements for the live news conferences for which Kennedy became so well known.

By the time my transfer back to Washington had become finalized, an occasion came along that called for Secret Service participation on a journey with the vice president. There was no detail assigned to Lyndon Johnson, for the law specified that Secret Service protection for the vice president was to be provided "at his request," and shortly after taking office, Johnson had taken the prerogative of doing without.

This controversial phrase regarding the protection of the vice president had been unacceptable to the Secret Service from the moment it was put on the lawbooks in 1951. It was unfair to the man for whom the protection was intended. In the first place, he could hardly be expected to make expert evaluations of intelligence relating to his own security, while at the same time carrying out the many tasks required of his position. And while the vice presidency had not entirely emerged from the shadows of anonymity, it was long since a far cry from the satirical role portrayed by Vice President Throttlebottom in the play *Of Thee I Sing*. Harry Truman's abrupt ascendancy under wartime conditions had a sobering effect on the nation concerning the man who was "only a heartbeat away from the presidency."

Secondly—and this applied especially to Lyndon Johnson—periodic criticisms by members of the other Party to the effect that the vice president had too many Secret Service agents put an additional burden on the man since the agents were there only at his bidding. The complainers, for the most part, seemed motivated by thoughts of how their moneysaving efforts would look in the hometown paper, with no regard for the possibility that they were, in effect, declaring the vice president expendable.

However, in March, President Kennedy had assigned a foreign trip to Vice President Johnson, and this called for Secret Service involvement. A basic two-man detail was then formed, consisting of Special Agents H. Stuart Knight and Rufus W. Youngblood.

Lyndon Johnson, of course, was not a complete stranger to us. His years of prominence on Capitol Hill had occasioned many visits to the White House and to various functions where our assignments carried us. But we never had the job of protecting him. On March 24, a summons to the Capitol, where the vice president maintained offices in his capacity as presiding officer of the Senate, ended our wait. Colonel Howard Burris, Johnson's Air Force aide, met with us.

"We've got a little trip coming up, gentlemen," Burris told Stu and me. "The African nation of Senegal is celebrating its independence, and Vice President Johnson will head the United States delegation."

Burris went over the itinerary with us and we returned to our office to map out plans. I was put in charge of the advance, and two additional agents, Charlie Taylor and John Paul Jones, were assigned to beef up the detail for this trip.

Five days later, aching from booster shots for everything from Asian flu to bubonic plague, Charlie Taylor, Captain Earl "Spider" Dunn of the White House Communications Agency, and I were winging our way across the Atlantic aboard a Pan Am jet bound for Senegal. We met the sun rising out of the African continent as we touched down at Dakar, the capital city.

Working out of the U.S. Embassy, Charlie and I familiarized ourselves with the city and with every event scheduled for the three-day celebration. "Spider" Dunn set up the communications capability, which included everything from local walkie-talkies to direct contact with the White House. When *Air Force Two* settled on the runway just before midnight a few days later, we were ready. We especially wanted the vice president to have a smooth operation the first time out, and we thought we had left nothing to chance.

Along with Vice President Johnson the usual entourage arrived, secretaries, aides, and a few congressmen, as well as Lady Bird Johnson and the other members of the Secret Service detail—Stu Knight and John Paul Jones.

For two days it went beautifully. We moved Mr. Johnson painlessly from one event to another—receptions, luncheons, cocktail parties at embassies, formal meetings with President Léopold Senghor and Prime Minister Mamadou Dia, and back and forth to his quarters at the ambassador's residence.

The Embassy report had supplied us with such details as the inadvisability of drinking Dakar's tap water, and when the African heat built a Texas-size thirst in the vice president, we would produce bottled water, or we knew precisely where the nearest Coke machine was, and we had the necessary change to operate it.

And so it went until the last day and one of the last events, a reception and luncheon at the National Assembly, which was scheduled from noon until two. Throughout the visit, the ambassador's personal car and chauffeur had been at Mr. Johnson's disposal, and it was in this car that the Johnsons, the ambassador and his wife, and Stu Knight arrived for the luncheon.

I was waiting at the curb when they pulled up, and as Stu and I walked into the building with them, I thought for the first time that I detected signs of fatigue in the vice president. We were leaving the next morning for a brief rest stop in Geneva, and I thought that we were all ready for it.

Halfway through the luncheon, however, Vice President Johnson motioned to Stu. There were a few whispered words, and Stu nodded and walked over to me.

"He says he wants to go back to the residence now to take a short nap. Get the car."

I went outside, and the first thing I saw was a vacant parking place where the ambassador's car and chauffeur were supposed to be. A policeman on duty informed me that the chauffeur got hungry, and the ambassador's wife had given him permission to go home for lunch, but had ordered him to be back by the time the official luncheon ended.

I hurried back inside. "We've got a problem," I told Stu and repeated what I had just learned. "But," I added, not wanting things to foul up now, "we *do* have a car, if you don't think he'll mind riding in it."

Charlie Taylor and I had been getting around in an old but serviceable Plymouth sedan that one of the Embassy aides had provided. It was parked on the street, with a driver and our Embassy friend, Frank Jeton, patiently waiting.

"I'll ask him," Stu replied. There was another whispered conversation, and I saw Vice President Johnson nod almost imperceptibly, then lean to say something to Lady Bird. Apparently she had elected to stay. He shook a few hands, and with Stu and me flanking him, he left the building. When we reached the car, Stu opened the rear door for Johnson, climbed into the front alongside Jeton and the driver, and instructed the driver to go to the ambassador's residence.

Seeing that four in the front seat would be a crowd, I told Stu I'd catch up later, and I stepped back onto the curb.

"Hold it," Mr. Johnson said to the driver, then leaned toward the window. "Come on, son, hop in. No use you standing out there in the hot sun."

"All right, sir." I opened the door and started to squeeze in beside Stu, but Johnson flung the back door open. "Climb in back here. No use crowding."

Who was I to question the vice president? I got in, sat down, and closed the door. It occurred to me that in the nearly ten years I had been riding with presidents—and an occasional vice president—this was the first time I had ever shared the back seat with one of them. And one I had not formally met, to boot.

Stu handled the formalities, turning as the driver pulled out into the stream of traffic. "Mr. Vice President, this is Special Agent Rufus Youngblood. He was in charge of doing our advance work for this trip."

Johnson stuck out his right hand and grinned. "Course, I've seen you working with Mr. Knight. Pleased to meet you, Mr. Youngblood. You and your men did a nice job getting set for this."

"My pleasure, sir. And thank you," I said as we shook hands.

"Where're you from?" he went on conversationally.

"Atlanta, Georgia, sir."

"Great state, Georgia. You folks have got one of the ablest men who ever came to Washington in Senator Dick Russell."

We drove on, the midday African air blasting in through the open windows like gusts from a furnace. I thought to myself that the people along the streets, if they noticed us at all, probably thought that the five perspiring, windblown characters driving along in the dented and faded sedan were nothing more than some not-too-successful businessmen on their way to lunch.

"How'd you fellows get over here?" Johnson asked.

"Sir?"

"Your advance group, how'd you get here to Dakar?"

"Commercial airline, sir. Pan Am."

He pursed his lips. "What'd your ticket cost?"

There were questions I might have expected him to ask, and even questions I might not have expected him to ask. But the price of my airline ticket was not in either category. Actually, I had no idea what the individual fare was, and I told him so. "We travel on GTRs, sir, government travel requests. The payment is handled by accounting."

I gathered from his expression that he was not entirely satisfied with my answer, so I added, "But I'll find out."

And I did. When he awoke from his nap, I handed him a typewritten note showing the exact fare from Washington, D.C., to Dakar, Senegal, and I underlined the notation that the three of us had traveled tourist class.

It was not until sometime later that I came to realize what lay behind his question. He never lost sight of the fact that government costs have to be met with tax dollars, and he respected the taxpayer.

The first overseas trip with Lyndon Johnson really amounted to little more than a routine courtesy extended to one country by another, a minor part of the continuing international game of trying to make and keep friends. But it introduced the Secret Service to the man it was destined to work with for many years to come. And if Lyndon Johnson did not feel that he really needed protection in a friendly country on a mission of goodwill, there was no doubt that he appreciated the logistics value we had shown him.

The role of vice president had undergone a change that was more than subtle in the relatively short span between Alben Barkley and Lyndon Johnson. If Mr. Barkley ever made a visit of state for President Truman, I do not know of it. Barkley could, I suppose, be called the last of the old-time vice presidents. Beginning with Richard Nixon in the Eisenhower administration, the job had begun to take on an active role, even rising to some prominence of its own.

As the role of the vice president grew, it became apparent that a great deal of unjustified risk reposed in those three words, "at his request," qualifying his Secret Service protection. Nixon himself was a classic example of this. He seemed oblivious to personal danger. Former Secret Service Chief U. E. Baughman scarcely mentioned Barkley's name in his book, *Secret Service Chief*, yet he devoted an entire chapter to Richard Nixon—and entitled it "Nixon—An Assassin's Dreamboat."

This is not to say that Vice President Barkley would not have been an assassin's dreamboat as well, if he had had the exposure. He didn't. The vice president is only as active as the president wants him to be, or needs him to be, and Ike put Nixon to work.

Chief Baughman met with Vice President Nixon in 1953, at the start of his first term as vice president, and Baughman came away shaking his head. Nixon refused Secret Service protection while he was in Washington and agreed only to minimal coverage elsewhere. Several years later, an incident that occurred in Caracas, Venezuela, which very nearly cost Nixon and those with him their lives, failed to bring about substantial change in his fatalistic attitude. In late April 1958, the vice president began a goodwill tour of South America. Despite intelligence that strong anti-American factions were also making plans for his tour, the vice president went ahead with the trip. Chief

Baughman made urgent appeals to Nixon to call off the trip entirely, but as Baughman put it, "It was like talking into a barrel."

Almost as a measure of compromise, Nixon agreed to substitute a closed limousine for the open car he preferred to use in motorcades.

The stop in Montevideo, Uruguay, was relatively mild, with only a few demonstrations and anti-American posters. The tempo increased in Lima, Peru, with the addition of spitting and rock throwing. The Secret Service agent in charge of the detail, John Sherwood, had a tooth chipped when a rock hit him, and Nixon was also hit, though not injured.

Anti-American feelings were known to be even stronger in Venezuela. Intelligence reports told of a massive demonstration, Communist-inspired and dominated, that would meet the American vice president in Caracas. CIA reports advised the Secret Service that the planned culmination of the Caracas demonstrations would be an attempt to assassinate Nixon.

The vice president was apprised of the reports but insisted on going through with the tour as planned. Long before his plane arrived at Caracas's Maiquetía International Airport, thousands of demonstrators were already on the scene, fired up, ready and waiting. The reception at the airport was sufficient to have made a change in the published itinerary. The Nixons were hooted, cursed, spit upon, and struck by objects thrown by the mob. Even the traditional nineteen-gun salute could not be heard for the noise of the crowd. The Secret Service agents were particularly hard-pressed, as the police and soldiers seemed to hang back when the going got rough.

The motorcade finally got under way, only to be harassed by cars filled with demonstrators until it reached the city itself. The situation, bad as it was, now became extremely serious. A steady stream of rocks, bottles, and other objects rained against Nixon's car from both sides of the street. The immediate objective of the motorcade had been the National Pantheon, where the vice president was to lay a wreath at the tomb of Simón Bolívar. Suddenly, only blocks from the destination, a large truck loomed directly in the path of the motorcade, parked crosswise in the street, completely blocking any passage. The drivers had no choice but to stop, which was the signal for hundreds of demonstrators to come swarming out of the alleys and byways to attack

Nixon's car. Inside the car were Nixon, Special Agents John Sherwood and Wade Rodham, Nixon's interpreter, Colonel Vernon Walters, Venezuelan Foreign Minister García Velutini, and a Venezuelan driver. Following this car was one carrying Mrs. Nixon and two Secret Service agents, and six other agents were in other cars.

For twelve long minutes it appeared that this might be the end of the line for Richard Nixon, and perhaps for others in the party as well. Agents Sherwood and Rodham had actually pulled the .38s as the pounding from outside began to break through the shatterproof glass, while the car rocked rhythmically from side to side as the mob attempted to turn it over and set it afire.

Then, like the cavalry in the cowboy movies, a contingent of Venezuelan troops arrived, plowed a narrow passageway through the howling mob, and allowed the cars to slip through.

They made straightaway for the American Embassy, and even in this sanctuary, the situation remained so serious that President Eisenhower had American troops readied in Puerto Rico and other Caribbean islands, as well as warships brought close inshore along the Venezuelan coast, prepared to do whatever became necessary to extricate the Nixon party.

Happily and almost miraculously, the entire fiasco ended with Nixon's successful escape from the country to which he had come, ironically, as an ambassador of goodwill.

Nixon credited his Secret Service detail with having saved his life, and each agent on the trip was presented the gold medal of the Treasury Exceptional Service Award. But there were many who felt that the whole matter could have been avoided in the first place if Vice President Nixon had heeded the advice of the Secret Service and passed up the Venezuelan stop, discretion still being the better part of valor.

Even this near assassination of a vice president did not bring about the change in the law that the Secret Service had been pleading for, that is, removing decisions regarding his own security from the hands of the vice president.

Lyndon Johnson, in a very real sense, was on the spot from a security standpoint when he took office. His predecessor had virtually disdained protection and had survived. It was like following Superman out of the telephone booth. Johnson could hardly be expected to fly in the face of this by ordering a large contingent of Secret Service agents for his own protection.

Chief Baughman, who seemed destined to confront stubborn vice presidents, held an almost identical meeting with Mr. Johnson as the one he had held eight years earlier with Mr. Nixon—and, predictably, with almost identical results. Also, it was springtime in Washington, and with the regularity of the blossoming cherry trees, there were the meetings of the Appropriations Committee. The Secret Service, along with other federal agencies, would annually trudge up Capitol Hill in spring and bare its proposed budget for the upcoming fiscal year.

Almost invariably, some committeeman would single out the expenditure for vice presidential protection. At one such hearing, a Republican congressman questioned the cost of protecting Lyndon Johnson by pointing out that it "would be used to protect a man who came from a state whose would-be tradition was wrapped in praise of the tough frontier spirit ... the land of the six-shooter and so many other things."

As absurd as such statements were, they never seemed to fail to touch a political switch somewhere inside Lyndon Johnson, for at budget time, we could expect word that he was either dropping his Secret Service protection altogether or cutting it back. On and off for two years and seven months, my assignment was "Lyndon Johnson, Vice President." And while he never indulged in the immutable the-show-must-go-on philosophy that nearly killed Richard Nixon in Venezuela, they were thirty-one months that were far from being humdrum.

The Senegal trip established us for a time with the new vice president, and President Kennedy soon had a bigger assignment for Mr. Johnson. On May 9, 1961, *Air Force Two* was on its way westward—first stop, Hickam Field, Hawaii. After an overnight stay, we continued on to Wake Island, Guam, and then to the heart of the mission—Saigon, South Vietnam. John Kennedy had come into office with the promise in his Inaugural Address that the United States would "pay any price, bear any burden, meet any hardship, support any friend, oppose any foe to assure the survival and the success of liberty." The situation in Southeast Asia had reached a point where he thought he should follow up on his promise, and Lyndon Johnson was given the task of personally conferring with South Vietnam's President Ngo Dinh Diem regarding American assistance in his country's struggle with the Communists.

As Stu Knight and I escorted Vice President Johnson and U.S. Ambassador Nolting to Independence Palace on the morning of May 12, 1961, I do not believe anyone at that meeting anticipated where this offer of help to an ally would eventually take the United States. In fact, with this particular trip scheduled to take us around the world, the Saigon stopover seemed at the time to be of more or less equal importance with several others we would make.

At Independence Palace that morning, there were the customary greetings at such occasions, followed by a brief ceremony on the grounds, after which Johnson, Diem, and their aides and advisers went inside to hold the meeting. It lasted through most of the morning, and when it ended, Vice President Johnson and Diem both seemed pleased with what had been accomplished.

With the business over, the vice president expressed a desire to have a look around. The countryside in the vicinity of Saigon was fairly safe for travelers at that time, and so after lunch, an impromptu motorcade wound its way out of the city. We stopped occasionally—in a hamlet for Johnson to have a few words with the people through his interpreter, or alongside a rice paddy to observe the farmers at work.

As we rounded a bend several miles out in the country, Johnson's face suddenly brightened. There to our right was a field in which a dozen or so head of cattle were contentedly grazing.

"Pull over!" Vice President Johnson ordered the driver. We eased off onto the roadside, the vehicles behind following suit. Johnson was out almost before the car stopped, loping off with his big Texas cattleman's gait to inspect the local stock. Stu Knight and I dutifully trotted along with him, not feeling too easy about a prolonged stop, and keeping an eye out toward the forest beyond the field. Battles were not being fought in the area, but sniping was not uncommon.

I had never had much contact with beef in the live state. My first brief visit to the LBJ Ranch in Texas, shortly before this trip, had shown me that the vice president was no stranger to the beasts, and as we made our way toward the assembled cattle, I assumed these were the same as those in Texas. Still, I preferred my cattle disassembled, preferably broken down into T-bone steaks, lightly salted and peppered, and done medium rare over charcoal. These, I noticed, had ceased their grazing and were eying the oncoming group with suspicion.

The next thing I noticed was that they were no longer simply standing there; they were coming to meet us, a couple of them at a steady trot.

"Mr. Vice President," I said, "I don't think it's advisable for us to get too far from the cars." What I was thinking was that I did not want to be the first Secret Service agent to get hoof marks in the line of duty.

Lyndon Johnson was a man who knew when to back off, and he knew it now. "Whatever you think is best, Rufus," he replied, and doing an about-face, we headed for the cars, trying not to break into a dead run because of the ever-present reporters and photographers who had come along with us.

We reached the cars about ten feet ahead of the cows, and as they strolled victoriously back into their field, the vice president suggested that he had seen enough of the countryside for this visit, and we headed back into Saigon.

It was around the world in fourteen days, with stops at Manila, Taipei, Hong Kong, Bangkok, New Delhi, Karachi, Athens, and a final rest stop in Bermuda, where the Johnsons hosted a nice party for the entire entourage and presented some of us with a special "LBJ watch" as a trip memento.

He was fond of giving presents of this sort, and almost everywhere he went, if time was available, he would get in some shopping. LBJ was a born horse trader. To him there was nothing final about a price tag. He might go into Neiman Marcus and pick up half a dozen expensive shirts, some slacks, a few ties, and socks, and when he had them all piled up, he would say, "Okay, now how much'll you take for all of 'em?"—obviously implying that he was not interested in an adding-machine tape of the price tags. As a haggler, he excelled in curio and art shops, and if it took an order of three dozen of something to get the price right, he would buy three dozen.

The vice president's assignment in all these countries had been primarily to establish personal contact for the new administration and to carry John

Kennedy's message to their leaders. In Karachi, Pakistan, however, he made a contact of a different kind, which turned out to be the most newsworthy item of the whole trip. Somewhere in his travels, Mr. Johnson had developed a curiosity about the camels that are used as beasts of burden in many parts of the world. Camels were abundant in Karachi, and Stu Knight and I had been on the lookout for a likely camel driver for the vice president to meet.

Stu spotted what seemed to be just what the doctor ordered as we toured a suburban area of Karachi, and he brought it to Vice President Johnson's attention. The vice president agreed, and we stopped to have a chat with the driver. It was not what could be called an auspicious meeting: the tall, lanky Johnson chatting with the small, brown camel driver, whose name, we learned through the interpreter, was Bashir Ahmed, and the huge camel standing placidly behind them attached to a wagon piled high with bags of straw. As they parted, however, amid the clicking of camera shutters, the vice president made an innocent remark that was to change Bashir Ahmed's life. He said, "Now, y'all come to see us," which is the standard farewell in Texas and the South and is not normally construed as a formal invitation.

But it was picked up somewhere, probably by the press and the State Department as a natural public relations ploy, and the following October, financed by private funds, Bashir Ahmed, camel driver, paid the unlikeliest visit of the decade to the United States. He came as a celebrity, met President Kennedy, was seen and read about in newspapers from coast to coast, visited the LBJ Ranch, got a three-page spread in *Life* magazine, and was even sent back home via Mecca.

Among the many gifts that went home with him was a pickup truck. So the camel, which had brought all this fame and fortune to Bashir in the first place, was replaced by the pickup truck and was sold.

Bashir, apparently, would have been better off if he had stayed in bed that day in 1961. The last thing I read about him was a news item almost eight years later. Unable to drive, he leased the truck to our embassy. It was returned to him in "bad shape," and he spent most of his time trying to gain entry into the U.S. Embassy to complain.

The Vice Presidential Detail in the summer of 1961 seemed to be more or less a full-time job. Stu Knight was the SAIC; I was the assistant SAIC. When we needed help, we drew on the manpower of the field offices. We called for help in August. Our operating instructions at the time were to check daily with the vice president's office, and one morning, I called his secretary, Mary Margaret Wiley, and inquired if anything was on the agenda that would include us.

"Well, we might have a trip to Berlin coming up," she said.

"Okay. What's the approximate date?"

"Today."

There is no way to advance a trip that begins on the day you find out about it, other than establishing contact with some United States agency already there. In most cases, our Embassy serves this purpose. This was a trip that had come up suddenly and could not be postponed. Access to Berlin was again being threatened by the Russians and the East Germans, and President Kennedy was sending Johnson to West Germany and Berlin to reassure the people of our government's full support.

We flew out of Andrews Air Force Base that night aboard *Air Force Two*— Vice President Johnson; General Lucius Clay, former military governor of Germany; and various State Department people and other aides. We landed in Bonn before noon the next day, and immediately some of the bread that Stu and I had cast upon the waters came back to us. Shortly after our trip to Dakar with LBJ, we had made our first visit to the LBJ ranch in Texas. German Chancellor Konrad Adenauer had dropped in for a couple of days after talks in Washington with President Kennedy, and we—Stu and I—had done everything we could to make the visit easy and pleasant for the chancellor's security men, headed by Dr. "Fritz" Brueckner.

Now, deplaning in Bonn under wet, gray skies, less than twenty-four hours after learning we were coming, who should we find at the airport but Dr. Brueckner, waving and calling, "Stu! Rufe! Over here!" What had begun as a sticky assignment for us now became as smooth as if we had had a month to prepare for it.

Johnson conferred with Adenauer, and later in the afternoon, we flew on to Tempelhof Airport in West Berlin. Dr. Brueckner insisted on sending two of his best men along to give any help we might want, and we made no effort to decline his offer.

Vice President Johnson met with Mayor Willy Brandt and addressed the city parliament, delivering President Kennedy's personal pledge that the freedom of the city and access to it would be maintained. The two leaders went on a joyous winding motorcade through the streets of Berlin. That it was a rainy, dull afternoon apparently did not keep any Berliner capable of getting into the streets from doing so. It was Lyndon Johnson's kind of crowd, where he could "press the flesh," and every few blocks, he would get out and wade into the throng, shaking hands, kissing babies, and even turning up a bottle of German beer thrust into his hands by a happy *hausfrau*.

The next day, Sunday, LBJ visited the border where the eastern and western sectors of the divided city met, and where the Communists had begun to build what was to be known as the Berlin Wall. When LBJ got going, he wanted to go everywhere. He had already overridden several nervous State Department types who had attempted to dissuade him from going out to the Autobahn to watch the American troops coming into the city. "Who says I can't go out there?" he demanded. "The hell I can't! With Stu and Rufe, I can go anywhere!"

But there was one place he could not go, and that was into the eastern sector of the city. Stu and I managed a brief tour into the Communist-controlled area with a group of American officers, and LBJ had to content himself with our "report."

Johnson had made the United States position clear. The mission was accomplished, and on Monday night, just three days after leaving, *Air Force Two* touched down at Andrews.

This might be a good place to clear up a minor point of confusion concerning the designation of airplanes as *Air Force One* and *Air Force Two*. Neither of these applies to a specific aircraft; they are simply code words used primarily for air traffic control, meaning that the particular aircraft that is so designated is carrying either the president or the vice president. The helicopters of the Army and the Marine Corps that transport the president to or from the White

House grounds are designated *Army One* or *Marine One* while the president is aboard. All these aircraft, when being operated without the president or vice president on board, use their regular number designations.

The code word *Valley* was used to identify the Washington residence of Vice President and Mrs. Johnson. During the summer of 1961, *Valley* was in the process of being relocated. The Johnsons had purchased Perle Mesta's home, The Elms, located in a prestigious northwestern Washington neighborhood. While the new owners remodeled it to suit their tastes, Stu Knight and I, assisted by Bob Bouck of the Protective Research Section, began to plan for security. This included such obvious things as fencing the parts of the property that were unfenced; putting outside lights at strategic places; and installing additional locks, automatic alarms, and a direct line to the White House security switchboard. Since the cost of such security measures was paid out of Secret Service funds, we had a selling job to convince LBJ that they were necessary. When we were able to show him that this would cut down on manpower requirements, that did it.

In October, after LBJ had entertained the Pakistani camel driver, Bashir Ahmed, down at the ranch, the alarm system at the unfinished residence in Washington got an unplanned test. At about eleven thirty one night, an alarm signal alerted our security switchboard. The Metropolitan Police were notified, and the men in blue hurried to the house to find a group of happy teenagers about to enjoy the vice president's pool.

Although the kids never made a splash in the pool, the incident did make a splash in the newspapers. This, in turn, provoked LBJ to land on Stu Knight like a duck on a June bug.

"I want you to get all that damn alarm equipment off the place!" he roared.

So we had to sell him all over again. We pointed out that this had, among other things, proved the equipment was functional and effective, and if nothing else, would prevent unauthorized skinny-dipping out of season.

The Secret Service underwent some key personnel changes in the latter part of 1961. Chief U. E. Baughman retired after a distinguished thirty-three-year career, and Jim Rowley, SAIC of the White House Detail, moved up to become chief. Jerry Behn, Rowley's deputy, was elevated to Rowley's former post.

The Vice Presidential Detail, however, still remained the stepchild of the protective forces. The Secret Service is a career organization, and assignment to this detail was not one of the more sought-after jobs, with its now-you-see-it-now-you-don't character. A change in the law would be the only thing that could alter the situation, and now we seemed to have something in our favor in our efforts to get this done. And that was Lyndon Johnson. I do not believe he felt that there was any real threat hanging over him, such as exists for the president. For every one who writes a letter saying he is going to shoot the vice president on sight, a thousand write the same letter to the president.

But protective work does not involve only protection from intentional harm; it means protection from any contingency, such things as being in communication with the White House and being able to respond immediately should the president or some emergency require the vice president.

At about the time these changes were being made, Stu and I accompanied LBJ to Kansas City, where he was to speak at a function of William Jewell College to be held in the banquet room of the Muehlebach Hotel. We checked the vice president into his customary corner room on the eleventh floor, and we set up shop in the adjoining room. Working with us were two special agents from the Kansas City Field Office, Maurice Martineau and Don Bell.

One of the secrets of LBJ's apparent boundless energy was his ability to relax. Like Harry Truman, Johnson would utilize a half an hour after lunch for a nap, except where Truman would simply strip down to his shorts and lie on his bed, LBJ would take it all off, put on his pajamas, and climb in under the covers, which is what he did after lunch that day at the Muehlebach.

Agent Don Bell had gone down to the coffee shop to get a sandwich while Stu and I stayed on duty on the eleventh floor. Don returned in a matter of minutes.

"Don't be surprised if you hear fire engines," he said, "because the coffee shop is on fire. It looks like just a grease fire with a lot of smoke but—"

"But we can't take a chance," Stu put in.

I trotted next door, tapped lightly, and then went in. LBJ was propped up on two pillows in his yellow pajamas, glasses down on the end of his nose, making some changes in the script of his speech. He gave me a look that plainly said, "What the hell are you doing in here?" and I answered the unspoken question with, "Mr. Vice President, you'd better get your clothes on because there's a fire in the hotel. Nothing bad yet, but we feel it's advisable to evacuate."

We had a sort of tacit agreement, the vice president and his Secret Service detail. We never told him how to be vice president and he never—well, hardly ever—told us how to be Secret Service. He laid the script aside.

"Okay, pardner," he said as he threw back the covers and ambled briefly into the bathroom. In less than five minutes, with the smell of smoke strong in the hallways, we rode down to the ground floor and calmly escorted LBJ out to the street where the car had been summoned by walkie-talkie. We were several blocks away before the first fire engine roared past us toward the hotel.

We later learned that the entire hotel had been evacuated shortly after our departure and that the quick action of the fire department had limited the damage mainly to smoke and water. The function was canceled, and we flew back to Washington—and there were no news photos of Vice President Johnson fleeing the premises in his yellow pajamas.

The limited staff available to Lyndon Johnson quite often cast us in a dual role, and our job at times included getting him to some destination on time or assuring him privacy when he wished it. These peripheral duties occasionally brought us both undeserved praise and blame. Another agent and I flew by commercial airline out of Baltimore's Friendship Airport one morning with LBJ on a purely political trip. Our departure was at a peak traffic period, and the vice president was becoming increasingly impatient as the plane crept along the taxi strip with agonizing slowness, awaiting its turn on the runway. We were behind schedule, and the pilot spoke on the public-address system to explain.

"Ladies and gentlemen, we regret the delay, which is being caused by a traffic mess-up in Washington. We should be taking off very soon now."

LBJ reached over and tapped me impatiently on the arm. "Son, go up there and get on the radio to Washington and straighten out that mess! We gotta get outta here!"

I glanced across the aisle at my fellow agent, who merely shrugged. Rather than attempt to explain that it was air traffic and not a "mess" in Washington, I hauled myself up and started forward to the cockpit. A stewardess met me at the door (this was pre-hijacking days), and I identified myself.

"We've just received clearance for takeoff, Mr. Youngblood," she said, "so please take your seat and fasten your seat belt."

I nodded and went back. I snapped the buckle just as the pilot shoved the throttles forward, and we roared down the runway. LBJ grinned at me.

"Nice going, pardner! Another job well done by your Secret Service in action!"

I gave a little shrug as if to say it was merely routine and glanced over at the other agent. I could see his lips forming the words "You lucky ..."—but I couldn't make out the last word, which was probably just as well.

It did not always go this way, however. A few months earlier, when we were in Austin, LBJ told me he wanted to fly over to Dallas and visit his old friend and political mentor, the venerable Speaker of the House Sam Rayburn, who lay dying in a Dallas hospital.

"I don't want any publicity, Rufus," he said. "Can you get somebody in your Dallas office to meet us and get us over to the hospital without any crowds or reporters?"

"Yes, sir," I assured him. I phoned SAIC Forrest Sorrels of our Dallas office, and he said he would take care of it and would personally meet us at the airport. The following morning we boarded LBJ's private plane and flew to Dallas. As Bill Willis, LBJ's pilot, taxied toward the gate where Sorrels was to meet us, Johnson suddenly leaned closer to the window.

"Rufus, I thought you said your people could handle a simple thing like getting me in and out of here without any fuss! What the hell is that crowd doing at our gate? Can't the Secret Service keep a secret?"

I peered ahead, and there was no doubt about it—there was a small crowd at the gate, and I had seen enough welcoming committees to know that's what it was. I could not understand it; Sorrels was not one to drop the ball.

I could only shrug as LBJ continued giving me hell until the plane came to a halt and the door was opened. "You boys haven't heard the last of this," he muttered before putting on his hat and a smile and walking down the steps with his hand outstretched to those in the forefront.

I glanced around apprehensively, wondering where Sorrels was. The man in the lead of the reception committee accepted LBJ's hand with a puzzled expression on his face.

"Well, Mr. Vice President, this is a surprise! We came out to meet the university chancellor! We had no idea we'd be running into you!"

At that moment I spied Sorrels, standing on his tiptoes at the back of the crowd, gesturing with his hat toward a plain black sedan parked near the gate.

"Excuse me, sir," I said to LBJ, "our party is waiting over there and we're running a little late."

"Oh? All right." He shook a few more hands and then we pressed on through the crowd, leaving the committee to welcome the chancellor.

I never told him I didn't get us out of Friendship Airport when all else was failing, and he never apologized for chewing me out for something I didn't do. I suppose we broke even.

Lyndon Johnson was a man of many moods. He seemed to draw strength simply from the presence of others. At meals, in particular, companionship and conversation were almost as important to him as food. On a number of occasions, I traveled with him as a protective detail of one. When mealtime came in some hotel or airport, and there was no one else with us, he would say, "Come on, Rufus, sit down and have a hamburger with me and let's talk."

He also had the capability of chewing you out in a way that would have been the envy of a seasoned Marine drill instructor. Yet when the mood was on him, he could be the most sentimental of men, sometimes almost to the point of becoming maudlin. If you could not adjust to this pendulum action, it could be unusually difficult working with him. There were many agents who would never have flinched under the assault of a thousand assassins, yet who wilted at the thought of LBJ. A young agent, Jerry Kivett, began working intermittently with us out of the Washington Field Office in the latter part of 1961, and I knew from the start that he was one of those who could roll with the punches.

For better or worse, his fate was sealed, and he became a member of the Vice Presidential Detail for next few months, until the annual budget hearings in the spring of 1962 put the detail back in limbo. In May, when the budget flak had settled and LBJ began to miss us again, I was called back from my interim assignment at the White House. Stu Knight elected to stay where he had gone—Special Investigations—and I was designated as SAIC. I signed Jerry Kivett on as my assistant.

That summer, I had my first big overseas trip as head of the detail. LBJ was to make a goodwill tour of several Middle Eastern countries, and on August 22, 1962, we were off to Beirut, Lebanon. There were the usual ceremonies, a motorcade into the city, meetings with the Lebanese leaders, and the next day on to Iran. The third day found us bushed, hot, and driving from the airport into Ankara, Turkey, through an eighteen-mile solid thicket of happy people. The vice president's penchant for "pressing the flesh" was never more apparent than on that day. He and Lady Bird rode in a convertible touring sedan that looked like something out of an early George Raft movie. An Embassy official sat in the front seat alongside Jerry Kivett and a uniformed chauffeur who was a dead ringer for General Pershing.

I worked from the follow-up car, and the way LBJ stopped the motorcade every few blocks—which meant I had to run up from the follow-up car to help handle the crowds—it seemed that I was going to run the whole eighteen miles into Ankara.

Georgia is hot in August. So are Texas, Washington, D.C., and New York City. But Turkey in August is *hot* hot. The heat was even getting to LBJ as we neared the city, and he made the stops fewer and farther between. But the wear and tear on me must have shown, because LBJ took a look at me and shook his head. "Come on, son," he said, "hop in here and ride with us."

"No, thank you, sir, there's no room and I'd better—"

Lady Bird interrupted, smiling and patting the seat. "Come on, Rufus. Now you ride back here with us."

My thoughts went back to a hot day in Dakar, Senegal. When we pulled up ten minutes later at the entrance of the Balin Hotel in downtown Ankara, there, lined up across the rear seat of the open touring car, accepting the accolades of the Turks, were Vice President and Mrs. Johnson and Special Agent Rufus W. Youngblood.

LBJ did not seem to realize how enervating the heat was; he wanted to do everything—visit crowded bazaars, take his usual rides out into the boondocks, and attend all the official functions staged in his honor. Lady Bird always kept an eye on him, and we would try to conspire with her whenever we could to cut things short when he began to tire. But we had not been able to do it that day in Ankara, and by nightfall, the heat and the pace he had set were definitely beginning to tell on him.

Frayed nerves, when they were Lyndon Johnson's, invariably meant chewing outs. Paul Glynn often found himself in the unfortunate position of getting the first blast. Paul was an Air Force sergeant who was a personal aide to the vice president, and Paul had committed the cardinal sin of leaving the vice president's pepper mill aboard the airplane, eighteen miles away. It would be a long time before Paul forgot the pepper mill again.

Jerry Kivett was next. Jerry had taken over with LBJ after we got in from the last function of the afternoon. I had gone to our quarters on the floor below the vice president's suite, taken a long, cold shower, and was going over the reading file in air-conditioned comfort when the door flew open and Jerry came in, his jaw set.

"That does it!" he said. "That *really* does it! Why the hell did I ever let you talk me into this job! I ain't working for that guy anymore—"

"Okay, okay," I said, "what happened?"

Kivett spun around. "He threw me out, that's what! He told everybody up there to go to their rooms! Everybody in the place is confined to quarters! He said we were under *house arrest*!"

I knew the symptoms, and I glanced at my watch. It was less than an hour before Vice President and Mrs. Johnson were due at a state banquet. "You're relieved," I told Jerry. "Take a shower. Have a cold drink sent up."

"Relieved? I'm under house arrest! And so are you, by the way!" He threw himself disgustedly on the bed.

I put my tuxedo on, made a final adjustment of the black tie, and went up to the vice president's suite. The agent on duty in the hall simply shook his head as I politely knocked and, without waiting overly long, opened the door and stuck my head in.

The vice president was sitting across the room at a desk, clad in his BVDs and glowering at me. "And just what the hell are you doing in here? Didn't you get my message?"

I stepped in and made a deep bow. "I am here, sir, to assist the Vice President of the United States in getting ready for the banquet."

It did not always work. If there was still a head of steam in the boiler, this kind of tomfoolery would bring on another explosion. This time I was lucky. Poor Jerry had caught the last of it. LBJ just stared at me for a moment, then gave me a tired grin and said, "Okay, pardner. Tell that sergeant to get back in here and let's get ready."

It was not a one-way street. A few days later we were at the Grand-Bretagne Hotel in Athens, Greece, beginning the homeward leg of the trip. Everybody was winding down from another long day when the phone rang in the Secret Service room. Jack Holtzhauer, our advance agent in Athens, answered it and held it out to me. "It's Mary Margaret, Rufe."

When his secretary calls, I said to myself, *that means the Man wants something.* I took the phone.

"The vice president would like you to come up to his suite, Rufus," she said.

I sighed, wondering whether there was anything chewable left in me or on me. "Okay. Coming."

Mary Margaret met me at the door. Across the room, LBJ stood at the open doors leading onto the balcony, his back toward me, a telephone in his hand. Beyond him, bathed in floodlights atop the hill of the Acropolis, I could see the Parthenon. It suggested durability, and I squared my shoulders and went in. I stood there quietly until he had finished his conversation and put the phone down.

"Thanks for coming up, son."

Son? I thought.

"Mary Margaret," he said, "fix us a couple of drinks, please. What'll you have, Rufus, scotch or bourbon?"

"Whatever you're having, sir."

He motioned me to a chair, and while Mary Margaret mixed the drinks, the vice president waxed mellow. "I want you to know what a good job you and your men have been doing, Rufus. This has been a rough trip, and nobody knows that any better than I do. I haven't seen the slightest sign that you or any man on your detail has wavered. I want all of you to know that I appreciate it."

Mary Margaret handed us the drinks, the vice president clinked glasses with me, and we all had, as they say down in Texas, a real nice visit.

We flew from Athens to Rome, where LBJ made the usual ceremonial visit to the Vatican. An opportunity to meet the pope is a momentous occasion for any good Catholic, and the vice president introduced members of his staff to Pope John. When he got to his personal aide, an upstanding Catholic lad, LBJ introduced him as "Sergeant Paul Glynn." The little pope smiled broadly at Paul and in his heavily accented English said, "You are a sergeant, eh? You know, I, too, was a sergeant before I became a pope!"

This really broke the ice and put everyone at ease.

The fall of 1962 brought with it off-year congressional elections, and LBJ did his share of stumping for the good of the Democratic Party. Often, it would be just Vice President Johnson, with me, traveling around the country to make a speech on behalf of some Democrat.

In October, Jerry Kivett and I flew out to Los Angeles with him for a big Democratic fund-raising dinner. At the hotel, LBJ was running late, and this was compounded by the absence of Paul Glynn, who would have had the vice president's clothes laid out neatly and ready. Into this breach stepped the intrepid Special Agent Jerry Kivett. I was waiting in the living room, and I soon began to hear a considerable amount of muttering from the bedroom. I opened the door, and there stood the vice president, red-faced, one trouser leg on while he hopped around trying to get the other one on, as Jerry crawled around on the floor picking up studs and cuff links. LBJ almost fell over him, and then he plopped down on the bed.

"Damn it, Jerry, you'd make a hell of a valet! It'll be midnight before I get dressed!"

Jerry drew himself up in righteous response. "Well, sir, you have to consider that this is the first time in my life I ever dressed another full-grown man!"

On the way back to Washington the following day, somewhere between Los Angeles and Albuquerque, as I recall, LBJ was sipping a cold drink and relaxing. He slapped me on the knee.

"Rufus, we're gonna get it this month. We're finally gonna pass that legislation. You boys won't have to check with Mary Margaret to find out if I want you, because I won't have any choice in the matter. There'll be Secret Service for the vice president, whether he requests it or not."

This was, of course, something of an inside problem, and would not have been newsworthy to the public even if, during the same month, World War III had not come close to starting—and ending. On October 16, missile sites were detected on the island of Cuba, and within a matter of days, Russia and the United States were eyeball to eyeball as Russian freighters were intercepted on their way to Cuba, bearing the missiles to arm the sites.

The vice president was called back from Honolulu where he was campaigning for the Democratic nominee for governor, Jack Burns. I had noticed that LBJ was suddenly getting an unusual amount of telephone traffic from Walter Jenkins and other aides in Washington. He took me aside, his campaign smile gone and a serious look on his face.

"Check the airlines and get us on the first thing back to Washington," he said.

Before nightfall, Jerry, LBJ, and I were streaking across the Pacific toward the capital. He did not tell us precisely what it was that had called him back in such haste, but he intimated that it was a national emergency. It was of sufficient importance to have a helicopter waiting for him when he touched down at Friendship Airport in Baltimore. Colonel Burris was standing by, and we boarded the chopper and were taken directly to the Pentagon and then on to the White House, where an emergency meeting of the National Security Council was being called.

While the top-level meetings were being held, the Secret Service beefed up the protective details assigned to both Kennedy and Johnson. We pulled in field agents for this duty, and after conferring with Major Ralph Stover, head of the White House Police, men from his organization were put on temporary duty at the Johnsons' residence.

People all over America were emptying supermarket shelves, building bomb shelters, listening to the frightening facts of how few minutes it took an intercontinental ballistic missile to get to the United States, and even discussing whether they would shoot their neighbor on sight or give warning if he tried to claw his way into the shelter. It was the ant and the grasshopper in the nuclear age.

When the showdown was over, and the ships had turned and headed back across the Atlantic with their cargoes still aboard, there were a lot of people who knew a lot more about their neighbors than they had before.

And very few people outside the Secret Service knew, or cared, that the day before the whole thing started, President Kennedy had signed H.R. 6691 into law, giving statutory responsibility to the Secret Service for the protection of vice president on a full-time nonrequest basis.

It had taken almost twelve years since the attempt on President Truman's life at Blair House had reminded the country of just how close the vice president can come to being president on a moment's notice. Out of this assassination attempt had come the watered-down legislation that provided Alben Barkley with Secret Service protection when he wanted it. One of the former Chief U. E. Baughman's long-sought goals was now a reality. It would have been highly appropriate if Baughman had been given the pen with which President Kennedy signed the bill.

It might have taken another few years if Jerry Kivett and I had not worked as smoothly as we had with LBJ, thereby enlisting the support of a man who was one of the most proficient at getting bills through Congress.

The two-man intermittent detail of Youngblood and Kivett was expanded to a permanent unit of twenty-six. Chief Rowley brought Stu Knight back as SAIC and I was dropped back once more to the number-two slot as his assistant. Jerry faded into the crowd as a journeyman agent on one of the shifts.

There were a lot of new faces around, some rookies and some veteran agents brought in from other positions. I had worked with many of them before—Thomas L. "Lem" Johns, Glenn Weaver, Paul Rundle, Jim Goodenough, Woody Taylor, Jerry Bechtle, and Don Bendickson, to name a few. Even with the new law, however, complaints of "too much Secret Service" for the vice president, emanating from the Appropriations Committee rooms, caused the old reflex action in LBJ, and at one point, the detail was cut back to fourteen men.

This was not for long. The president's extensive use of Lyndon Johnson as his personal emissary quieted these mutterings. Extended trips to such places as the Dominican Republic, Italy, and the Scandinavian countries, in addition to LBJ's usual busy schedule around Washington and the United States, kept both the vice president and his Secret Service detail busy through the summer and into the early autumn of 1963.

But the Vice Presidential Detail was soon to disappear again, for the worst of all reasons. There would be no vice president, therefore no Vice Presidential Detail.

CHAPTER 6

Preparing for Dallas

November 1963 began with an assassination. A coup in South Vietnam on November 1 and 2 culminated in the shooting of President Ngo Dinh Diem, the man Lyndon Johnson had visited in the spring of 1961 as John Kennedy's personal emissary. November 1963 also began with finalizing plans drawn up for a relatively important political trip for President Kennedy and Vice President Johnson. They were going to Texas, Johnson's home state. Much has been written about the purpose of this trip. Some have viewed it as an effort to repair the rift in the Democratic Party in Texas that had resulted from feuding between the liberal and conservative factions, led respectively by Senator Ralph Yarborough and Governor John Connally. A feud between Yarborough and Johnson has also been suggested.

Johnson himself has said the trip "was presidential politics, pure and simple. It was the opening of the 1964 campaign." And that is primarily what it was; the election of 1960 had provided the Democratic ticket with only a slim margin of victory in the vice president's own state, and Texas's twenty-five electoral votes were essential for the upcoming 1964 election. Thus, the Texas trip was not of small significance to Kennedy and Johnson, but as a news item it provided only regional interest at the time.

The general plan had been drawn up at a meeting in El Paso, Texas, the previous June. President Kennedy and Vice President Johnson had conferred there with Governor Connally, and a decision had been made tentatively to visit the state in November. By late September, the plans had firmed to the point that the *Dallas Morning News* was able to report to its readers that the president and vice president would jointly pay a visit to their city on either November 21 or 22.

In early November, the political strategists had made the dates definite, and the Secret Service was routinely advised. Special Assistant to the President Kenneth O'Donnell discussed the itinerary with Jerry Behn, SAIC of the White House Detail. The itinerary consisted of a simple two-page list, which began:

November 21, Thursday. 10:45 a.m. Leave White House lawn—helicopter
and ended:
November 22, Friday. 10:45 p.m. Arrive V. P. Ranch

Thirty-six hours in which the president was to leave Washington, visit five Texas cities, speak to thousands of Texans, be seen by thousands more, huddle with key political figures, and arrive at the LBJ Ranch for a night's rest before returning to Washington.

Along the way, there were to be visits to the Aerospace Medical Health Center in San Antonio, a dinner in honor of Texas congressman Albert Thomas in Houston, a breakfast address to the Fort Worth Chamber of Commerce on Friday morning, then a short hop to neighboring Dallas. In the embryonic stage, the Texas trip had been discussed as a one-day whirlwind affair, and as such, no motorcade had been planned for Dallas due to the shortage of time. Even in its final form, of the forty-seven items on the official itinerary, only six had to do with the Dallas stop. These were:

11:35 a.m. Arrive Dallas—Love Field
11:45 a.m. Leave airport—car
12:30 p.m. Arrive Trade Mart—Luncheon—Dallas Citizens Council
2:00 p.m. Leave Trade Mart—car
2:30 p.m. Arrive Love Field
2:35 p.m. Leave Love Field

The preparation for the three hours in Dallas would be painstaking and thorough, even though it was the sort of movement the president made routinely in any city he visited anywhere in the country. Jerry Behn, after his initial meeting with Ken O'Donnell, started the usual Secret Service procedure. The field offices in Texas were put on notice. Advance agents were assigned from the White House Detail to each segment of the trip. The Dallas advance became the job of Special Agent Winston Lawson.

Movements involving both the president and the vice president did not require duplication by both Secret Service details, so the advance work was left primarily to the White House Detail. In the meantime, while Win Lawson and others were preparing for the Texas trip, the Vice Presidential Detail had an advance of its own. LBJ, who had already done more traveling than any vice president before him, was scheduled to tour the Benelux countries—Belgium, the Netherlands, and Luxembourg—beginning on November 3. This was to be Stu Knight's last trip as head of the detail, as he had requested a transfer back to a headquarters unit, Special Investigations. A memo from Chief Rowley confirmed the transfer and announced my moving up—again—to the post of SAIC of the Vice Presidential Detail. Stu's transfer and my promotion were to become effective Monday, November 25.

The Benelux trip went smoothly, with the exception of a bomb threat at the Brussels airport while *Air Force Two* was en route. Like most such threats, it proved to be false, and we were back in Washington on November 9. The following week, Roy Kellerman, one of Jerry Behn's top assistants on the White House Detail, called and asked me to meet him in his office.

Roy had overall charge of the Texas trip, and he wanted to talk about our participation, and especially about the security arrangements at the final stop, the LBJ Ranch. He wanted to have an agent from the White House Detail familiarized with the ranch, and when I flew to Texas on November 18, Special Agent Bob Burke went along as their advance agent to the ranch.

Win Lawson, in the meantime, was in Dallas attending to the infinite details preparatory to the three hours the president was scheduled to be there. A presidential trip is as carefully planned and rehearsed as is a Broadway opening. Lawson's work began even before he left Washington. One of his first jobs had been to conduct a search of the files within the Protective Research Section, where dossiers are kept on thousands of individuals who have, in some manner, indicated they might be a potential threat to the security of the president. Such people come to the attention of the Secret Service in numerous ways, the most common being the U.S. mail. The president received thousands of letters every week. The vast majority were entirely innocent insofar as showing any violent hostility in the writer. But there was a residue of threatening mail that required actual investigation. There were also threatening phone calls to the White House, and often a mentally disturbed individual would appear at one of the White House gates or would be caught trying to climb the fence. Many of these people were found to have some mental imbalance that made it necessary that they be committed to an institution or at least that a file be kept on them in the Protective Research Section.

Information on possibly dangerous individuals also reached the files from field offices, from reports from other governmental agencies, like the FBI and the CIA or even the U.S. Postal Service such as the report on Richard Pavlick that came from a postal inspector, as well as from the thousands of nonfederal law enforcement agencies all across the country.

In addition to the general files, there was a file of higher priority that was maintained on individuals who were considered definite security risks and whose movements were unpredictable. Albums containing photographs and other identifying information on these people were kept in the offices of the White House Detail and were required reading for all agents.

At Lawson's request, the Protective Research Section's files were searched. This search revealed that there were no known individuals in the Dallas area who posed a direct threat to the president. Lawson then moved on to Dallas to continue the security preparations for the November 22 visit.

A political advance man, Jack Puterbaugh, flew to Dallas with Lawson on November 12. The following day, they met with Forrest Sorrels, the SAIC of the Dallas Field Office. Sorrels had been advised, as early as November 4, to inspect three potential sites for a luncheon at which the president would speak. These were the Trade Mart, Market Hall, and the Women's Building at the state fairgrounds. Market Hall, directly across Industrial Boulevard from the Trade Mart, was not available, thus narrowing the choice to two.

Sorrels reported that the Trade Mart posed considerable security problems, as there were three floors above the courtyard where the luncheon would be held, and that each of these floors had two suspended bridges, balconies around all four sides, and dozens of entrances. The fairgrounds site, on the other hand, was ideal from a security point of view, but it was low-ceilinged, had many supporting beams, and in general was an unattractive place for the intended purpose.

Lawson went over both locations with Sorrels, and although the easy security of the fairgrounds building would have simplified Secret Service problems during the luncheon, it was agreed that the Trade Mart would be recommended. With enough manpower, the building could be made secure.

The route from Love Field to the Trade Mart now had to be established. The itinerary called for a forty-five-minute motorcade—from 11:45 a.m. to 12:30 p.m. Lawson and Sorrels mapped out a tentative route of approximately ten miles, in compliance with White House specifications, which would take the president through areas of greatest exposure to the largest number of people. On November 18, the two Secret Service men, along with Dallas Assistant Police Chief Charles Batchelor, made a survey drive over the route. They discussed police requirements at intersections, details of crowd control, and the policing of underpasses and overpasses. The route appeared to be ideal, both in maximum public exposure and in meeting the time requirements.

Lawson advised the White House of the final routing. It was approved and released to the press. On November 20, the details of the motorcade route were published in both Dallas newspapers.

As in any city, there were hundreds of buildings and thousands of windows along the ten-mile route. Any kind of effective security check of all the buildings overlooking the motorcade was obviously impossible. Even if such an inspection had been feasible, it would have required that the buildings be sealed and guarded and not reopened until the president was safely passed. No such effort was made.

The FBI brought two pieces of information to Lawson's attention. One was intelligence of a possible problem with pickets; the other was a circular patterned after the WANTED posters seen on post office bulletin boards. Beneath two photographs of President Kennedy, one full face, one profile, were the words WANTED FOR TREASON, followed by seven accusations:

1. Betraying the Constitution (which he swore to uphold). He is turning the sovereignty of the U.S. over to the Communist-controlled United Nations. He is betraying our friends (Cuba, Katanga, Portugal) and befriending our enemies (Russia, Yugoslavia, Poland).

2. He has been WRONG on innumerable issues affecting the security of the U.S. (United Nations—Berlin Wall—Missile removal—Cuba—Wheat deals—Test Ban Treaty, etc.).

3. He has been lax in enforcing Communist-registration laws.

4. He has given support and encouragement to the Communist-inspired racial riots.

5. He has illegally invaded a sovereign state with federal troops.

6. He has consistently appointed anti-Christians to federal office: Upholds the Supreme Court in its anti-Christian rulings. Aliens and known Communists abound in federal offices.

7. He has been caught in fantastic LIES to the American people (including personal ones like his previous marriage and divorce).

The source of these handbills had not been discovered by the time the president arrived in Dallas. The author was later found to be a thirty-eight-year-old printing salesman, Robert A. Surrey, who was an associate of General Edwin Walker, a controversial and voluble right-winger who was a Dallas resident.

There were many other indications that the mood of Dallas was not what one might have wished it to be for a presidential visit, but certainly nothing sufficient to question the advisability of the trip.

There was one individual living and working in Dallas at the time whose name was in the files of the FBI and who had been interviewed and investigated by FBI agents because of a period of defection to the Soviet Union. However, the criteria for bringing this man to the attention of the Secret Service did not exist since he had never indicated any presidential interest. He remained in the background with hundreds of thousands of other Dallas citizens. His name was Lee Harvey Oswald.

Three days before the joint visit, Vice President Johnson addressed a bottlers' convention at Market Hall in Dallas, then returned to the ranch to await the arrival of the president. Jerry Kivett had advanced this brief trip, and I instructed him to stay in Dallas and work with Win Lawson in coordinating our activities for the November 22 visit.

In San Antonio, Houston, Fort Worth, Dallas, and Austin, the various Secret Service advance units were pulling together all the strings that would, hopefully, make the events of the upcoming two days mesh with the ease of precision gears. The weather seemed to be the only problem standing in the way of the trip's success. It had begun to rain the morning LBJ went to Dallas for the bottlers' convention, and by Wednesday, November 20, it still showed little sign of letting up.

On Thursday, we flew to San Antonio to meet the president—LBJ, Lady Bird, Liz Carpenter, Marie Fehmer, and myself in Johnson's Beechcraft piloted by Dale Meeks.

A huge crowd was on hand long before the scheduled 1:30 p.m. arrival of *Air Force One,* and for the first time in two days, the weather had taken a turn for the better. Right on schedule, the big blue-and-white jet touched down on the runway and taxied into position for the boarding ramp.

Vice President Johnson, Lady Bird, Governor and Mrs. Connally, and a number of other dignitaries made up the reception committee. The ramp was positioned at the door of the plane, the door opened, and two Air Force guards came quickly and took their positions on either side at the foot of the ramp. Jackie Kennedy stepped from inside the plane, smiling, and the crowd went wild. The president emerged out of the shadow of the plane's interior and the roar doubled. If there had been any lingering question about how he would be received on Texas soil, this settled it.

After the airport greeting, the motorcade moved out toward the Aerospace Medical Health Center, and, after a speech there by the president, continued on to Kelly Air Force Base, where the planes had been moved in the interim. The weeks of advance work were paying off as the entourage moved on to Houston and another motorcade into the city to the Rice Hotel. At 10:30 p.m. Thursday night, after the testimonial dinner for Congressman Albert Thomas at Houston Coliseum, the three jets—*Air Force One, Air Force Two,* and the chartered press plane—made a forty-five-minute flight to Fort Worth and the final motorcade of a motorcade-filled day. It was now close to midnight. A light drizzle was falling as the cars lined up for the ride into the city. It was reasonable to assume that only a few hardy souls would be out to watch the president go by, but this was not the case. Thousands of umbrellas and more thousands of bare heads lined the route into Fort Worth. Above the noise of the police motorcycles, I heard cries alongside the streets as our car passed— *"There's Lyndon!" "God bless you, Lady Bird!"*

By the time we reached the Texas Hotel, the lobby was packed and the crowd was spilling over into the streets. LBJ's grin, as we pried him through the happy crowd, told me that the Texas trip, all the prophets of gloom notwithstanding, was blossoming into a huge success.

Friday, November 22, dawned gray, but less threatening than the weather had been earlier in the week. Shortly after eight o'clock, the president, accompanied by LBJ, Connally, and others, went outside the hotel to a parking lot where he addressed a group of people who had not been able to get tickets to the Chamber of Commerce breakfast. When some of the crowd good-naturedly called for Jackie to put in an appearance, the president got a laugh when he replied, "Mrs. Kennedy is organizing herself. It takes her longer, but of course, she looks better than we do when she does it."

After the breakfast speech and a short rest, President and Mrs. Kennedy, the Johnsons, and the entire party started the day's movement with a motorcade to Carswell Air Force Base. Ahead of us lay Dallas, then Austin for the big fundraising dinner, and finally to Johnson City and the LBJ Ranch that night. Optimism abounded. San Antonio, Houston, and Fort Worth had turned out better than expected. Even the skies were beginning to clear. It promised to be a good day.

CHAPTER 7

Dallas

The rain had stopped and the sun was shining sporadically through the scattering clouds. The three airplanes were loaded and ready for the short hop from Carswell Air Force Base to Love Field. The official Texas highway map lists Fort Worth and Dallas as being thirty-one miles apart, but in reality the suburbs of one merge into the suburbs of the other. The possibility of moving to Dallas by automobile had been considered when the weather had seemed uncertain, but that alternative had been discarded, and now the three big jets moved along the taxi strips while all other air traffic in the area came to a temporary halt, as required when the president's aircraft is arriving or departing an airport.

The press plane was first off so that the reporters might be on hand to record the arrival of the other two. *Air Force Two* followed, climbing steeply over Lake Worth at the north end of the runway and banking to the right toward Dallas, which was already visible through the haze to the east. *Air Force One* followed minutes later.

It was a low-altitude flight, necessitated by the short distance to be covered. The Boeing 707s, designed for efficient operation at high altitude, scarcely reached seven thousand feet on the commuter-length run before beginning the descent into Love Field. They moved at slow speeds, rocking and yawing cumbersomely in the turbulence above small communities and open spaces on the semicircular swing.

The skies had almost cleared as we touched down at Dallas. It would be ideal weather for the motorcade into the city. At least it would be ideal from the political point of view, conducive for a large turnout of the citizenry. The Secret Service would have settled for rain, accompanied by high winds—anything to keep the people off the streets and behind closed doors and windows. It was not that we did not want the good people of Dallas to see their president; we did—on their television sets in the comfort of their living rooms.

The plane turned off the runway and began to make its way across the maze of taxiways toward the reception area near the terminal building. Special Agent Lem Johns peered out, squinting against the Texas sun.

"Good crowd," he said without enthusiasm.

"Wonderful crowd!" beamed one of the Texas congressmen. "Absolutely wonderful!" He slapped Lem on the shoulder. "Texas size!"

The plane stopped, the ramp was rolled into position, and the door swung open. I walked down with the two Air Force guards, and then Lady Bird and Vice President Johnson stepped out into the sunshine. The crowd roared, and the Johnsons came down the steps, smiling and waving, then went down the reception line of a dozen or so dignitaries, headed by Dallas Mayor Earl E. Cabell. The reception was hearty and warm, even though LBJ had seen many of the welcomers only three days before at the bottlers' convention. Beyond a low chain-link fence, along which were posted Dallas police officers and Secret Service agents, the crowd continued to wave and yell.

But they had not turned out to see only Lyndon Johnson. Now the attention of the crowd and the dignitaries alike was drawn to the graceful blue-and-white *Air Force One,* just settling on the distant runway. It was the only aircraft moving across the vast expanse of the usually bustling airport. On taxi strips and in assigned traffic patterns over the surrounding countryside, the normal flow of airliners and private planes waited for the signal to resume operations, impatient to continue on their way.

Jerry Kivett, who had stayed in Dallas to work with the White House advance group, joined us. "Everything's set, Rufe." He nodded toward the line of cars to be used for the motorcade. "That Lincoln convertible is the vice president's car."

Win Lawson paused briefly to confirm that we did not require any assistance, then we all moved to our assigned positions as Colonel Jim Swindal, the pilot of *Air Force One,* brought the plane to a gentle halt. There was a momentary quiet as the engines ceased their whine and the crowd took a deep breath for its greeting to the Kennedys. The ramp was placed in position and the Air Force guards came down and took their posts, standing stiffly at attention.

The Johnsons had not been billed as the stars of the day, and now the stars appeared. Jackie emerged first from the darkness of the cabin into the sunlight in the pink suit and box hat that would later be described in newspapers and newscasts the world over. The silence was shattered as the crowd found its voice, and then President Kennedy stepped out and stood beside his wife, both smiling, the president fingering his tie in an unconsciously characteristic movement.

Lem Johns, Woody Taylor, and I had moved Vice President Johnson and Lady Bird to the foot of the ramp while the Kennedys were accepting the adulation of the crowd. The young couple came down the steps for the official greeting, Jackie accepting a dozen red roses, while the president properly admired two charcoal portraits presented to him, then passed them on to the waiting hands of an aide for safekeeping.

President Kennedy was obviously pleased with the turnout and the enthusiasm of the crowd. When the welcoming ritual was over, he took Jackie's arm and moved impulsively toward the fence. Hundreds of eager arms stretched out, straining to touch President Kennedy and the First Lady. The Johnsons followed a few yards behind, speaking to friends in the crowd, shaking hands. Woody, Lem, Jerry, and I kept close. The closer the principal is to the crowd, the closer the Secret Service sticks to the principal. Roy Kellerman, Clint Hill, and other agents of the White House Detail were doing the same thing ahead of us, scanning the faces, watching for anything that might appear out of the ordinary.

The crowd was going wild, and in the crush to get within touching distance of the president, the pressure was more than the fence could withstand. It began to buckle, and it probably would have collapsed entirely if alert agents and police officers had not moved quickly to counteract the press of the crowd until after the Kennedys had passed.

The crowd was not entirely friendly. There were some demonstrators, but they were of the silent type, placards instead of catcalls. Beyond the rows of well-wishers, a number of handmade signs bobbed up and down for attention: HELP KENNEDY STAMP OUT DEMOCRACY, YOU'RE A TRAITOR, and others of the same tone. We had expected this. In fact, we had expected more than we saw.

President Kennedy had read the crowd from the moment he had stepped out onto the ramp, and he was in no hurry to break off this personal contact. He continued down the fence—talking, laughing, shaking or just touching hands, signing autographs—and then as he seemed about to make his way back to the car, the pleas of those who had failed to touch him brought him back for more.

I glanced at my watch. We were slightly behind schedule, but this was why they had come to Texas, and the schedule was not that inflexible. Politicians on purely political missions do not consult their watches in the same manner that Secret Service agents do. Their timing is set by the political advantage or disadvantage of the moment. If the airport crowd had been unexpectedly small, or surly, the motorcade would already have been well on its way toward the Trade Mart. As it was, the president was not ready to go, and the cars would stay where they were until he was ready. The motorcade could wait a few more minutes.

Special Agent Bill Greer, assigned to drive the president's car, eased the big parade limousine forward slowly so that the Kennedys would not have to walk back when they reached the end of the fence. Then, with a final wave, Jackie and the president broke away from the crowd and went to the car. Roy Kellerman held the door for the president as he got in and took his seat. Jackie sat in the rear seat to her husband's left, Governor and Mrs. Connally took the jump seats, and when Kellerman saw that the passengers were all in their places, he climbed into the front alongside Bill Greer.

The limousine, by Secret Service designation, *SS 100X*, was a seven-passenger Lincoln convertible, with certain special adaptations for its particular purpose. It had been tagged the "Bubbletop" by the press because of the bubble-like removable Plexiglas canopy designed to protect its occupants from inclement weather while leaving them visible to the public. Under the clear Texas sky, the bubbletop was stowed in the trunk, leaving those in the car completely exposed to the crowds. It was a situation the Secret Service had deplored for years, to no avail. The Plexiglas canopy, at best, would cause little more than the slight deflection of a high-velocity bullet, and offered no protection at all against a bomb.

Directly behind the president's limousine was his Secret Service follow-up car, an open Cadillac dubbed the *Queen Mary*. In it were Special Agents Sam Kinney, who was driving; Emory Roberts; Paul Landis; Jack Ready; Clint Hill; Tim McIntyre; Glen Bennett; and George Hickey; plus two Kennedy staffers, Dave Powers and Ken O'Donnell.

The vice president's Lincoln was next in line, with Senator Ralph Yarborough on the left side of the rear seat, Lady Bird in the middle, and LBJ on the right, directly behind me.

In our follow-up car were Special Agents Lem Johns, Jerry Kivett, and Woody Taylor, along with LBJ staffer Cliff Carter and the driver, Joe Rich, a Texas highway patrolman.

The president was ready to go. Roy Kellerman, over our short-wave radio network, gave the order to move out. Ahead of us, the *Queen Mary* began to roll. I nodded to our driver, Texas highway patrolman Hurchel Jacks, and he touched the accelerator and eased forward.

The motorcade was on the move: twenty-two cars, three buses, plus numerous Dallas police motorcycles—a caravan half a mile long when strung out. The lead car, driven by Dallas Police Chief Jesse Curry and carrying agents Win Lawson and Forrest Sorrels, eased through an opening in the fence and snaked through the airport complex. My watch read 11:55 a.m., approximately ten minutes behind schedule, as we turned left onto Mockingbird Lane and were on our way into Dallas.

As we made a right turn onto Lemmon Avenue, the crowd grew thicker with each passing block. The route had been laid out so that the people would have no trouble finding a spot to watch President and Mrs. Kennedy go by.

The official itinerary had stated it simply: *"The motorcade is taking a longer route than necessary to the Trade Mart where the luncheon is being held to afford the people of Dallas a chance to see the President."*

At the intersection of Lemmon and Lomo Alto Drive, we made our first unscheduled stop. A group of children was frantically waving a long, crudely lettered banner: MR. PRESIDENT, PLEASE STOP AND SHAKE OUR HANDS. The bright little Texan who came up with that idea knew what he was doing; it caught Kennedy's eye, and he called to Bill Greer to stop. Kellerman radioed advice of the stop to the rest of the motorcade, and cars bearing Vice President Johnson, a senator, several congressmen, police, newsmen, and assorted aides came to a standstill in the middle of Lemmon Avenue while President Kennedy got out of his car and waded into the throng of delighted kids.

The stop was brief, and an even briefer one was made at the corner of Reagan, half a dozen blocks later, where Kennedy, without getting out, exchanged a few words with a nun presiding over another cluster of children.

Lem Johns radioed me from our follow-up car that even with these two stops we were now only five minutes behind schedule. I passed the information back to LBJ, who was always interested in such matters.

We reached Turtle Creek Boulevard where we swung right off Lemmon, then angled left onto Cedar Springs Road and left again onto Harwood. On the map, we were moving obliquely away from our destination, but now we made a hard right onto Main Street, the Dallas jail looming to our left on the southeast corner, and we began to lessen the distance to the Trade Mart.

The time was 12:21 p.m. We were in the heart of downtown Dallas and the crowds were huge. People leaned out of office windows, confetti rained down, and a shout from half a dozen feet away would have been drowned out by the steady roar of the crowd. On several occasions, Clint Hill and Jack Ready dropped from their positions on the running boards of the presidential follow-up car and jogged forward to their assigned posts at the left and right rear of the president's limousine.

Normally, a motorcycle escort would ride to the right and left of the president's car, but Kennedy did not like the noise, or the fact that this obscured him somewhat from the crowd, so the officers had been instructed to fall back. This, in turn, provided an obstacle for Jack Ready in moving forward to take his position on the rear bumper step just behind the president.

The motorcade crawled along Main Street, often almost brought to a standstill by the crowds overflowing from the sidewalks. Several times I pushed my door open at a forty-five-degree angle, which is an effective method of fending people away from the side of a car. This was as much for the protection of the public as the protection of the vice president. A Lincoln limousine rolling over a foot can be a painful experience, as more than one Secret Service agent can attest to from personal experience.

It took eight minutes to go the length of Main Street. At 12:29 we passed between the Criminal Court and the Old Courthouse Buildings and turned right onto Houston. The smell of burning rubber permeated the air because of the necessity of the motorcycle police having to ride their clutches at such slow speeds.

The heaviest congestion was now behind us, and with only a short distance to Stemmons Freeway, we were almost through with the parade route, as a freeway is a poor place for a crowd to gather.

As we swung onto Houston, Dealey Plaza lay to our left, with reflecting pools and peristyles on both sides where Main Street split the plaza, and pergolas spread wider along the streets that converged below the plaza to pass beneath the triple railroad underpass at the bottom of an incline.

We were now approaching the final turn that would take us down the incline and into the cloverleaf that would swing us onto the freeway and to the Trade Mart.

Lem's voice came over my radio. "Five minutes to the Trade Mart."

I acknowledged and passed the information back to the vice president. Ahead, as I scanned the many faces in the windows of the Texas School Book Depository, I noticed the time on a large sign atop the building: 12:30 p.m., which I probably took note of only because that was our scheduled time of arrival at the Trade Mart.

The lead car had already made the acute left turn onto Elm Street in front of the depository. The president's limousine slowed as Bill Greer negotiated the turn. The turn's sharpness made it clumsy for such a large vehicle, but now the car was around, and Greer straightened and began the glide down the incline, slowly picking up momentum.

The follow-up car completed its turn, and Hurchel Jacks turned the wheel of our car. The crowds along either side were spread thinly over the grassy slopes of the plaza. Here, it was more on the order of individuals or small clumps of people, a man with a camera to the right, one on the left holding a child up to see the president. The Kennedys were acknowledging the accolades here as warmly as they had those of the thousands along Main Street. We had straightened on Elm now and were beginning to move easily down the incline in the wake of the cars ahead.

Suddenly, there was an explosive noise—distinct, sharp, resounding. Nothing that could be mistaken for the incessant popping and backfiring of the motorcycles, but in the instant I heard it, I could not be certain if it had been a firecracker, bullet, bomb, or some other explosive. I looked around quickly and saw nothing to indicate its source.

But the movements in the president's car were not normal. Kennedy seemed to be falling to his left, and there was sudden movement among the agents in the car directly ahead of us. I turned instinctively in my seat and with my left hand I grasped Lyndon Johnson's right shoulder, and with all the leverage I could exert from a sitting position, I forced him downward.

"Get down!" I shouted. *"Get down!"*

Vice President Johnson reacted immediately. Still not seeing the source of the explosion, I swung across the seat back and sat on top of him. There were two more explosions in rapid succession, only seconds after the first. From my crouched position I saw a grayish blur in the air above the right side of the president's car. George Hickey, standing in the follow-up car just ahead of us, was poised with the AR-15 rifle, swinging back toward the building we had just passed. People along the sides of the street were scattering in panic.

There were shouts from ahead, then the cars in front of us lurched forward toward the underpass. I yelled to our driver, Jacks, "Stay with them, and keep close!" Then I radioed back to Kivett in our follow-up car. "I'm switching to Charlie frequency!" We had been alternately using two frequencies, and the instant I flicked the switch to the primary channel I heard urgent transmission.

"*Halfback* (code name for the presidential follow-up car; this was Emory Roberts's voice)! *Halfback* to Lawson! The president's been hit! Get us to a hospital, fast but safe!"

We roared through the underpass, Vice President Johnson half on, half off the seat, sprawled uncomfortably under my weight. Lady Bird and Yarborough were crouched low beside us. I could see an agent spread-eagled across the trunk of the president's car.

"What's happened, Rufus?" Johnson asked. "Where are we going?"

Yarborough, huddled on the left of the seat, echoed the questions.

"The president must have been shot or wounded, sir," I replied. "We're being directed to a hospital."

"*Shot!*" someone said. "*Oh my God!*"

"I haven't heard anything about his condition or any details other than Roberts saying the president was hit," I said. "I want everybody to stay down until we find out what this is all about!"

"All right, Rufus," I heard Johnson say.

Jacks was an expert driver, tight-lipped and cool behind the wheel. We had roared up the cloverleaf, the wind whipping through the open car, and now we were almost bumper to bumper with the presidential follow-up car, speeding along Stemmons Freeway at seventy to eighty miles an hour.

I heard Emory Roberts call back to our follow-up car, apparently thinking I was still operating on the secondary frequency. "Tell Rufus to keep his man down! Keep him covered!"

I broke in as Kivett started to reply. "He's down and covered!" Then I leaned down toward the vice president. "When we get to the hospital, I want you and Mrs. Johnson to stick with me and the other agents as close as you can. We don't know the extent of the emergency in the president's car, but it may be necessary for you to be acting president." I had to shout against the noise of the wind and the wail of dozens of sirens from front and rear. "We are going into the hospital, and we aren't gonna stop for anything or anybody. Do you understand? We will separate from the other party the moment we stop!"

"Okay, pardner, I understand."

I shifted my weight to lessen the pressure on him, still keeping my body over him and holding him below window level. For all I—or anyone else— knew, whatever had happened could be part of a widespread conspiracy. Even the route we were taking to the hospital was entirely predictable. Simply because the explosions were behind us did not necessarily mean that there could not be more at any moment.

The speeding motorcade had swung off the freeway now and a sign loomed on the roadside: PARKLAND MEMORIAL HOSPITAL. I recalled from the map of the motorcade route that this was off Harry Hines Boulevard, beyond our intended destination, the Trade Mart.

Jacks was braking. The car decelerated rapidly and our momentum pushed both the vice president and myself hard against the seat back.

"Get ready," I said, "we're almost there."

"You ready, Bird?" Johnson said to his wife.

"I'm ready."

The car lurched to a halt. Sirens all around were winding down; people were shouting instructions and moving quickly from the cars ahead of us toward an entrance marked EMERGENCY CASES ONLY. I grabbed the door handle; Woody Taylor and Jerry Kivett, who had apparently hit the ground running before our follow-up car stopped rolling, were already along- side us, and Tim McIntyre and Glen Bennett were running back from the presidential follow-up car.

There was a moment's frustration as Jerry and I were apparently work- ing against each other on the inside and outside door handles, then we had the door open, and surrounding Vice President Johnson and Lady Bird, we rushed them headlong into the building.

Emory Roberts had preceded us and was holding a hurried conversation with a nurse as we moved quickly down the corridor, the vice president twist- ing and rubbing his shoulder to get the kinks out.

The nurse indicated a doorway across the hall and Emory motioned for us. As we went in, I stationed Glen Bennett at the door. "Nobody comes in here unless you know who he is and you know he's got a damn good reason to be here!"

It was a large room, divided into small treatment areas, each with an examination table and a chair, with a white, sheetlike curtain to offer privacy. In one cubicle, a nurse was attending to a patient, and both of them had turned to stare in amazement at this sudden massive intrusion.

I instructed Jerry Kivett to have them moved as we continued farther into the room until we reached a corner. There was a window that, surprisingly, looked out into the entranceway where we had just come in through the emergency ambulance bays. Woody Taylor closed the window blinds.

"I'm sticking to you like glue," I told Vice President Johnson. "We're staying right here until we find out what's happened."

Emory Roberts joined us. He had seen President Kennedy as the agents and hospital attendants had been getting him out of the car. "It looks bad," Emory said flatly. "Both President Kennedy and Governor Connally have suffered gunshot wounds. I don't know the governor's condition, but I have seen the president, and I don't believe he can make it."

I turned to Johnson. "We should leave here immediately and get you back to Washington. We don't know whether or not this is some kind of conspiracy, and until we know what's happening, the White House is the safest place for you."

Emory and I were in complete agreement on this point, but LBJ was shaking his head even before I finished speaking.

"No. It would be unthinkable for me to leave with President Kennedy's life hanging in the balance."

He understood our point of view and we understood his.

His prevailed. We would have to wait. Meanwhile, several people had been passed through Glen Bennett's checkpoint at the door. Cliff Carter had joined Vice President Johnson, as had Congressmen Jack Brooks and Homer Thornberry. Thornberry was a particularly close friend of Johnson's, and I heard Johnson say to him, "This is a time for prayer, Homer, if ever there was one."

Emory's statement that he did not believe Kennedy could make it meant that LBJ might become president at any moment—if he had not already. While their father was vice president, the Johnson daughters did not receive Secret Service protection. If he became president, they would get this protection. We needed to assign men to them as quickly as possible. I asked Mrs. Johnson for their precise whereabouts and then told Jerry Kivett to inform headquarters and arrange protection for them at once.

As Jerry hurried out, Vice President Johnson motioned to me. "Rufus, would it be all right if Mrs. Johnson and I went to see Mrs. Kennedy and Mrs. Connally?"

"No, sir," I said emphatically. "We don't want you out of this room until we're ready to leave the hospital."

He did not question this, but he added, "Can Mrs. Johnson go to them?"

"Yes, sir, that will be all right."

Lady Bird and Jack Brooks went out, accompanied by two agents. I continued to press Johnson for a decision to leave the hospital, if not for Washington, at least to the airplane. He remained adamant about staying put until there was some definite word on President Kennedy's condition. We discussed moving *Air Force One* to Carswell Air Force Base in nearby Fort Worth on the assumption that the military base would inherently be a more secure location than Love Field. This was discarded as entailing too long a drive. Additional security was ordered for the plane at its present location while it was being fueled for the inevitable cross-country flight to Washington.

Lem Johns joined us in the hospital room. He had been momentarily stranded in Dealey Plaza when he had tried to run from our follow-up car and had failed to reach the Lincoln before we accelerated. He had gotten a ride in a press car, and now Lem and I discussed with LBJ the plan for evacuation to Love Field when the time came.

"Get two unmarked cars," I told Lem, "with drivers who can move around this city blindfolded. When we leave, we don't want any hesitation, and if we have to take back streets, we want drivers who know them."

This was Lem's cup of tea. If you sent Lem Johns for a glass of water in the middle of the Sahara, he would be back in ten minutes with a pitcher and two glasses. I knew the cars were as good as there.

In the meantime, Emory Roberts had been reporting back to us on the president's condition. Each report was less encouraging than the one preceding it. At approximately 1:15 p.m., Roy Kellerman and Ken O'Donnell came into the room. Their faces conveyed the message even before O'Donnell spoke.

"He's gone" was all he said, and Roy could only nod.

Emory came back in with the same message, but he saw at once that it had already been delivered.

"Sir, we *must* leave here immediately!" I said to Johnson. President Kennedy's life was no longer hanging in the balance. The reason for staying at the hospital no longer existed.

"I can't leave without Mrs. Kennedy," Johnson replied.

O'Donnell said, "She won't leave without the body. A casket has been ordered, but it isn't here yet."

"We can wait for her on the plane," I said. O'Donnell agreed that Johnson should go to *Air Force One* at once. Months later, amid all the sniping and second-guessing, Johnson was criticized for "usurping" the presidential aircraft. What these critics chose to ignore was the simple fact that *Air Force One*—or to more correctly identify the plane in question, Number 26000—had superior communications capabilities that were absolutely essential in the uncertain conditions that prevailed at the time. Lyndon Johnson *was* president, even though the formality of the swearing in had not yet taken place. As president, his duty to the country was to take every possible measure to ensure the safety of the nation. In Dallas, *Air Force One* was an extension of the White House, and as Johnson said himself, he saw nothing strange about the president using the president's plane.

Johnson agreed now that it was time to leave the hospital. As I sent an agent out to alert the drivers that we were coming out shortly, Assistant Press Secretary Malcolm Kilduff came into the room.

"Mr. President," he said. He was the first to address him by the title, and there was a flicker of surprise on Johnson's face as Kilduff went on. "Mr. President, I have to announce the death of President Kennedy. Is it all right with you if the public announcement is made now?"

Johnson glanced quickly at me. Apparently his thoughts were the same as mine, for without asking me, he turned back to Kilduff.

"For security reasons, I think you had better wait until we leave the hospital," he said.

"And we're leaving now," I told Kilduff. We moved out quickly, turning left in the corridor past the nurses' triage desk, then left again to follow the red center stripe down the bustling corridor and out through the ambulance bays.

There were two unmarked automobiles waiting. Police Chief Jesse Curry was at the wheel of the lead car. I opened the rear door and assisted Johnson in. "Keep down below window level, sir," I said as I climbed in with him, taking the right side of the seat, normally occupied by the president or vice president, as an added security measure.

Homer Thornberry got into the front. I looked back, saw that Woody Taylor and Jerry Kivett were getting into the second car with Lady Bird and Jack Brooks, and told Curry, "Let's go!"

The car slid quickly from the curb, moving down the narrow drive toward the street. Cars were jammed into every available parking place.

Ahead, I recognized Congressman Albert Thomas as he stepped between two parked cars. He had apparently recognized Thornberry in the front seat and was flagging him down.

"Keep going," I instructed Curry. But Johnson saw him now and countermanded my order.

"Stop and let him in. It's all right."

Curry obeyed, and Thomas slid into the front seat alongside Thornberry. I do not think he saw Johnson until he was getting in.

"Hurry up, Albert!" Johnson said. "Close the door!"

The car lunged ahead and Johnson told Thornberry to climb across into the back. I motioned for him to sit by the left window so that we would have Johnson sandwiched between us. There was another brief halt as we were confronted by a delivery truck headed toward us on the narrow and crowded drive. Curry made his way around it, out of the hospital complex, picked up a couple of motorcycles as escorts, and headed for Love Field.

Throughout the entire time, I had carried my shoulder-strap walkie-talkie radio, and now I raised *Air Force One* on it and advised the personnel that we would be arriving shortly.

"About two minutes," Curry called back to me.

"Two minutes," I repeated. "And we're coming up the ramp in a hurry."

One of the motorcycle officers ahead of us had begun to sound his siren, and I quickly told Curry to have him stop. Unlike the trip into Dallas from Love Field, we had no desire to attract attention. I felt that if we could get through the next few minutes, then conspiracy or no conspiracy, we would have Lyndon Johnson in a secure situation.

We reached the outskirts of the airport, Chief Curry threaded the car smoothly through the airport maze, and suddenly there before us was one of the most welcome sights I had ever seen—the big, gleaming blue-and-white jet, with UNITED STATES OF AMERICA painted along the fuselage above the long row of windows and the number 26000 gracing the tall rudder.

The car slid to a halt at the foot of the ramp, with Mrs. Johnson's car pulling up directly behind us. I opened the car door and went up the steps, almost running, with LBJ. Lady Bird, the congressmen, Jerry, Woody, and other agents followed. The interior of the plane was stiflingly hot. But it was secure. I had one final thought of security—a sniper atop one of the airport buildings could conceivably get a shot at LBJ through the plane's windows.

"Jerry, Woody," I said, "let's get all the shades pulled!"

Physically, of course, we were still in Dallas. But *Air Force One*, no matter where it is, is a nerve ending of the White House, a miniaturized outpost. For the first time since the shots rang out across Dealey Plaza, I felt reasonably comfortable about Lyndon Johnson's security.

I looked at my watch. It was slightly past 1:40 p.m., only an hour and ten minutes since the President of the United States had been assassinated.

CHAPTER 8

The Flight Home

In the more secure environment of the presidential aircraft, the impact of what had taken place now seemed to settle in. A stream of cars began converging on Love Field, some carrying people who would be indispensable to Lyndon Johnson in the crucial hours to come, some who came because everyone else seemed headed in that direction.

The original passenger manifest of *Air Force One* was meaningless. There was no definitive list of who would now be returning to the capital aboard this plane or the backup plane—formerly *Air Force Two*—or come later by other means. The business of the nation was uppermost, the effective continuation of the presidency with a minimum of slack. For this, Johnson needed immediate and close contact not only with members of his own staff but with the key figures who had surrounded John Kennedy.

In our effort to maintain the tightest security, and, at the same time, make Johnson accessible to those he needed aboard, I stationed Secret Service agents at the ramps of the plane along with the usual Air Force guards. If there was a question of admittance, they were to check with me.

I continued to stick close by Johnson's side. Emory Roberts, who had been in charge of the duty shift that day for the White House Detail, had informed the pilot and others of the plane's crew that the aircraft was not to be moved unless the decision to do so had been cleared with me. This was not to say the decision itself rested in my hands, but as the SAIC of the Johnson Detail, it was my job to make absolutely certain that any movements met with his approval.

In the flood of printed and spoken comment that filled the days, months, and years that followed, there were statements to the effect that Secret Service men were "switching allegiance" almost before President Kennedy was rushed into the emergency room at Parkland. Nothing could have been further from the truth. The agents in Dallas did not have allegiance, in this sense, to an individual. Their allegiance was to the mission itself. John Kennedy was dead. He was beyond the protective efforts of the Secret Service.

As of the time we boarded the plane, we had not heard the name of Lee Harvey Oswald. The possibility that the death of John Kennedy was part of a far-ranging conspiracy that had not yet run its course was very real indeed and was in the thoughts of everyone—especially in the thoughts of the Secret Service. We did not know what we might yet encounter, but we knew that Lyndon Johnson was the president, and our mission of presidential protection was no less clearly defined simply because he had not yet taken the oath of office.

After boarding the plane, one of the first things LBJ did was to decline the use of the presidential quarters. My orders were clear: "I want this kept strictly for the use of Mrs. Kennedy, Rufus. See to that."

Forward of this suite aboard the plane was a stateroom that served as an office and sitting room for the president. It was the width of the plane and contained a chair, desk, a large worktable, sofas, and a television set. I walked into the crowded compartment with Johnson, a simple act that would have caused no stir whatever if it had taken place the previous day. He had been vice president then; close friends did not hesitate to call him Lyndon. The difference now was almost palpable. As crowded as the compartment was, no one remained sitting when he came in. It was a dramatic moment. As Johnson later wrote: "It was at that moment that I realized nothing would ever be the same again. A wall—high, forbidding, historic—separated us now, a wall that derives from the Office of the Presidency of the United States. No one but my family would ever penetrate it, as long as I held the office."

He put everyone at ease, and someone turned the sound up on the television. The familiar face of Walter Cronkite was on the screen, telling of the shooting in Dallas, and suddenly, he was interrupted by the local station for the bulletin Malcolm Kilduff had just issued to the press at Parkland.

"President John F. Kennedy died at approximately one o'clock, Central Standard Time, today, here in Dallas. He died of a gunshot wound in the brain. There are no other details at this time regarding the assassination of the president."

Johnson began to confer with key people concerning the administering of the oath of office. For the sake of national security, I felt that we should not remain parked at Love Field any longer than was absolutely necessary. If it was felt that the oath was an immediate necessity, and not something we could attend to when we reached Washington, there were people aboard the plane who were empowered to administer it—among them, every Secret Service agent. My own feeling was that this was a formality that could be taken care of later.

However, we already were faced with a delay that no one questioned. The plane would not leave Dallas until Jacqueline Kennedy and the late President Kennedy's body were aboard. Those who favored swearing Johnson in immediately pointed out that it might be done while the plane was waiting. Other reasons were put forward to strengthen the argument. "Suppose we were to run into bad weather?" one of the congressmen suggested. "It could take three or four hours to get to Washington. I don't think it's fair to the country to delay. The world must know that we do not have a break in leadership."

Continuity was the key word. There was a real basis for fear, other than the possibility of a conspiracy. Reports had already been received telling of a panic in the New York Stock Exchange that had forced the closing of the Exchange after an unprecedented $11 billion drop in stock values in less than half an hour after news of the shooting reached New York.

Johnson agreed tentatively. "I want to talk to the attorney general. I want his opinion."

The radioman put a call through the White House switchboard to Robert Kennedy at his home in McLean, Virginia. Johnson made one exception to his order regarding the use of the presidential suite, and that was his own use of it for this conversation with Bobby Kennedy.

I stood at his side as he spoke to the grieving brother. He gave his condolences for the terrible thing that had happened, and then he talked of the matter of the oath. The attorney general, among his other duties, is counsel to the president.

"I need your opinion on this," Johnson told him frankly.

He sat for a time, listening, gazing past me at the bulkhead. He nodded almost imperceptibly, and obviously paraphrasing the words that he alone could hear, he said, "You feel it should be administered as soon as possible, then. Who in Dallas should administer it?"

There was apparently some question about this, and Johnson said, "Then you'll check with Mr. Katzenbach and let us know. All right. Goodbye."

Minutes later Bobby Kennedy called back, and Johnson again repeated what was said to him. "Any judicial officer of the United States can officiate, is that right? Thank you."

The remainder of the conversation was brief; it was certainly no occasion for small talk. Johnson went back into the stateroom where the discussion continued for several minutes. He decided that a longtime political supporter Federal District Court Judge Sarah T. Hughes should officiate, and a call was placed to her in Dallas. She was located at home, where she had just arrived from the Trade Mart, and the luncheon that was never held.

While the judge was hurrying toward Love Field, the radioman aboard the plane was being swamped with requests for outgoing calls, running the gamut from "Get my wife on the phone and tell her I'll be late" to "Get the attorney general for the president." We immediately made it known that the communications capability of the plane was to be used only for essential traffic. Even so, the load was tremendous, and radioman John Trimble has to be one of the heroes of that day for the job he did.

Meanwhile, word had been received from Parkland Memorial Hospital that there had been some unexpected difficulty with local authorities regarding the release of President Kennedy's body, but that the ambulance bearing the casket was now on its way. Lem Johns and the air crew removed several seats on the port side of the plane, near the rear door, to accommodate the casket. This would position it near the bedroom that was being held for Jacqueline Kennedy and would offer complete privacy from the forward compartments where the urgent business of government had to be conducted.

The rear ramp was in position at the door as the ambulance was cleared into the heavily guarded area. A solemn group of Secret Service agents, Air Force personnel, and Kennedy staffers slid the dull bronze casket out of the ambulance as Jacqueline Kennedy, still wearing the clothes she had worn in the motorcade, stood to one side.

The men gripped the handles and moved up the steep stairs of the ramp. It was a clumsy operation; the steps were too narrow, and the incline forced those in the rear to push the casket up almost at arm's length so that it would not tip backward. For an instant, it seemed that it might fall. Then, with a final effort, it was eased through the doorway and was gently moved into position where the seats had been removed.

It was a moment of utter sadness. Jackie Kennedy, in the pink dress she wore when she had stepped smiling out of this same plane less than three hours earlier, the fabric now smeared and caked with the blood of her husband, stood abjectly at the side of his casket. Lady Bird and Lyndon Johnson stood before her, trying to find the words that had to be said.

It was Lady Bird who found her voice. "Oh, Mrs. Kennedy, you know we never even wanted to be vice president, and now, dear God, it's come to this!"

Jackie Kennedy, her eyes dulled by the shock of what she was going through, took Mrs. Johnson's hands. "Oh, Lady Bird, we've liked you two so much. Oh, what if I had not been there? I'm so glad I was there."

Lady Bird asked if she could get someone to help her change her clothes, and Jackie shook her head. "No. Perhaps later I'll get Mary [Gallagher] to help me, but not right now." She turned her eyes toward the heavy casket. "I want them to see what they have done to Jack."

My mission was in seeing to the security of Lyndon Johnson, and perhaps I would have paid less attention to things that did not seem to bear directly on this mission if he had not already instructed me to have everyone around him take notes. Perhaps he already anticipated the complexity of the investigation that would have to come in one form or another. Perhaps he also realized that the magnitude of what had happened would inevitably bring forth such a torrent of comment in the days to come that our exposure to this could easily taint the memory of what we had actually seen and experienced. He wanted our memories committed to paper while they were fresh.

Many of the things later written by people who were not within a thousand miles of *Air Force One* on that day were as incredible as they were damaging to the already difficult job of keeping the executive branch of our government functioning. I had my own job to do, and while I do not claim that I was able to detect the motivations behind every individual aboard that airplane, I know there was one overpowering and understandable emotion in every face I saw, and that was grief. Grief and shock. We were scarcely two hours past an act of such unspeakable brutality that even the most self-interested could not have had the time to recover. The maneuverings for position and power that are integral to a political environment would resume, but they were not evident on *Air Force One* that day.

There was a certain amount of confusion and a few misunderstandings. Brigadier General Godfrey T. McHugh, Kennedy's Air Force aide, had arrived at the plane with the Kennedy entourage. After seeing that the casket was properly placed on board, he gave the order for the pilot, Colonel Swindal, to get the plane airborne. This was a perfectly normal order, as McHugh was not aware of what had taken place and that LBJ was waiting for Judge Hughes. This momentary misunderstanding was badly distorted in subsequent reports, as were others.

As we waited for the arrival of Judge Hughes, Johnson took me aside for a moment. "I think it would be appropriate for you to keep some of your Secret Service men with the casket, Rufus, as a courtesy."

I told him it would be done. He then conferred briefly with Ken O'Donnell and Larry O'Brien. These men were at the nucleus of those John Kennedy had surrounded himself with, intensely loyal to him both as an individual and as a president. In their grief and shock, they were in no frame of mind to consider the future. But talk of the future could not be delayed, and they knew it.

"The Constitution of the United States is putting me into the White House," Johnson said, leaning across the table toward them. He had purposely not used the chair in the stateroom that had been Kennedy's habitual seat, and this in itself did not go unnoticed. "But there's no law to make you stay there with me. But I need your help. I need it badly. There is no one for me to turn to with the experience of these past three years that you have."

Both men assured him that he had their support for as long as he needed it. As this brief but important meeting ended, Malcolm Kilduff informed me that Judge Hughes was being cleared through the gate and would be aboard shortly. I took him into the stateroom as O'Brien and O'Donnell moved back through the passageway toward the casket.

"Mr. President," Kilduff said, "I need to talk to you about the press coverage of the swearing in."

Johnson asked him flatly if press coverage was absolutely necessary.

"Absolutely, sir," he said strongly, "I think it's extremely important!"

"All right," Johnson replied. "In that case, I think we should ask everyone on the plane who wants to come, to be present."

Kilduff brought in the three-man press pool, Merriman Smith, Charles Roberts, and Sid Davis. Judge Hughes was escorted aboard and was ushered quickly into the stateroom. Johnson greeted her somberly but warmly.

People began moving into the compartment. *Air Force One* was a big plane, but even on the biggest there are no large rooms. Captain Cecil Stoughton, the official White House photographer, moved to the rear of the room where he climbed onto the sofa against the bulkhead. I stood beside him. Larry O'Brien squeezed in through the narrow passageway and put a small Catholic missal in Judge Hughes's hands. The small room was packed. Jacqueline Kennedy, her expression dazed, almost slack-jawed, stood just to Johnson's left, Lady Bird to his right. Judge Hughes, dwarfed by the towering figure of Lyndon Johnson, stood just below Stoughton's camera.

"Everybody's in," Johnson said to Stoughton. "Is this all right?"

"No, sir," Cecil said. "You'll have to move back a bit." He peered through the camera as they pressed back. In the open doorway leading forward to the staff area, I saw Roy Kellerman and Lem Johns, both looking toward the president rather than away from him as they normally would have been doing while on protective duty. Now there was nowhere else to look, and no reason to look away.

Stoughton indicated that he was ready. Malcolm Kilduff, for lack of better recording equipment, held the microphone of a portable office dictating machine to record what was spoken, and Judge Hughes began to read the typed copy of the oath. Lyndon Johnson repeated the words after her, his voice sober and with little inflection.

"I do solemnly swear that I will faithfully execute the Office of President of the United States, and will to the best of my ability, preserve, protect and defend the Constitution of the United States."

That was all, as the oath is written in the Constitution, but Judge Hughes added, "So help me God."

And President Johnson repeated after her, "So help me God." Johnson turned to his left and kissed Jacqueline Kennedy's cheek. "You're very brave to do this," he said in an almost inaudible voice, "and I'll ever be grateful to you."

Then he turned to his right and kissed his wife, after which he gave his first official order as president. "Let's get this plane back to Washington."

Jacqueline Kennedy, along with Ken O'Donnell, Larry O'Brien, Dave Powers, and others who had been close to President Kennedy, moved back to the aft compartment to maintain their vigil. At 2:47 p.m., Colonel Jim Swindal lined the big jet up with the long runway and advanced the throttles, and *Air Force One* was on its way to the capital. The ETA at Andrews Air Force Base was 6:00 p.m., Eastern Standard Time.

President Johnson sat quietly for some time after the takeoff while the plane streaked upward, leaving the mottled Texas countryside far below and Dallas far behind. The closeness and discomfort that had prevailed on the ground disappeared now that the air-conditioning system was functioning.

"Have the radioman get Mrs. Rose Kennedy for me, Rufus," he said.

The first attempt resulted in a poor connection. Radioman John Trimble rerouted the call, and President Kennedy's mother was on the line.

"I wish to God I could do something to help you," Johnson said, his voice thick. He seemed to want to say more, but found himself incapable of it, and he said simply, "Here's Lady Bird," and handed the phone to his wife.

She spoke for a short time, saying the things that women say to each other in times of grief. Then a call was made back to Dallas, to Parkland Memorial

Hospital, to learn of Governor Connally's condition. Nellie Connally told them that her husband was in surgery and that the doctors had expressed optimism on his chances of pulling through. This was the first good news.

There was much to be done before reaching Washington, however, and Johnson began conferring with the three Texas congressmen, Brooks, Thornberry, and Thomas, and with Bill Moyers and other aides. His concern for the moment was with the urgent matters remaining for that day. A statement would have to be made upon arrival at Andrews, and meetings would have to be set up with key people in Washington.

"I want McNamara, Rusk, and McGeorge Bundy to be on the helicopter with me when we fly to the White House," he told Bill Moyers.

In the pressure of the moment, however, President Johnson had forgotten that Secretary of State Dean Rusk and several other cabinet members were aboard an Air Force plane en route to Japan. The plane had turned back as soon as the news of the assassination was received, but it had been far out over the Pacific, beyond Hawaii, and it would be the following morning before it would reach Washington.

As he went over the items of first priority, some of which were arranged, some of which would have to be postponed, the question came up of where President and Mrs. Johnson would stay upon reaching Washington. The Secret Service strongly recommended the White House because it is the one place that is complete in its readiness for the president. Communications, security—everything is there.

But Johnson was adamant on this point. "There will be no hurry involving Mrs. Kennedy. She will have as long as she wants." He looked at me and said bluntly, "Can't the Secret Service secure The Elms?"

His deference to Jackie Kennedy was entirely appropriate and understandable, and his decision seemed even more correct in light of later comments accusing him of "taking over" *Air Force One* at Love Field.

I nodded. "Yes, sir, Mr. President, we will secure The Elms."

I immediately radioed ahead to Jerry Behn, SAIC of the White House Detail, and my new boss. "Jerry, the president will chopper from Andrews to the White House south grounds. He'll go to his offices in the Executive Office

Building, but he is very strong about not rushing Mrs. Kennedy. He feels this would be an intrusion on her privacy and would be entirely inappropriate, so he will go to The Elms when he leaves his office. I suggest that you make the necessary arrangements to secure his residence. Also, the telephone capability at The Elms should be beefed up."

Jerry acknowledged and said he would have it done by the time we arrived.

Lem Johns and I contacted Special Agent Clarence Knetsch at the LBJ Ranch and advised him that the agents who were in Johnson City should be kept there for the security of the area.

I had several conferences with Roy Kellerman coordinating the assignment of our agents on arrival in Washington, and Roy radioed these plans ahead to Behn.

As I made my way back into the stateroom, someone said, "They've just picked up a man in Dallas in connection with the assassination. His name's Oswald. Lee Harvey Oswald." There was also a report that a Dallas police officer, J. D. Tippit, had been killed by the fleeing assassin. We later learned that this report caused a shock in Jerry Kivett's hometown, Burlington, North Carolina, because of the similarity of names—J. D. Kivett and J. D. Tippit. In the confusion, it was several hours before his friends and relatives knew that Jerry was alive.

Streaking eastward with the aid of a strong tail wind, night came quickly. The lights of Washington blinked below as *Air Force One* made its approach to Andrews, touching down at 6:05 p.m., two hours and eighteen minutes after taking off from Love Field. Colonel Swindal taxied to the reception area, where scores of newsmen and hundreds of VIPs—senators, congressmen, members of the diplomatic corps, and others—waited. For obvious security reasons, admittance to the area was extremely tight. But the general public was not excluded from what went on, for when the big plane came to a halt, and the rear door opened, viewers across the nation saw a yellow forklift truck, in the brilliant glare of the television lights, gently lower the bronze casket bearing the late president. O'Donnell, O'Brien, Dave Powers, and two men from the honor guard that had awaited the arrival of the plane lifted the casket off the forklift and placed it in a gray Navy ambulance. Jacqueline Kennedy, Bobby Kennedy, and General Godfrey McHugh got into the rear with the casket. Agents Keller-man and Greer, who had been in President Kennedy's car in Dallas, along with Special Agent Paul Landis and Rear Admiral George Burkley, John Kennedy's physician, rode in front as the ambulance slowly moved out for Bethesda Naval Hospital where an autopsy was to be performed.

As the ambulance moved away, President Johnson glanced around the stateroom, obviously looking for something. "Rufus," he said, "where's my hat?"

"Your hat, sir?"

"It was in the car during the motorcade."

"Then that's where it probably still is, sir," I said. "I didn't get it."

"Well, get the damn thing! Call back to Dallas and have one of your men get it!"

His *hat* at a time like this? Then the incident struck me as the first indica-tion of a return to normalcy. This was LBJ, the president, giving me a chewing out. Through the almost unbelievable pressures since turning onto Elm Street in Dallas, this man had kept his composure. He had been forceful, but coopera-tive, and now the safety valve eased open for a moment, and I had the dubious honor of being the first to be chewed out by the new president.

But it was more than that. It was a brief, object lesson in not forgetting the little things. You really had to know Johnson to understand this.

"I'll see to the hat, sir," I replied.

He nodded, then turned toward his wife. "Bird?" he said. And Lyndon Johnson, bareheaded, with Lady Bird at his side, moved down the ramp into the blaze of lights and, before a forest of microphones, spoke to the stunned nation.

"This is a sad time for all people. We have suffered a loss that cannot be weighed. For me it is a deep personal tragedy. I know the world shares the sor-row that Mrs. Kennedy and her family bear. I will do my best. That is all I can do. I ask for your help—and God's."

In my job, I had flown in and out of Andrews Air Force Base countless times, but it had never been like this. I preceded the president past clusters of solemn, silent people, some of whom he nodded to gravely in recognition, and with Lady Bird, Secretary McNamara, McGeorge Bundy, Under Secretary of State George Ball, and others, we boarded a helicopter, and within a few minutes of our arrival, we lifted off the pad and banked off toward the White House. We passed close by the lighted Washington Monument, which somehow seemed more symbolic than ever before, then settled over the trees and put down on the White House lawn.

Lady Bird, along with her press secretary, Liz Carpenter, and others, was immediately whisked off under tight Secret Service security to The Elms. I moved quickly across the lawn with President Johnson and directly to his offices in the Executive Office Building. For the next few hours, a stream of top government officials met with him. Under Secretary of State Averell Harriman; Senator William Fulbright, chairman of the Foreign Relations Committee; Senator Richard Russell, of the Armed Services Committee; and Sargent Shriver, brother-in-law of the slain president and head of the Peace Corps, moved in and out of the office. Johnson consulted by phone with former Presidents Harry Truman and Dwight Eisenhower.

Congressional leaders were summoned, and Johnson told them that he needed the help of all of them and called for a truce along Party lines. Among those present was House Speaker John W. McCormack who was now the next man in line of succession to the presidency.

During this time, while urgent meetings and briefings that normally would have taken days or weeks were concentrated into hours, reports began to grow more conclusive that the man who had been captured in Dallas, Lee Harvey Oswald, was the assassin. There was still no evidence, one way or the other, whether the assassination was part of a conspiracy that might have further aims. Throughout the whole tragic day, I had been close to Johnson. I remained close at the Executive Office Building, hovering in and out of his office or in my own across the hall.

At about 9 p.m., Cliff Carter poked his head into my office and said, "Rufe, he's about ready to go home."

The simpler the movement in this case, the better. I rode in the follow-up car, while Jerry Behn rode with President Johnson, and with a police escort, our small motorcade moved across the city as quickly and quietly as possible.

I stayed at The Elms until long after midnight, checked with the duty shift, and then drove to my home in nearby Vienna, Virginia. My thoughts went back over the whole horrible day that had begun with Lyndon Johnson as vice president and had ended with him as president. It seemed hardly possible that it had been only slightly more than twelve hours since we had taken off from Fort Worth, with only two more stops scheduled at Dallas and Austin before we went on to the LBJ Ranch. I thought, *That's where we should be now, at the ranch* ...

Thinking about the ranch reminded me of the hat. I made a mental note to get in touch with Forrest Sorrels in Dallas first thing the next morning. The hat arrived in Washington two days later.

CHAPTER 9

The Aftermath

Saturday dawned cold, with dismal gray skies and a light, freezing rain sifting down over Washington. During the predawn hours, John Kennedy's casket had been brought from Bethesda Naval Hospital to be placed on a catafalque in the East Room of the White House, where the body was to lie in state until the following day.

The Secret Service had maintained extremely tight security at the Johnsons' home throughout the night. I arrived at The Elms at 8:00 a.m., now one of the top four supervisors of the White House Detail. The former Vice Presidential Detail had been merged into the White House Detail.

There was only light traffic as we drove toward the White House, where we were met by a strangely touching sight as the big car turned into the drive. Hundreds of people stood in the rain along the sidewalk beside the White House fence and across the street in Lafayette Square, silent, with little discernible movement beneath the sea of umbrellas.

There was to be no public viewing of the casket at the White House; that was to be on Sunday when the body would be moved to the Capitol Rotunda. Yet they stood there, ordinary citizens, some with cameras, others simply standing and looking toward the White House. All through the day they stood, some moving away only to be replaced by others, silently watching the stream of dignitaries who came to pay their respects to John Kennedy.

President Johnson went directly to the West Wing where he held a private meeting with Bobby Kennedy. Following this, he moved quickly to the west basement and the top-secret Situation Room, the intelligence nerve center of the White House, with its windowless, map-covered walls, where the president was briefed by CIA Director John McCone and McGeorge Bundy on the current situation in critical areas all over the globe.

The plane that had been en route to Japan at the time of the assassination had reached Washington during the night, and Secretary of State Dean Rusk was waiting when Johnson strode quickly through the rain, surrounded by Secret Service agents and numerous aides, to the Executive Office Building. He and Rusk conferred for nearly an hour, and this was followed by a long meeting with Defense Secretary McNamara and another with congressional leaders.

Outside, a slow procession of limousines was moving into the White House drive and pausing beneath the north portico to discharge the dignitaries who had come to view the casket in the East Room. Former President Dwight Eisenhower was among them, arriving with Senator Everett Dirksen and John Eisenhower. Johnson greeted Eisenhower in the Blue Room, and together they paid their respects at the flag-draped bier of the dead president.

In the early afternoon, after a hurried luncheon, Johnson held his first cabinet meeting, after which he went into the Fish Room to issue a proclamation declaring Monday, November 25, the day of John Kennedy's funeral, to be a day of national mourning.

Into a bank of microphones, he read in a somber voice: "I earnestly recommend the people to assemble on that day in their respective places of divine worship, there to bow down in submission to the will of Almighty God, and to pay their homage of love and reverence to the memory of a great and good man. I invite the people of the world who share our grief to join us in this day of mourning and rededication."

It was a long, tiring day, and I was seldom more than a few yards from President Johnson from the time we left The Elms that morning until we took him home again late that night.

As incredible as the two preceding days had been, Sunday would bring another shock. By Sunday morning, there seemed to be little question that Oswald, whether acting alone or as a member of a conspiracy, had fired the shots that killed President Kennedy. Dallas police were reporting that the case was "cinched," that the man they had captured in the Texas Theatre was the man who had killed Officer J. D. Tippit and the president. Steps were being taken to protect Oswald from possible mob action, and these steps included transferring him from the city to the county jail. This movement was to take place at about the same time John Kennedy's body was to be moved from the White House to the Capitol Rotunda, where it was to lie in state until the funeral on Monday. At The Elms, President Johnson held a morning briefing with CIA Director McCone, after which he attended St. Marks Church and went to the White House for a final viewing of the casket before the procession to the Capitol. Unlike Saturday, the skies over Washington were clear and blue. Ice still sheathed the bare limbs of the trees along the drive that curved beneath the north portico as the traditional caisson, drawn by six horses, stood waiting for the casket to be placed on it.

While the honor guard assembled and the long, black limousines lined up in the drive, President and Mrs. Johnson went into the Green Room to await the Kennedy family. According to protocol, President and Mrs. Johnson were to ride in the lead limousine, along with Jacqueline Kennedy, her two children, and Bobby Kennedy. It was almost time for the procession to begin. I stood at the door of the Green Room, waiting to escort the president to the car.

Elsewhere in the White House, just as in millions of homes all over the country, television sets were showing the removal of the accused assassin from the Dallas jail, under heavy security. A figure suddenly moved out of the crowd of police and newsmen in the basement corridor of the jail, shoved a gun into Lee Harvey Oswald's stomach, and pulled the trigger.

A White House police officer came quickly down the hallway toward me. He had just heard the report of what had happened in Dallas.

"Oswald!" he said. "He's just been shot! At the jail, while they were moving him!"

A murmur spread through the quiet room as the incredible news was passed from person to person. It was time to go. The president had heard the report by the time I got to him. He closed his eyes for a moment, then he said, "Keep me posted on this."

And then we went out into the cold sunlight, and the slow procession to the Capitol began. We moved down the flag-lined drive and out onto Pennsylvania Avenue. In the cold glare of midday, hundreds of thousands of people stood ten or more deep along both sides of the route, and even as the body of their fallen president moved slowly past them, the word of what had just taken place in Dallas spread, creating new questions and uncertainties. Before the procession reached its destination, thousands of transistor radios in the hands of the crowd told of Oswald's death at Parkland Memorial Hospital.

Oswald had been a Marxist, a defector who had gone to the Soviet Union and had attempted to renounce his United States citizenship. He had worked for the cause of Cuban Communism, and scarcely a year had gone by since President Kennedy had come to the brink with Russia over the Cuban missiles.

And now, the accused assassin was dead. The questions flew thick and fast. What or who had been behind Oswald's alleged act? His killer, cabaret owner Jack Ruby, had said he shot Oswald to spare Jackie Kennedy the pain of a prolonged public trial, but the fact that he killed Oswald within forty-eight hours of John Kennedy's death was far too coincidental for many.

The answers to these questions would have to wait until after the funeral. Throughout Sunday afternoon, through the long night, and into Monday morning, the people moved in a slow, steady stream up the steps of the Capitol and into the Rotunda to say goodbye to the young president who had served them less than three years.

On Monday, November 25, three related funerals took place. In Dallas, some four hundred people attended the burial of Patrolman J. D. Tippit, who had been gunned down while attempting to question Lee Harvey Oswald following the assassination. In nearby Fort Worth, five mourners, a hundred policemen, and some forty newsmen attended the unpublicized burial of Oswald. The police were there only to protect the mourners and the body itself against possible actions of the crowd that somehow found out about the funeral and showed up. There was no eulogy as Oswald was lowered into the earth. The Reverend Louis Saunders, executive secretary of the Fort Worth Council of Churches, had volunteered to officiate. "We are not here to judge," he intoned, "we are here to lay him away before an understanding God."

The third funeral was held in Washington, with presidents, kings, and the leaders of nations all around the globe in attendance. At 10:50 a.m., the nine pallbearers brought the casket down the Capitol steps that they had taken it up the day before. It was placed once more on the caisson to start the long journey across the city for services at St. Matthew's Cathedral and then on to Arlington National Cemetery. Behind the caisson was a serviceman bearing the presidential flag, and then a riderless black horse, being led behind the casket, empty boots reversed in the stirrups, symbolic of a fallen leader.

On Friday, November 29, 1963, one week after the assassination, President Johnson issued an executive order that named the commission that was "to ascertain, evaluate, and report" on the facts surrounding the assassination of President John F. Kennedy and the subsequent murder of Lee Harvey Oswald. The seven-man commission, headed by U.S. Supreme Court Chief Justice Earl Warren, was given the broadest of powers, being left virtually to its own devices in the conduct of the investigation. Even the most outspoken Johnson critic could not reasonably call it biased. The other six members were to be Georgia Senator Richard B. Russell, Senator John S. Cooper of Kentucky, Representative Hale Boggs of Louisiana, Representative Gerald R. Ford of Michigan, and two men from private life, both of whom had served their country under Democratic and Republican administrations: former CIA Director Allen W. Dulles and John J. McCloy. Thus, the spread was north to south, Republican and Democratic, men widely respected for their integrity.

The Secret Service found itself under fire almost before the echoes had died in Dealey Plaza. The Service, in the loss of its number-one protective responsibility, had flunked the course and was fair game for anyone who wanted to take a crack at it. Columnist Drew Pearson, in the December 2 edition of the *Washington Post*, reported that six Secret Service agents had been drinking in the Fort Worth Press Club until 3:00 a.m. on the morning of the assassination. The report was picked up by certain political figures while cooler heads noted that this was one of the many things that should be left to the Warren Commission.

All comment about the Secret Service, however, was not adverse. On December 3, at the main Treasury Building, Special Agent Clinton J. Hill was presented the Exceptional Service Award. Mrs. Jacqueline Kennedy, Clint Hill's family, officials of the Treasury Department and of the Secret Service, and others were present when Secretary Dillon read the citation.

> This Award is conferred upon Special Agent Clinton J. Hill of the Secret Service for exceptional bravery in his effort to protect the President and First Lady of the United States at the time of President John F. Kennedy's assassination in Dallas, Texas, on November 22, 1963.
>
> Agent Hill was standing on the left front running board of the Secret Service car located directly behind the Presidential limousine when the assassin fired his first shot. Agent Hill immediately ran from his vehicle while the bullets were still being fired, climbed on the rear of the President's rapidly moving limousine, and shielded the President and Mrs. Kennedy with his own body. His extraordinary courage and heroic effort in the face of maximum danger reflect great credit on the United States of America, which can produce such men. His dedication to the highest traditions of the United States makes him a deserving recipient of this Award.

The following morning, December 4, in the Rose Garden at the White House, Secretary Dillon also presented me with the Exceptional Service Award, in the presence of President Johnson, Treasury and Secret Service officials, my family, and others. The secretary read the citation.

> This Award is made in recognition of Agent Youngblood's outstanding courage and voluntary risk of personal safety in protecting the Vice President of the United States at the time of President John F. Kennedy's assassination in Dallas, Texas, on November 22, 1963.
>
> Mr. Youngblood was riding in the front seat of the Vice President's limousine within close proximity to the Presi-

dent's limousine when the assassination occurred. Upon hearing the first shot, Mr. Youngblood instantly vaulted across the front seat of the car, pushed the Vice President to the floor, and shielded the Vice President's body with his own. His prompt response in the face of great danger and his readiness to sacrifice his life to save the Vice President were in the highest traditions of the Secret Service. His valor and example make him a worthy recipient of this Award.

After the secretary had presented the award, the president stepped before the microphone.

There is no more heroic act than offering your life to save another, and in that awful moment of confusion when all about him were losing their heads, Rufus Youngblood never lost his. Without hesitation, he volunteered his life to save mine. Nothing makes a man feel better than being an American and to be witness to this kind of noble patriotism. Rufus, there is no prouder person here this morning than I. You are a brave soldier in the highest American tradition of love for country and for duty. You are a proud son of Georgia. You are an excellent example of all the honored and brave and dedicated and diligent men and the women who work with them who make up what we proudly call the United States Secret Service. A more dedicated group of men I have never known from the Chief to the most humble employee.

I am glad to know that Chief Rowley has made it possible for you to continue to serve the President as you did the Vice President, and I know in so doing that I will have one of the most noble and most able public servants I have ever known.

The awards notwithstanding, the Secret Service was still on shaky ground, and the FBI, the CIA, and the Defense Department were all reportedly looking into the business of presidential protection as a possible addition to their own jobs.

The tragedy in Dallas, however, carried with it a subtle but strong point that was an effective deterrent to anyone wanting to take over the Service's chief responsibility. The Secret Service had shouldered this awesome burden for more than sixty years, not without serious incident, but without its mission being thwarted. Now, after one volley of gunfire by a man whose reasons we would probably never know, the Secret Service was fighting for its very existence as a protective unit because there are no small losses in this line of work. Bank robbers may roam the country, spies may abound, wars may flare, and the agencies and departments responsible for containing these activities are seldom, if ever, called summarily on the carpet with an attitude of "If you can't cut the mustard, we'll get somebody who can."

The headlines made on November 22 and the days that followed would be a long time getting to page two. Why would anyone seek a job whose failure, regardless of the manner in which it happened, would inevitably cause such an upheaval? I felt then, and I feel now, that this question was evaluated and came up with no enthusiastic takers.

This and the fact that Lyndon Johnson, in the main, backed the Secret Service were largely responsible for the job remaining where it was. The feeling seemed to have been, "Give them some lumps, do some revising and reorganizing, but let them keep it." The hot potato went around the circle and came back to where it started.

Understandably, morale was not at an all-time high in the Secret Service. Many career agents in protective assignments felt that this mandate might pass to other hands, and they sought transfers to the field. The necessary merging of the Vice Presidential Detail into the White House Detail disturbed the normal upward flow of promotions. It was a time of uncertainty, and in a surprisingly short time, it came to the attention of President Johnson himself. Less than two months in office, and with the monumental responsibility and workload that had been thrust on him, he considered the matter of sufficient importance to deal with personally which is exactly what he did on January 6, 1964.

I was just sitting down to supper with my wife, Peggy, and the children when the phone rang. There was no aide or secretary saying, "Hold the line please for the president." It was LBJ himself, and he minced no words.

"I've received a memorandum that disturbs me, Rufus. I'll read you some of it. 'Morale in the Secret Service is at an all-time low. A number of agents of the White House Detail have been asking for transfers. This is a great body of men. These men feel they are being prevented from doing their job properly. They do not want favors; they just want to be accepted. We need them badly, especially in campaign years.' And it goes on."

"Sir," I said, "may I ask who wrote the memorandum?"

"I don't think I ought to name him, but it was one of Kennedy's top people, and somebody in your outfit has been bellyaching to him."

The case in point, the president told me, was a small write-up in a national magazine to the effect that LBJ, while driving his own car at the ranch, had told a Secret Service agent in the follow-up car that he was going to shoot out a tire if he did not stop following too close. The incident itself was not important. It was a simple example of LBJ being himself. The fact that a magazine found out about it was important.

"There's enough truth in it to see that somebody talked," the president went on. "You know I can't have disloyalty, and I can't talk in front of your people and have them repeat it. I told Chief Rowley that, to call 'em in and take the resignations of anybody who wanted out, and I'll be glad to have his or yours or anybody else's. If they don't want to handle it, we can get the FBI to do it. So, you get ahold of Rowley, and you all hold a meeting, and if you want to resign, I'll be glad to accept it forthwith. If Secret Service wants to go back to counterfeiting, then I'll get Hoover to assign me a couple of men to stand by my side without all this damn fuss!"

"Well, sir," I put in, "you're absolutely right. You can't have disloyalty, and I don't want any transfer, reassignment, or any other damn thing."

He went on, chewing me out for the incident itself and the fact that it came to his attention from a third party. He had a point. I don't know how long I sat there in my kitchen with the phone in my hand, saying "Yes, sir, Mr. President" every now and then.

At last, he began to wind down. "Get ahold of Rowley and find out who the hell has been doing all this bellyaching and get it straightened out. Take their resignations, get them out of here, and get Lem Johns back and you and Lem handle me. (Lem had been put on shift work when we got back from Dallas.) And if you don't want it, just honestly say so, and I'll get Hoover to send me over a couple of twenty-one-year-old accountants, and they'll probably do as good a job!"

I winced on that one, but he finally had it off his chest. I said, "We'll stick with you, sir."

There was a pause. "Okay. But I want something done about it, you understand? Good night, Rufus." And he hung up.

I lowered the phone and sat there staring at it. Peggy came and stood in the kitchen doorway. "I fed the children," she said. "I didn't know how long you'd be, so I put our plates in the oven."

I looked up. "Can you see the teeth marks on me?"

She shrugged and smiled. "Well, for three years the vice president's been chewing you out. Now it's the president. You've come up in the world."

The FBI dart was going to be thrown at us more than once, and there was a lot that went unsaid when we would hear about the two twenty-one-year-old accountants who were going to be sent over to replace the Secret Service. J. Edgar Hoover was a permanent fixture as FBI director, and if he did not begin with the confidence of a particular president, he eventually gained it, even if grudgingly. Under the conditions that prevailed in the months following the assassination, if Hoover had wanted his outfit to assume the protective responsibility at the White House, he could have had it with little difficulty. He chose to remain in the support role, where there was little chance of the FBI's reputation becoming tarnished.

And so the arduous task of sorting the whole thing out began. The Warren Commission began its monumental task, which would, within ten months, come to fill twenty-six volumes. The muckrakers began their work, disdaining fact for sensationalism for the most part. At the everyday, practical level, the Secret Service also started its self-examination. This began with a look at the omission that had allowed the assassination to happen as it did—and that was the automobile in which the president had been riding. Traditionally, the president often rode in an open automobile. He is there to be seen, and there is nothing about an open car to obstruct the view of the public—or the aim of an assassin.

The exception to this had been closed, armored automobiles provided for President Franklin D. Roosevelt during World War II. Shortly after the Japanese attack on Pearl Harbor, Secret Service Agent Mike Reilly acquired an armored car for the president's use. In the tradition of great Secret Service scroungers, Reilly had ferreted it out of the depths of a Treasury Department garage, where it had been gathering dust since being confiscated from a gentleman by the name of Al Capone. This was, of course, an interim measure while the Secret Service ordered several specially built Packards and Lincolns for Roosevelt's protection from possible harm at the hands of Axis sympathizers or foreign agents.

After the war, these cars were phased out and were not budgeted for replacement. Presidents resumed riding in open cars during public motorcades when weather permitted, and the Secret Service resumed having its pleas for new armored cars fall on deaf ears. Apparently, no one wanted to believe the President of the United States was as vulnerable as the Secret Service made him out to be.

With all the rhetorical blaming of a city, a state, or a country for the assassination of a president, it had always boiled down to one man carrying out the deed. Regardless of the detail of preparation for a presidential motorcade, the one thing that is unalterable is the agonizingly long, slow drive over a highly publicized route. From the security point of view, this has always been considered one of the more difficult and risky assignments.

The possibility of an assassination attempt from a distance, using a high-powered rifle, had also been a longtime nightmare. This is not an exercise in hindsight. Chief U. E. Baughman found it almost impossible to convince President Eisenhower that the observation tower overlooking the Gettysburg farm offered an ideal place from which to make such an attack.

In Fort Worth on the morning of November 22, 1963, President Kennedy had been discussing the risks inherent in the president's public appearances with his wife and Ken O'Donnell, and he had said, "If anybody really wanted to shoot the President of the United States, it would not be a very difficult job—all one would have to do is get on a high building someday with a telescopic rifle, and there is nothing anybody could do to defend against such an attempt."

And then John F. Kennedy had boarded *Air Force One* and flown off to Dallas. Yet Kennedy, like his predecessors, had not supported any effort to obtain the single protective device that could have prevented his death—an armored parade car.

As with Mike Reilly in 1941, the urgency of the moment brought forth a similar vehicle for the use of President Johnson. The FBI provided armored cars for the use of J. Edgar Hoover, and the FBI director offered one of these for the president's use. Although I appreciated Mr. Hoover's generosity in doing this, it seemed to me more than slightly ironic that the President of the United States should have to borrow an armored car from one of his subordinates. At the same time, a series of planning sessions began with representatives of the Ford Motor Company, which supplied Lincoln limousines for the White House, for the construction of armored cars.

A month after the assassination, the Secretary of the Treasury formally requested that Chief Rowley begin a study of the procedures used by the Secret Service in protecting the president and that reports and recommendations for changes be submitted to him.

Secretary Dillon recognized fully that the protective mission of the Secret Service would always be in conflict with the demands of an open society and that any changes suggested would have to take this into consideration. He did not limit the scope of the study, but he specifically touched on several of the factors that, in combination, had provided Lee Harvey Oswald with the opportunity to shoot the president. These included the security of the presidential vehicle, the procedures used for selection of motorcade sources and methods of identifying individuals who might pose a danger to the president, and the Secret Service's liaison with other intelligence and law enforcement agencies, such as the FBI, which had a file on Oswald.

While the enormous task of investigating and reporting on the assassination got under way, the routine work had to continue. The nation was without a vice president for the first time since 1945. John W. McCormack, the seventy-one-year-old Speaker of the House, who was now first in line of succession to the presidency, was provided with Secret Service protection immediately after the assassination. But, for personal reasons, he soon requested that it be discontinued. The Service had no choice but to withdraw the men assigned to him.

President Johnson, while he stated that he would make no trips outside the United States so long as the country was without a vice president, soon began to show us that, in one respect, he was little different from any other president we had had to deal with. He had that same peculiar fatalistic attitude about his own safety.

The Secret Service could study forever on the security of presidential protection, and even if it came up with the perfect assassin-proof device, there would remain the even more difficult task of getting the president to use it.

CHAPTER 10

LBJ 1964: Unfinished Business

Early in December, Jacqueline, Caroline, and John-John Kennedy left the White House for their new home in nearby Georgetown. The Johnsons began moving from The Elms to 1600 Pennsylvania Avenue, the thirty-fourth family to call it home since President and Mrs. John Adams set up housekeeping there in 1800.

As vice president, Lyndon Johnson had been the only member of his family officially to receive Secret Service protection. During the past three years, of course, those of us who worked with the Vice Presidential Detail had come to know Lady Bird and the two daughters, Lucy and Lynda. Now we were officially charged with their protection. Jerry Kivett, Woody Taylor, and Jerry Bechtle, all of the old Vice Presidential Detail, were assigned as Lady Bird's protective unit. They dubbed themselves the KTBC group (Kivett, Taylor, Bechtle, and Lady Bird's given name, Claudia), which were the call letters of the Johnson television station in Austin.

Lucy had been living at The Elms and was attending school in Washington. But Lynda, at the time of the assassination, had been enrolled at the University of Texas in Austin. Shortly after her father became president, she had been badly advised that, for security reasons, she should transfer to a school in the capital area so that she could live at the White House.

The day of John Kennedy's funeral, she had mentioned this to me at The Elms. This was the first time I had seen her since the tragedy had occurred, and she greeted me warmly, giving me a hug and a kiss on the cheek. She thanked me for "protecting Daddy," and then she asked me if I agreed that she should move back to Washington.

"Do you want to stay in Austin?" I asked her.

"Well, yes ... but—"

"Then stay there. The law provides you with Secret Service protection, but this doesn't mean that you have to adapt to us. It's the other way around; we adapt to you."

Lynda stayed in Austin, and her Secret Service detail soon became a familiar sight on the university campus. She did not move back to Washington until after she graduated.

The presidency had deprived Lyndon Johnson of something he had grown accustomed to over the years, and that was the services of his longtime chauffeur, Norman Edwards. Norman was an employee of the Senate, and as majority leader and later as presiding officer of the Senate, LBJ had grown quite fond of Norman. To bring Norman to the White House would mean a change of employer from the U.S. Senate to the Secret Service.

A few days after he became president, LBJ held a conference with me. "I've got a lot of important things to do, Rufus, and I'm gonna assign one of the most important projects to you. Get Norman for me. I need him as much as I need you and Lady Bird."

Conferences with Senate officials, with Chief Rowley, and—most importantly—with Norman followed, and on December 9, Norman took the oath as a special officer, U.S. Secret Service. After that Norman could be found, on most occasions, behind the wheel when the car pulled up the White House drive to take the president somewhere in the city.

Long hours never seemed to bother Norman. He could come on duty at eight o'clock in the morning and still be ready to drive the president long after midnight. I once asked him how he managed this. He laughed. "Well, when the Man is in town, I'll take him any place he wants to go, any time. But when he's outta town, I'm hard to find!"

With the exception of his usual Christmas stay at the LBJ Ranch in Texas, the president was not out of Washington often during his first few months in office. With no vice president, he had to mind the store, and the store was in Washington. The transition of the presidency, after the traumatic days of late November and early December, was as smooth as such an abrupt change could reasonably be expected to be. John Kennedy's key personnel assured LBJ that they would stay on for as long as he wanted or needed them, and he assured them—and the world— that it was his intent to carry forward the programs and policies the late president had begun, especially those aimed at eliminating racial injustice.

Just as I had told Lynda that the Secret Service had the job of adapting to her, it had an even bigger job of adapting to the new president. LBJ possessed a streak of impetuosity that could knock the best-laid plans into a cocked hat and send even the coolest agent climbing the walls. For years, the Service had dealt with men who would make no great changes in their itineraries unless something of major importance called for it. Harry Truman, for example, was the most punctual of men. If he had a noon appointment, it would not begin at 11:59 or 12:01. Eisenhower's life in the Army had built clocks into him. The youthful exuberance of John Kennedy, not keeping him as tightly bound as his predecessors, did not allow for sudden or unexpected changes.

Lyndon Johnson, on occasion, would literally change plans in midair. A few months after he became president, we were bound for Washington aboard *Air Force One*, returning from the West Coast, when LBJ motioned to me.

"Rufus, I feel like sleeping with my head on my own pillow tonight. Tell 'em up front that we're going to the ranch."

In my years with him as vice president, I had adjusted to this sort of thing. But there are far fewer ramifications in a last-minute rerouting for a vice president than there are for a president. *Air Force One* was already on a flight plan to Andrews Air Force Base. The presidential helicopter was alerted and was waiting for the flight to the White House. Air Force personnel, Secret Service agents, and White House staffers were already involved in the preparations for the president's arrival in the capital. The shift would be on duty at the White House. The shift would be off duty in Johnson City.

President Theodore Roosevelt once referred to the Secret Service as a "very small but very necessary thorn in the flesh." Unless there is some very apparent security risk involved, the thorn does not tell the president what pillow he will sleep on. The radios aboard *Air Force One* sent out a stream of messages to Washington, to Austin, and to Johnson City. That night the president laid his head on his own pillow while hundreds of people were either taking sleeping pills or drinking black coffee, depending on which end of the switch they were on.

Spontaneous changes of this sort, while they bring on all sorts of logistical problems, are not necessarily security risks. They may actually lessen the normal risks that have to be taken with any announced movement of the president. A basic requirement of an assassin is the knowledge of where his intended victim will be and when. To fly into Austin's Bergstrom Air Force Base virtually unannounced in the middle of the night, and then to go by chopper to the ranch, another secure area, is as free of this particular danger as the president is likely to get.

After John Kennedy was killed, the cranks across the country who were getting out pen and paper at the time to write him a threatening letter merely changed the name and mailed it to Lyndon Johnson. In addition to the predictable flow of such mail, there was an additional inpouring from those who were convinced Johnson was somehow implicated in the assassination.

But one of the strangest threats to a president that ever came to light occurred in February 1964. A big Democratic fund-raising dinner was to be held at the plush Fontainebleau Hotel in Miami Beach on February 27. The president was scheduled as the principal speaker. The presidential airplane was readied for the flight south, and all was routine until the FBI informed the Secret Service that it had received intelligence that a Cuban pilot might attempt to intercept *Air Force One* over Florida and either shoot it down or ram it.

Bizarre as it was, it was not outside the realm of possibility, especially since Cuba was known to be equipped with modern military jets, and with Cuba lying just ninety miles off the Florida coast, this was a flight of only a few minutes by such aircraft. Of course, the trip could not be canceled on such sketchy information. If the president's movements were predicated on the threats he received, he would never set foot out of the White House. Also, as head of the Democratic Party, and with the 1964 elections looming, LBJ would probably have flown directly over Havana if it had been necessary to reach the Fontainebleau Hotel.

On the other hand, the report could not be summarily dismissed, and steps were taken accordingly. The primary presidential aircraft, number 26000, being more easily identifiable than the other 707s in the squadron, was sidelined. Three of the big jets, outwardly alike, were readied for the flight south, with LBJ to be aboard one and the others to be used as decoys, flying over approximately the same route.

Air Force fighter planes were to fly cover, and Navy vessels were positioned along the Florida coast to supplement the radar stations ashore that might detect a blip coming out of Cuba. There was also a slight shift in the schedule, with LBJ to land in Palm Beach rather than Miami.

As we flew south on the twenty-seventh, I thought back to the days in World War II when I stood freezing in the open gun port of *Jack the Ripper* as my B-17 squadron flew over Germany. But a 1942 Messerschmitt was a far cry from a 1964 MIG, and there are no waist gunners aboard 707s, so we sat and talked and occasionally looked out at the fighter escort flanking us.

The Cuban pilot never showed up, whether due to the elaborate precautions that were taken or because he never existed. The important thing was that the mission of getting the president to his destination was successfully completed.

From the airport in Palm Beach, LBJ was taken by chopper to a prearranged spot on Miami Beach's Bay Shore Golf Club. After the greeting by the official welcoming committee, Johnson, in his typical fashion, moved through the security lines and across the street into the crowd to "press the flesh." Newspapers invariably reported such incidents as "causing jitters" among the Secret Service agents, and in this case, they were not far from wrong. We had just brought him from Washington under a heavy threat, and it had been in Miami that a little man by the name of Zangara had leaped up on a chair and sprayed bullets at President-elect Franklin D. Roosevelt in 1933.

We tried to discourage this, even when we took him to a place that was not publicly announced beforehand. But public exposure and hand-to-hand contact are as vital to the metabolism of most politicians as the air they breathe or the food they eat. There were some three thousand loyal Democrats in Miami Beach, each plunking down his hundred dollars for a plate of Chicken à la King and a speech from the president. LBJ was not about to sneak into town so long as the *News* and the *Herald* had the presses rolling.

LBJ stuck by his resolve to see the Kennedy programs through as best he could, and no doubt, this kept many of the key people at the White House who, having a personal allegiance to Jack Kennedy rather than to the presidency, might have left sooner than they did.

With his legislative prowess, LBJ pushed the Civil Rights Act through Congress. After the longest filibuster in its history, he signed it into law on July 2, 1964.

Poverty in America was another one of the problems Kennedy had vowed to attack, and Johnson, under the banner of the War on Poverty, went full steam ahead. In May of 1964, he made a tour of the Appalachia area to see firsthand some of the most severe pockets of poverty in the country. He combined this with some politicking by making a stop in my hometown of Atlanta where he addressed a breakfast of the state legislature at the Dinkler-Plaza Hotel. The Kennedy-Johnson administration was not too popular in Georgia, but the turnout for the president was proper and polite. At the speakers' table with President Johnson were Governor Carl Sanders, Atlanta Mayor Ivan Allen, Senator Herman Talmadge, and a number of congressmen and other political figures.

But LBJ had not simply been content with inviting the political leaders. He had personally telephoned my mother, who lived in Atlanta, and invited her. I was not aware of it at the time, but he had run into some difficulty with Mother. She was elderly and quite dependent upon my sister, Ann, to assist her in almost everything she did. She responded to the presidential invitation by telling him that she wasn't sure, that she "would have to talk to Ann first."

"I'll come out myself and pick you up, Mrs. Youngblood," he urged.

"I don't know," Mother hedged. "I'd better see what Ann says."

Ann, of course, said it would be just fine, so Mother was taken down to the Dinkler-Plaza to meet the president. But it took some doing.

President Johnson spoke of the War on Poverty and was heard attentively but without great enthusiasm. I must admit I was not unappreciative when he glanced at me during his speech and told the audience, "My life is in the hands of Georgia, and it is twenty-four hours a day under the direction of Rufus Youngblood, and no greater or more noble son has this state ever produced, and no braver or more courageous man." In fact, I may even have blushed a bit as the legislators gave me a standing ovation.

Almost at the end of the festivities, however, as all heads were bowed for the benediction (except those of the Secret Service, who trusted that the Lord understood), Special Agent Bill Payne, our advance agent at this stop, moved quietly to my side and whispered, "I just received a report of a fire in the hotel. It hasn't been confirmed yet."

If there had to be such a report, this was about the best time it could have happened, at least from a security standpoint. The banquet hall was on the ground floor, the vehicles were lined up outside on Forsyth Street ready for the motorcade to the airport, and the program was winding up. Even if a raging holocaust developed, the president was in no imminent danger.

But it was standard procedure to evacuate him as quickly as possible on any such report, and I moved over, touched his arm lightly, and passed the information on. "I've received a report, sir, that there may be a fire in the hotel. As soon as the prayer is over, I think it would be advisable for you to follow me directly out to the car, and don't stop to shake hands."

Without opening his eyes, he nodded slightly. "Okay, pardner."

I do not know the effect it had on the assembled Georgia legislators when the president moved from the speakers' table, through the banquet hall, and out through the lobby and into his parade car without shaking a hand, but there was no doubt in my mind that a confirmed fire would be much better than an unconfirmed fire when it came to explaining having to whisk him past that many politicians without letting him "press the flesh" of so much as one.

As we pulled away from the hotel my ears were keenly attuned for the sound of fire engines. We were only a few blocks along the motorcade route to the airport when LBJ leaned forward from the back seat.

"What's the latest report on that fire?"

"Nothing yet, Mr. President. I'll let you know as soon as I hear."

This motorcade was to let the people see the president, so it avoided the freeways, moving out of the downtown area, out Peters Street to Lee Street and, by the purest of coincidences, through the area of West End, where I grew up, and where, unbeknownst to me, a lot of people I knew were waiting along the route. The crowds were good, and when we were out of the area of the tall downtown buildings, the president insisted on transferring from the enclosed limousine to an open car (which we tried vainly to discourage), and with me riding in the right front seat, approached a place known as McCall's Crossing, only a few blocks from my old high school.

Riding with the president, you grow accustomed to the calls of the people along the way. But now I began to hear something I had never before heard in a motorcade. I heard cries of "*Hey, Wayne!*" My middle name is Wayne, and that was what folks called me when I was growing up and going to school in West End.

I began to see familiar faces as I routinely scanned the crowd, and from time to time, I tried to wave back when someone yelled, "*Hey, Wayne!*" in such a manner that the president and the VIPs riding in the back could not see. Up ahead, the Joe Brown High band was blaring away on the corner, and somebody held up a homemade placard that settled the question of who "Wayne" was. It read: WELCOME HOME WAYNE YOUNGBLOOD!

LBJ was chuckling. "Rufus," he said, "would you like to get back here and let me ride up front?"

The little personal incident did not take his mind off what had happened back at the hotel. As we pulled in to the airport to board the chopper for a scheduled stop at nearby Gainesville, he asked me again, "When am I gonna get a report on that fire?"

"The minute I get it, sir," I replied. Just before we boarded the chopper I talked with Bill Payne. "Look, he keeps bugging me about that fire, and I want a report! Damn it, if you don't have a fire, *make* one! Even if it's in a wastebasket, so you can put it out!"

LBJ continued launching programs to establish a "Great Society" which, in addition to eliminating poverty and racial injustice, included Medicare, Medicaid, and environmental protection, among others. As the summer of 1964 wore on, the protection of the president began to crop up more and more in the press. LBJ's public exposure during his first six months in office had been minimal. During this same time, the Secret Service had augmented its procedures in a number of ways. First, of course, were the armored cars. We still had the 1961 limousine provided by J. Edgar Hoover, and we had put the first armored Lincoln delivered by Ford into service and were planning more improvements on the second, which was in production.

We had begun to use helicopter surveillance along motorcade routes, and since Dallas, local police had never balked at providing any and all help that we asked for. It was obvious that nobody wanted a "Dallas" to happen in their town. In response to this abundance of cooperation, I would always pass along a word of praise from the president to the well-deserving local police chief. In one city, as we drove to the airport preparatory to leaving, I picked up the microphone and called the chief of police, who was riding in the lead car.

"Chief, this is Youngblood of the Secret Service. The president has asked me to tell you how much he appreciates the great job you and your men did while he was here. He said to tell you what a fine group of men and well-run police department you have here, and he looks forward to coming back again."

I noticed that there was silence in the back seat while I was talking, and when I broke off with the chief, the president tapped me on the shoulder.

"You know, I don't remember saying what you just said I said."

I turned around, grinning sheepishly at him. "That's right, Mr. President, but after all, there are a lot of policemen, and they all vote."

He looked at me for a moment. "Rufus, have you ever thought about going into politics?"

On one of his visits to Texas, the president was observed driving his own car on a public highway at what were said to be "excessive speeds." This hit the newspapers all over the country and immediately resulted in protests from the public.

Letters were even addressed to me, personally, appealing for a stop to this. One young lady in Denver wrote: "We read in this morning's paper with a great deal of concern that President Johnson was driving at very dangerous speeds on the highway in Texas. As he is the only President this country has, and a very good one at that, we implore you to put obstacles in his way so that this type of excursion will not be repeated again. If necessary, keep him out of Texas."

Press Secretary George Reedy, one of the most difficult of men to put on the spot, was put on the spot at a press conference when the speeding story came up. Merriman Smith, dean of the White House press corps, pounded away at him.

"George, what happens when the Secret Service people want one thing done for the president's safety and he wants something else? The president overrides the Secret Service, doesn't he?"

"I would think that in any question involving safety, the Secret Service, which is rather experienced in this matter, would be able to work out whatever necessary details fitted the president's desires and were within the prudent limits of safety," George replied in a masterful nonanswer.

"In other words," Smitty went on, "that means that if the president desires not to have them with him, they can't do anything about it. Is that right?"

"Not necessarily," George hedged. "As I said, I would assume on any occasion like that, and that is somewhat of a hypothetical question, that a prudent arrangement would be arrived at which would permit the president's desires to be carried out within the prudent bounds of safety."

It was times like this that we could appreciate our standing order to make "no comment" on our duties. Of course the president was not as disdainful of his own safety as it might have seemed. It was simply that more attention was being focused in this direction than ever before.

On other occasions, the president's desires were carried considerably beyond his intent. When I was a boy, the last person to leave a room always turned out the light. It must have been the same with LBJ because he began to notice lights burning late into the night in the windows of the White House complex. When he remarked to one of the members of his staff about the hard workers he had, he was told that the lights did not necessarily mean anyone was working.

"Then why are they on?" he wanted to know. "Why don't they turn them off? Don't they know electricity costs money?"

The order went out, and with hardly a pause at the reasonable point LBJ had intended, the pendulum swung to near-total darkness. Ushers, White House police, and agents stumbled around in the dark. The Executive Office Building was as blacked out as it might have been in expectation of an air raid. When someone would ask about the necessity of turning *all* the lights out, the answer would simply be "President's orders."

LBJ, unfairly, received considerable ridicule in some segments of the press for this, and soon the lights were back on. The incident does bring up the question of how divergent intent and result may be in the extremely complex chain of command, when such a simple matter can go so far astray.

After Senator Barry Goldwater won the nomination at the 1964 Republican Convention and the campaign began in earnest, our security around the president was tightened even more. The work of the Protective Research Section paid off on many occasions. In October, agents in Buffalo, New York, went to question an individual who had come to the attention of the Secret Service. The man was found at a machine in the shop where he worked, a rifle lying on the ledge of a window overlooking the street below, and a single cartridge in his pocket. A published report had stated that the president was to drive past the building on his way to the airport, although the plan had later been changed. The suspect claimed that he was a brigadier general in the army of the minutemen and that he needed "only one bullet to do the job." He was committed for mental observation.

In a Midwestern city, agents kept under surveillance the home of a man who was known to have a large collection of military weapons and ammunition and whose house was less than three hundred yards from the inn where President Johnson was scheduled to stay during his visit to that city. The man admitted that the inn was within easy rifle shot of any military firearm and that the 25 mm cannon he kept in his garage would have little difficulty penetrating a concrete wall.

At the time, Senator Goldwater; his running mate, Representative William E. Miller; and Democratic vice presidential nominee Hubert Humphrey had to provide whatever protective forces they felt they might need, as there was no provision for Secret Service protection for nominees. This protection had been proposed from time to time, as recently as August 1964, when Representative Charles E. Goodell introduced a bill to "authorize the United States Secret Service to protect the persons of the nominees of the two major political parties for President and Vice President of the United States."

The bill had failed to pass. It was going to take another assassination to get it through.

The anniversary of John Kennedy's assassination was approaching, and the tension was apparent even in the press corps. In Providence, Rhode Island, on September 28, LBJ's campaign motorcade was moving through the city. I was riding in the right front seat of the president's open car, and LBJ was sitting atop the seat back in the rear, with his feet on the seat, waving at the crowds. We were moving up a hill when I received a radio report that there was a car on fire in the motorcade. It was behind us, but when I looked back and saw smoke rising from one of the staff cars, I had no way of knowing what had caused it and no time to speculate. I turned and grabbed both of the president's ankles and pulled. He slid down onto the seat. Evacuation in such a case is the role of the Secret Service, and evacuate we did.

I shouted to our driver: "Get the hell outta here!"

He responded immediately, and three cars—the lead car, the president's, and our follow-up car—roared up the hill, splitting off from the rest of the motorcade to a point of apparent safety.

We learned shortly by radio that the fire was under control, the occupants had loaded into a spare car, and the motorcade would be joining us. But the memory of Dallas and of the suddenness with which disaster can strike were still fresh. One veteran reporter in the press bus behind the burning car later said, "When I saw that fire and smoke shoot up, I remember thinking, 'Oh, God, this time they used a bomb!' When I saw that it wasn't the president's car, but one behind it, and learned that it wasn't a bomb, but an electrical fire, I just sat there for a moment bathed in sweat."

On a stumping tour through Florida during the campaign, we were moving across a broad parking area to a speaking engagement for the president. I was in the open follow-up car with other agents of the shift; Lem Johns was just ahead of us with the president in the armored limousine, along with several local dignitaries.

Suddenly, there was a loud explosion, I saw President Johnson turn quickly, looking back, startled.

But I had seen what caused this one, and I grabbed the microphone. "It's okay. Your right rear tire just blew out."

But it was another example of what the gunfire in Dealey Plaza had etched into the minds of those who were there.

There were other incidents during the hectic campaign, but no shots were fired and no bombs were thrown, at least that we knew about. We would soon be resuming a job that had ended abruptly in Dallas, and that was vice presidential protection. I was among those at the time who urged that the Vice Presidential Detail not be allowed to become even temporarily extinct, but office space was always at a premium in the Executive Office Building, where the detail was headquartered, and since governmental agencies abhor empty offices as much as nature abhors a vacuum, they were soon taken over.

Temporary contingent details were assigned to the various unprotected nominees to be at their sides on November 3 when the vote count would begin. Glenn Weaver was selected as SAIC of the Vice Presidential (elect) Detail, and agents were sent to Minneapolis to be on hand if Hubert Humphrey got the job and to Buffalo in the event William Miller came out on top. Agents were also dispatched to Phoenix, the home of Senator Barry Goldwater.

On November 4, the Secret Service quietly slipped out of Phoenix and Buffalo. It hadn't even been close. Johnson and Humphrey got the highest percentage of the popular vote since the keeping of such records had begun, and that went all the way back to 1824.

LBJ had voted in Johnson City and had waited out the results at the ranch. On election eve, I hitched a flight on a cargo plane moving some Secret Service cars back east from Austin, voted at my home in Vienna, Virginia, and caught another flight back to Texas. I had forgotten a small mistake I made until I saw LBJ walking toward me, grinning, his wallet in one hand and his other hand out, the fingers rubbing together in the time-honored gesture that means money.

I had said he would carry my native state of Georgia. He had said, according to the polls, he wouldn't.

"Okay," I said, "you've got the polls, I've got history."

"Five dollars?" he said.

"Five dollars!" I said.

And for the first time since Reconstruction, Georgia went Republican. It cost five dollars to learn not to bet on anything political with a president. However, to LBJ, the way Georgia went was a matter of public record. He never asked me how I voted. To him, that was my business and mine alone.

He had completed John Kennedy's unfinished term. Now he had the mandate of the people, and for better or worse, Lyndon Johnson was going to put his personal stamp on the presidency.

CHAPTER 11

The Warren Report

On February 3, 1964, Marina Oswald, the widow of the accused assassin, became the first of 552 witnesses—ranging from spectators in the street to Mrs. Jacqueline Kennedy and the President of the United States—to give testimony to the Warren Commission. The FBI conducted some 25,000 interviews and submitted 2,300 reports to the commission. The Secret Service interviewed approximately 1,500 people and submitted 800 reports. Constant contact with the commission was maintained by the assignment of Inspector Thomas J. Kelley as the Secret Service's liaison officer, and Special Agents Elmer Moore and Robert Newbrand were assigned to provide limited physical protection to Chief Justice Warren when he traveled about.

In the days immediately following the assassination, Secret Service personnel who had been assigned in Dallas on the day of the tragedy made written reports to Chief Jim Rowley. My own report, dated November 29, was compiled from notes I made during and immediately after the events in Dallas. These statements were also made available to the commission.

On March 9, 1964, Roy Kellerman, Bill Greer, Clint Hill, and I—whose roles had been of particular significance—appeared before the commission, and a number of other Secret Service personnel were later called to testify.

Of necessity, a great deal of time was spent in hearing from individuals who were in no position to contribute any constructive or pertinent information, but whose exclusion, because of theories they had advanced or positions they had taken, would inevitably have brought forth cries of suppression.

Ten months after President Johnson had signed the executive order creating it, the Warren Commission published its report. The 888-page document, distilled and sifted from a mountain of data, was released on September 27, 1964. Anyone seeking some sensational new revelation was due for a disappointment. Almost from the moment the shots were fired in Dallas, speculation had ranged in every conceivable direction as to what lay behind the shooting of President Kennedy and the subsequent murder of his accused assassin. The commission reached the conclusion that Lee Harvey Oswald, acting alone and without involvement in any conspiracy, had assassinated the president. It also concluded that Jack Ruby, equally uninvolved in any conspiracy, had acted alone in the murder of Oswald.

But even the massive weight of the evidence would never convince some that there was not more to this than the Warren Commission reported. Even ten years later, people still asked me if it was true that John Kennedy was still alive, hidden in a secret room at Parkland Memorial Hospital. Such thoughts are ridiculous; still, there is no question that the assassination of President Kennedy will remain fertile ground to be plowed by sensationalists, muckrakers, and some honest skeptics for a long time to come.

In addition to reporting its conclusions about the assassination, the commission made a great many recommendations intended to lessen the possibility of such a thing happening again. Among them were extensive comments and recommendations to the Secret Service. The commission was not unrealistic about the problems inherent in presidential protection. The report stated:

> This Commission can recommend no procedures for the future protection of our Presidents which will guarantee security. The demands on the President in the execution of his responsibilities in today's world are so varied and complex and the traditions of the office in a democracy such as ours are so deepseated as to preclude absolute security.

Still, the commission and the Secret Service were in complete accord in that they sought the most secure environment possible, under the stated conditions. The report also stated:

> The Commission recognizes that the varied responsibilities of the President require that he make frequent trips to all parts of the United States and abroad. Consistent with their high responsibilities Presidents can never be protected from every potential threat. The Secret Service's difficulty in meeting its protective responsibility varies with the activities and the nature of the occupant of the Office of the Presidency and his willingness to conform to plans for his safety. In appraising the performance of the Secret Service it should be understood that it has to do its work within such limitations. Nevertheless, the Commission believes that recommendations for improvements in Presidential protection are compelled by the facts disclosed in this investigation.

Almost simultaneously with the publication of the report, the Secret Service was operating under the very limitations it referred to. The activities and the nature of Lyndon Johnson resulted in his riding through heavily populated metropolitan areas all across the country, campaigning by sitting on the back seats of open sedans, waving and smiling at the thousands of voters, and not failing to give a salute to those watching from the windows of the buildings along his route. All that was missing was another Lee Harvey Oswald.

The Secret Service began taking steps to tighten presidential security long before the Warren Commission report was published. There were a number of things that were self-evident. The commission pointed out that the Secret Service had not been able to develop or secure adequate resources of personnel and facilities to keep pace with the rapidly increasing complexity of the presidency. We were well aware of this, and we knew that the remedy would have to start with a larger budget. Our reception at the annual Appropriations hearings in the spring of 1964 was unlike any we had encountered on Capitol Hill before.

It would have been political suicide that year for committee members to be tightfisted with the Secret Service.

The fact that Lee Harvey Oswald was known to the FBI and not to the Secret Service was another area the commission delved into. This involved the criteria used in one agency making its files available to another. Oswald's Communist activities and the fact that he had lived in Russia and had attempted to renounce his United States citizenship had brought him to the attention of the FBI. But the FBI had files on a great many Communists and fellow travelers, and unless these individuals had indicated in some way that they were a potential danger to the president, they were not brought to the attention of the Secret Service.

In regard to criteria, the report simply said that "the criteria and procedures of the Secret Service designed to identify and protect against persons considered threats to the President were not adequate prior to the assassination."

The criteria now would mean that the Secret Service would, at the least, maintain surveillance on a man with Oswald's record. He would not be able to secrete himself behind stacks of boxes high in a building overlooking the motorcade route and be ready with a high-powered rifle as the president passed below.

During the hearings, this became a point of contention between the FBI and the Secret Service. In the words of the report:

> There were no Secret Service criteria which specifically required the referral of Oswald's case to the Secret Service; nor was there any requirement to report the names of defectors. However, there was much material in the hands of the FBI about Oswald: the knowledge of his defection, his arrogance and hostility to the United States, his pro-Castro tendencies, his lies when interrogated by the FBI, his trip to Mexico where he was in contact with Soviet authorities, his presence in the School Book Depository job and its location along the route of the motorcade. All this does seem to amount to enough to have induced an alert agency, such

as the FBI, possessed of this information to list Oswald as a potential threat to the safety of the President. This conclusion may be tinged with hindsight, but it is stated primarily to direct the thought of those responsible for the future safety of our Presidents to the need for a more imaginative and less narrow interpretation of their responsibilities. ...

The formal FBI instructions to its agents outlining the information to be referred to the Secret Service were too narrow at the time of the assassination. While the Secret Service bears the principal responsibility for this failure, the FBI instructions did not reflect fully the Secret Service's need for information regarding potential threats.

Testifying for the FBI, Alan H. Belmont, an assistant to Director Hoover, said:

This man came back from Russia; he indicated that he had learned his lesson, was disenchanted with Russia, and had a renewed concept—I am paraphrasing, a renewed concept—of the American free society. He gave evidence of settling down. Nowhere during the course of this investigation or the information that came to us from other agencies was there any indication of a potential for violence on his part.

Robert I. Bouck, SAIC of the Secret Service's Protective Research Section, which had the task of gathering information on people who represented a possible danger to the president, presented another view.

I would think his continued association with the Russian Embassy after his return, his association with Castro groups would have been of concern to us, a knowledge that he had, I believe, been court-martialed for illegal possession of a handgun in the Marines, that he owned a weapon and did a good deal of hunting or use of it, perhaps in Russia, plus a number of items about his disposition and unreliability of character, I think all of those, if we had them altogether, would have added up to pointing out a pretty bad individual, and I think that, together, had we known that he had a vantage point would seem somewhat serious to us, even though I must admit that none of them in themselves would meet our specific criteria—none of them alone.

The fact that the man who killed the president was known to one federal law enforcement agency but not to the agency responsible for the president's security had to be explained. The commission, on many occasions, pointed out that it was not trying to operate on the basis of hindsight, and this was obviously an area in which hindsight could easily have prevented the assassination. The commission, wisely I think, chose to express a need for broader criteria on the part of the Secret Service, as well as for broader interpretation of the criteria on the part of agencies receiving information.

No one reasonably expects the broadening of criteria to provide the final solution to assassination. In 1972, Arthur Herman Bremer pumped five pistol shots at presidential candidate George C. Wallace as a second choice since he had been unable to find the opportunity to assassinate President Nixon. Wallace was crippled and Secret Service Special Agent Nick Zarvos was wounded, yet to my knowledge, Bremer was on no one's list of potentially dangerous individuals.

Not unexpectedly, in the flood of criticism in the months following the assassination, there was much that was unjustified and unfair. A number of uninformed observers found fault in the fact that Jerry Behn, head of the White House Detail, was in Washington and not in Dallas at the time of the assassination. What critics of this sort fail to realize is that presidential protection is a job that never stops; it goes on twenty-four hours a day, every day. No one man is physically present on every presidential movement as a part of the Secret Service detail. Behn made his share of the trips and delegated others to his assistants.

Particularly caustic and unfair were the criticisms heaped upon the two Secret Service agents in the president's car, Bill Greer and Roy Kellerman, apparently for not having pulled some miracle out of a hat to save the president.

The Warren Commission, which did not hesitate to point out fault where it found it, was clear in its appraisal of the situation in the president's car.

> The configuration of the Presidential car and the seating arrangements of the Secret Service agents in the car did not afford the Secret Service agents the opportunity they should have had to be of immediate assistance to the President at the first sign of danger. Within these limitations, however, the Commission finds that the agents most immediately responsible for the President's safety reacted promptly at the time the shots were fired from the Texas School Book Depository Building.

As an outgrowth of the Warren Commission's recommendations, the Dillon Committee was formed, consisting of Treasury Secretary Douglas Dillon, Attorney General Nicholas Katzenbach, John A. McCone of the CIA, and National Security Adviser McGeorge Bundy. This group was to review and oversee the protective activities of the Secret Service and the other federal agencies that assist in safeguarding the president.

The Warren Commission was dealing with one of the most prejudged events in history, and the fact that it carefully examined every scrap of evidence relating to the assassination and reached its conclusions on the basis of this evidence seemed to carry little weight with a lot of people. Even the most casual acquaintance would still occasionally ask me, "Do you believe the findings of the Warren Commission?" What they were asking was, Do I believe Lee Harvey Oswald, acting alone, killed President Kennedy, and do I believe Jack Ruby, acting alone, killed Oswald? My answer is yes. The Warren Commission, in my opinion, accomplished its mission, and dug until it reached the truth.

CHAPTER 12

LBJ: 1965–1967

There were new faces around the White House. A dynamic young Texan, Marvin Watson, now filled Ken O'Donnell's shoes as special assistant to the president, one of the most powerful jobs in the White House. Bobby Kennedy had gone to New York and had been elected to the Senate. Nicholas Katzenbach replaced him as attorney general, with Ramsey Clark as his assistant. Other Kennedy appointees and aides who had stayed on at LBJ's request were now moving on. The Air Force pilot who had done most of the flying with Johnson as vice president, Colonel Jim Cross, was appointed Armed Forces aide to the president.

Top-level changes were also being made in the Secret Service. Jerry Behn and Floyd Boring, respectively the number-one and two men of the White House Detail, moved up to headquarters and to assignments as inspectors. I was promoted to SAIC of the White House Detail, with Roy Kellerman my deputy and Lem Johns and Bob Taylor my top assistants.

Ahead of us lay the single biggest security job the Secret Service faces—the Inauguration. There are two ways of looking at the Inauguration from the security standpoint. It comes along, without fail, every four years, occurs at the same time and place, and moves over an unvarying route, which allows us all the time we could possibly want to prepare for it. On the other hand, this same set of specifications could be used advantageously by a would-be assassin.

For the 1965 Inauguration, the parade route of approximately two miles from the White House to the Capitol and back was checked more thoroughly than ever before. Every building along Constitution and Pennsylvania Avenues was inspected, windows overlooking the route were ordered closed during the parade, manhole covers in the streets were sealed, and agents flew overhead in helicopters, in constant radio contact with those on the ground. Agents were brought in from the field offices on temporary assignment, and additional thousands of police and service personnel were to participate.

The Inaugural stand constructed on the steps of the Capitol had, for the first time, a barrier of bulletproof glass installed around the podium where Johnson and Humphrey were to take the oath. The reviewing stand in front of the White House also had protective glass installed.

Special Agent Bill Duncan had been supervising these intricate preparations for several months, and by Inauguration Day, January 20, everything was ready. Lady Bird had one item she wanted me to attend to. A couple of nights before the big day, she asked me to join them in their living quarters upstairs at the White House. She took an old family Bible from a bookcase.

"Rufe, this is the Bible that will be used when Lyndon takes the oath." She held it out to me. "You'll be there, I'm sure, and I'm depending on you to have this for us."

I tucked it under my arm. "Don't worry, Mrs. Johnson. It'll be there."

I had been with LBJ—on and off—for almost four years, and beginning with the trip to Dakar, I had been impressed with his stamina. But I had never seen him as active as he was during the days surrounding the Inauguration. The weekend preceding it, there had been festivities at the ranch. Something called an Inaugural Gala was held in Washington on Monday at the National Guard Armory and a concert and a governors' reception on Tuesday. All this in addition to business as usual.

Wednesday, January 20, at noon, he stood behind the bulletproof glass on the Capitol steps, bareheaded and without a topcoat, with a wintry wind whipping around him and a pale sun shining down. I handed the Bible to Lady Bird and LBJ placed his left hand on it as Chief Justice Warren administered the oath. It was a far different scene, as he repeated the words, than it had been fourteen months before, standing in the packed, sweltering cabin of *Air Force One*, with the body of John Kennedy lying in a casket only a few yards away.

The massive security arrangements proved to be adequate, as no serious incidents occurred. But with all due respect to the theorists who lay out a plan on paper and think that will do it, presidential protection on paper and presidential protection in the flesh are two different things—especially when the president is Lyndon Johnson.

Everything involved in the Inauguration is as tradition bound and predetermined as a ceremony can be. To the best of my knowledge, no president ever got out of his limousine during the Inaugural Parade to walk into the crowd and "press the flesh." No president, that is, until LBJ. With President and Mrs. Johnson, and Senator Everett Jordan in the rear seat of the limousine, we pulled away from the Capitol after the ceremony, turned left onto Constitution Avenue, and fell into line behind the lead cars, the Army Band, the Old Guard, the color guard, and the television and photographic vehicles.

The limousine came to a halt while these units began to stretch out along the route. LBJ did not like to sit still, and after a couple of minutes, he was getting restless.

He leaned toward the front. "Let's get out and talk to the folks while we're waiting, Rufus. When this thing's ready to move, we'll get back in."

I did not feel that the request involved any great security risk; it was completely spontaneous, and there were no buildings along that part of the avenue, so I climbed out and opened the door for him. Still hatless and without a topcoat, he waded out into the delighted crowd, talking and shaking hands, and as soon as the parade showed signs of moving, he obediently got back in and we continued on to the White House.

The next few hours were spent in the near-freezing weather in the reviewing stand, as the floats, bands, baton twirlers, and marching units passed in review beyond the bulletproof glass. That night, the Johnsons attended all five Inaugural Balls. He was up early the next morning with the usual tight work schedule.

But the hyperactivity of the week caught up with him Friday night. His personal physician, Admiral George G. Burkley, was called sometime after midnight. He found LBJ to be suffering from a severe cold, and as a precautionary measure, he ordered him taken to Bethesda Naval Hospital. For the next several days, the president recuperated, and the Secret Service and everyone else around the White House had an unexpected, but most welcome, rest.

The president's stay at Bethesda did prevent him from doing something that he felt very strongly he should do, and that was to attend the funeral of Winston Churchill, who died on January 24. Dr. Burkley flatly vetoed the trip because of LBJ's health, and that was that.

When he assumed the presidency after Kennedy's death, Johnson had vowed to remain in the United States until the country once again had a vice president. This was to continue for some time, however, after Hubert Humphrey filled the vacancy because of national and world conditions and LBJ's desire to get his domestic programs rolling in Congress.

The war in Vietnam was escalating. Early in February, after Viet Cong attacks on a helicopter base and U.S. Army advisers' barracks near Pleiku, South Vietnam, President Johnson decided that the situation was such that U.S. servicemen's dependents were no longer safe in that country and would have to be withdrawn. He also ordered retaliatory air strikes on targets in North Vietnam, which, in turn, roused students in Moscow to attack the U.S. Embassy there.

This was the start of the really rough years. While we continued to become more deeply involved in Asia, the home front was far from calm. Pickets outside the White House became an almost daily occurrence. A situation was developing in Selma, Alabama, that required the president's action. Black people in Selma were protesting unjust obstacles being placed in the way of their voter-registration efforts. Civil rights groups organized for a march on the capitol in Montgomery, and during the march, a woman was murdered by Ku Klux Klansmen.

Pickets and demonstrators homed in on the White House. In addition to being the presidential residence and office complex, the White House was administered by the National Park Service, and certain areas were open to public view. Tours were conducted every day except Sunday, Monday, and holidays. One morning in March, during a routine tour of the White House, fourteen civil rights demonstrators fell to the floor in a hallway on the ground floor and refused to move, although two did leave later voluntarily.

Protest activity of this sort had been anticipated, and procedures had been planned to cope with it. First, it was necessary to isolate the group, thereby preventing reinforcements from joining or supplying them and avoiding friction with other tourists.

I was notified of what was happening. In days gone by, such a thing would have been handled simply and directly by picking them up off the floor, putting them in a paddy wagon, and hauling them off to the nearest precinct house to be booked on a charge of unlawful entry. But those days were gone. While I went up to the president's bedroom to apprise him of the situation, the very able and efficient White House Police Chief Major Ralph Stover explained to the demonstrators that they were in violation of the law and duly asked that they get up and leave. They, just as duly, told him what he could do with his law and continued to lie on the floor.

At first, the president suggested that he go down and reason with them.

"I don't think you should, sir," I said. "With your permission, I'll have them arrested and removed."

Jack Valenti, Bill Moyers, Cliff Alexander, and several other presidential aides had been summoned. The protest was taking on the proportions of a national crisis. Valenti opposed my solution. Bill Moyers said he would go down and talk to them, and he and Cliff Alexander went downstairs, got the same reaction Stover had, and returned. That my view was entirely nonpolitical may have led to oversimplification, but it seemed to clearly be a case of the minority infringing on the rights of the majority. The White House belonging to all the citizens was being obstructed by a dozen demonstrators.

For nearly seven hours, they lay there on the floor, the routine of the White House being routed around this section of hallway. A reception was scheduled for that night, however, and it would require the use of this hallway. LBJ had an appointment at 6:00 p.m. at the Rayburn Building, and as he prepared to leave, he took me aside.

"This damn thing has gone on long enough, Rufus. Get 'em outta here while we're gone. I don't have to tell you that they're the ones who would like to see this on page one of the *Post* tomorrow, not us."

I smiled, thinking that this *could* have been done seven hours ago. "They'll be gone when you get back, Mr. President."

There was no violence, no pictures, nothing but an orderly removal to several police vehicles that were waiting discreetly off the rear drive. When several of them were found guilty a few months later of the charge Ralph Stover had explained to them, unlawful entry, the prosecuting attorney told the jury: "One thing that is not on trial here is the reasonableness or the justness of the cause, but the defendants chose the wrong way to express their views."

These were busy times for the Secret Service. We had the routine movements with the president in and out of Washington, and at the same time, we were strengthening the organization along the lines of the Warren Commission recommendations. We had a larger budget, more personnel, better equipment, increased office space, and improved communications support.

The armored-car program had been broadened, and working with General Motors, Ford, Pittsburgh Plate Glass, and others, designs for future models were being constantly improved and refined.

That summer, on July 5, 1965, the Secret Service celebrated its one hundredth anniversary, in honor of which the president proclaimed July 5 through 11 to be Secret Service Week. A medallion commemorating the occasion was struck at the U.S. Mint.

The protective mission, by requiring people to be in close proximity with one another over extended periods of time, often creates genuine friendships. And out of this, a question of propriety may occasionally arise. When the Johnson girls came under Secret Service protection, Special Agent Bob Kollar and two other agents were assigned to Luci (she had streamlined the spelling by changing the *y* to *i*).

Luci tested the agents once or twice, getting into her car and driving away from the White House, leaving her Secret Service detail the job of tracking her down.

Bob's solution to this was simple. Once, when Luci hopped into the car and reached to turn the key, it was not there.

"Looking for something, Luci?"

She glanced across the drive where Bob Kollar was standing, a set of car keys dangling from his hand. From then on, it was no Secret Service, no car keys. If she had not fully realized it before, she did now. Bob Kollar was going to look after her security, whether she liked it or not. No more tricks were played on Bob. Luci respected his judgment and looked on him as a real friend.

This friendship brought Bob into my office one day. "Rufe, Luci is planning to convert to Catholicism, and she's asked me to be one of her sponsors. What do you think I should do?"

We both realized that this could easily be misinterpreted and become a sticky item indeed.

"It's a personal decision for you," I said. "And I don't need to tell you that she's paid you one of the highest compliments she could. But for professional reasons, I think you should respectfully decline."

Bob agreed, and when he talked to Luci, she understood.

As firmly founded as the protective procedures of the Secret Service are, certain exceptions can be made in the light of reason. And occasionally, reason does not prevail. The handling of food that comes to the White House in the form of gifts has always been a routine matter. One of the classic methods of assassination has been the poisoning of food or drink, and the surest and simplest way to prevent this from happening is to destroy such gifts.

Lady Bird Johnson, one of the most cooperative and uncomplaining women we ever had the privilege of serving, occasionally found fault with this indiscriminate destruction, and when special friends wished to send her some edible gift, she would have them send it to her secretary, thus circumventing the Secret Service.

Even so, there remained obvious cases that could not involve a security risk. One bright Sunday morning, Secretary of Defense Robert McNamara arrived alone in his station wagon at the southwest gate of the White House. Rather than go into the mansion in his casual attire, he handed a package of Mrs. McNamara's cheese blintzes—a gourmet specialty for which she was well known—to the policeman with instructions to have them delivered to the Johnsons.

The officer, following his written orders, advised the Secret Service. The package was picked up shortly afterward and went the way of all food gifts. This might well have been the end of it except that a few days later, Mrs. McNamara asked the president if he had liked the cheese blintzes she sent him. At this point, the blintzes hit the fan.

"What the hell happened to the cheese blintzes Mrs. McNamara sent me?" the president roared at the nearest Secret Service agent, who happened to be Lem Johns. Lem relayed the question through channels, and it very quickly settled on my desk.

I checked it out and went straight to the Man with my answer. "Sir," I told him, "about Mrs. McNamara's cheese blintzes ..." I took a deep breath. "We just fouled up."

He couldn't argue with that, and that was the last of it, except that a few internal changes were made in the handling of food gifts.

In September 1965, the Secret Service was assigned additional duties. The president signed legislation that extended Secret Service protection to former presidents and their wives. We were to resume coverage of the Trumans and the Eisenhowers, unless they declined it. Bess and Harry Truman, after a short trial period, did decline. They had been without Secret Service protection for twelve years and felt that it was not necessary at this late date.

Mamie and Ike were pleased with it. Herb Dixon was assigned as SAIC of the Eisenhower Detail, with Jim McCown as his top assistant.

A few weeks after this, the president's doctors advised him to undergo surgery for a gallbladder condition. While the operation itself was not considered especially serious, it had to be handled carefully so that the public did not think any sort of crisis might be approaching. Before making a public announcement, LBJ wisely consulted with former President Eisenhower to get his views on how it should best be done, as Ike had been through this twice during his tenure of office.

When it was announced, it was without fanfare, pointing out the minimal danger of the operation itself and the fact that Vice President Humphrey had specific instructions in the event major decisions were required while the president was under anesthesia. As soon as we had the time and the place—October 8, at Bethesda Naval Hospital—the Secret Service began getting ready for security at the hospital.

For the operation itself, I scrubbed up along with the doctors and nurses, donned a hospital mask and gown, and joined Dr. Willis Hurst on an elevated observation area just off the main floor of the operating room. We had taken every precaution to keep any unauthorized personnel out of the operating-room area. Even so, as I watched in fascination while a masked surgeon poked his arm elbow deep inside the belly of the President of the United States, it occurred to me that the high cost of hospital care was understandable if a relatively simple gallbladder operation required the presence of more than twenty doctors and nurses moving in and out of the operating room.

When the operation was completed and LBJ was safely in the recovery room, I struck up a conversation with the head nurse. "You know, it was really surprising just how many people it takes to perform an operation. I counted more than twenty in that operating room."

"Sure you did. Come here, let me show you something." She led me down the corridor where she stopped outside an operating room. There was a small, rectangular glass window in the door. "Take a look through there. They're doing a gallbladder."

I peered in. Clustered around the still form on the table were no more than half a dozen masked and gowned figures. I looked around at the nurse. "The same operation?"

She nodded. "The same."

"But ..." I pointed down the hall to where LBJ's gallbladder had been worked on.

"Mr. Youngblood," she said flatly, "who's going to tell the chief of surgery, the commanding officer of the hospital, the chief of medicine, the head radiologist—"

I was nodding. "That they can't be there while the president is being operated on."

Whether because of, or in spite of, the crowded operating room, LBJ made a speedy recovery. He even proudly displayed his scar to newsmen and photographers a few days later while sunning on the lawn at Bethesda, which earned him an irreverent tag, "The Abdominal Showman."

The restructuring of the Secret Service took another step in the fall of 1965. David Acheson, who became a special assistant to Treasury Secretary Henry Fowler in August, was given the job of overseeing the activities of the Secret Service and of furthering the reorganization. At this time, Jim Rowley's designation was changed from chief to director. At the next level, four assistant directorships were formed. One of these, assistant director of protective forces, encompassed all the protective details, as well as the White House Police and the Treasury Guard forces. I was promoted to this post, and Roy Kellerman remained with me as my deputy. Lem Johns moved up to become SAIC of the White House Detail, with Bob Taylor as his deputy.

In this new job, the Eisenhower Detail, being a protective unit, came under my direction. Before dawn on November 9, I was awakened by a phone call from Herb Dixon, who was with Ike and Mamie in Augusta.

"The General's had another heart attack, Rufe," he said. "We've got him at Fort Gordon Army Hospital."

The detail with Ike had only recently been activated, and in my position as director over all such details, I felt that, in a situation such as this, I should be there with them. Herb went on to tell me that, while everything possible was being done for Ike, Mamie, understandably, was quite distraught. This added weight to my decision, and I told him I would fly down as a headquarters representative as soon as I could get out of Washington to help out if I was needed.

Shortly after I got to Augusta, I met with Mamie in a room at Fort Gordon Army Hospital, just down a corridor from where the General was being cared for.

"I want you to know, Mr. Youngblood," she told me, "that if it had not been for Mr. Dixon and the other agents, this could have been much more serious. They knew exactly what to do when the attack began, and they got medical assistance immediately. I intend to write President Johnson and Director Row-ley and let them know what a fine job the Secret Service did."

As we talked, I began to notice an unusual amount of activity around Ike's room, doctors and nurses moving in and out the door in the sort of controlled run they seem to have during emergencies. Mamie had also noticed this, and as she started up from her chair, one of the doctors came down the hall.

"What is it, Doctor?" Mamie said, her voice tight. "What's happened?"

"Don't be alarmed, Mrs. Eisenhower," he told her. "The General just had another seizure, but we're working with him, and we'll keep you informed. We're doing everything that can be done." He took her arm. "Please sit down."

She sank slowly back down on the chair, "Thank you, Doctor. I'll be all right. You go back to the General ..."

I sat there, feeling helpless, but not wanting to leave her alone. Shortly, one of her close friends came and sat beside her.

I stood up. "I'm sure he'll be just fine, Mrs. Eisenhower," I said awkwardly. "If there's anything at all that Mr. Rowley, I, or any of the men can do, you just say the word. We'll all be praying for you."

She smiled at me, and I moved back, said my farewell, and then turned and walked down the hall.

But Ike was tough, and he proved it by pulling through again.

While I was in Augusta, a reporter for one of the Washington papers saw me and created his own minor scoop. When I got back to the capital a few days later, a clipping was on my desk. "Youngblood Replaced as LBJ Bodyguard," the headline read, and the article went on to tell of my fall from grace. "A new Secret Service agent has been placed in charge of the detail that guards President Johnson. Rufus Youngblood, the agent who protected Mr. Johnson in Dallas when President Kennedy was assassinated two years ago, is no longer assigned as the President's personal bodyguard."

Well, you can't win 'em all. My "fall from grace" had landed me in a new post as an assistant director.

The incident with Ike showed the real value of having agents with our former presidents, and there was growing concern on the part of LBJ and the Secret Service over the safety and well-being of the Trumans. Since they had declined protection, it certainly would not be forced on them. We had an office in Kansas City, though, only a short distance from the Trumans' home in Independence, and Special Agent Paul Burns was transferred from the White House Detail to the Kansas City Field Office to be on hand for any assignment involving the Trumans. It took time and patience, but Bess and Harry Truman finally accepted limited protection, and Paul became head of the detail.

It was more than a year after his Inauguration when LBJ made a trip outside the United States. He had requested that I go along on any foreign trips, and one came up almost by accident in April 1966. In the planning stages, it was to have been a visit to Mexico City by Lady Bird. But LBJ became interested, included himself, and inevitably took over. A trip like this with Lyndon Johnson either had to be a logistical masterpiece or a disaster. First came the "rendezvous" at Randolph Field in San Antonio. I flew in by chopper from Johnson City with other Secret Service men. Next, Lady Bird and her party arrived from Washington aboard the presidential 707. Then came Lynda via the family Beechcraft from the University of Texas, and last, but far from least, LBJ roared in from the ranch on an Air Force JetStar.

It all meshed beautifully, and without undue delay, everybody got aboard the 707—now *Air Force One*—and off we flew to Mexico City. It was good to be out again, but the motorcade from the airport into Mexico City immediately became a security nightmare. It would have been a perfect example of what the Warren Report said not to do. But in Mexico City, we were the guests, and we did as the Mexicans said to do.

It began with an open car, with President Johnson and President Díaz Ordaz standing and waving as we drove slowly through a city filled with balconied buildings. Estimates of the crowd ran to two million or more.

"Don't worry, señor," the Mexican security chief kept telling us. "Nothing is going to happen! Don't look so worried!"

He was right. Nothing did happen. But once was enough.

In the late summer of 1966, Luci Johnson became the bride of Patrick Nugent, of Waukegan. A gala reception was held at the White House. In addition to our routine security plans for an affair of this magnitude, we were delegated the job of smuggling the newlyweds out of the mansion and on their way to a secret honeymoon hideaway in the Bahama Islands. To effect this, Luci was disguised in a blond wig for the commercial airline flight south, using initialed luggage belonging to Special Agent Bob Kollar's wife, Eve. The most important task was to get the Nugents out of the White House without a battalion of newsmen tagging along, and this was done by spiriting them away through one of the tunnels leading from the White House basement to the Treasury Building. It went like clockwork, and Luci, Pat, and Luci's Secret Service detail flew off undetected.

In October 1966, LBJ began his first overseas trip in almost three years— since the Benelux trip as vice president, only weeks before Dallas. The primary purpose of this trip was a seven-nation summit conference to be held in the Philippines to grapple with the mounting problems of Vietnam. The president also intended visiting a number of countries, which meant Secret Service advance teams would be scattered all over the Pacific, from New Zealand to Australia, the Philippines, Thailand, Malaysia, and South Korea, plus the outgoing U.S. stops at Honolulu and Samoa and the return stop in Alaska.

It would be the first time an American president while in office set foot in these countries, except for Korea and the Philippines, which Ike had visited in his 1960 odyssey.

As head of the White House Detail, Lem Johns was directly in charge of the overall trip. But as his boss, and to the extent it required help from headquarters, I went along.

Vietnam was not only the subject to be discussed in Manila; it was to crop up almost as soon as the trip began in the form of protesters to the war. New Zealand, the first foreign stop, was not entirely devoid of demonstrators, but we had no major problem with them. In Australia, however, our first stop gave us a sampling of what lay ahead. At dusk on October 20, *Air Force One* settled to earth at the Canberra airport. The capital was a small city, less than one hundred thousand at that time, but the turnout seemed to include everybody in town as we drove to the hotel where the president's party was staying. Amidst the crowds, placards protesting the war were much more in evidence than they had been in New Zealand, but there was no physical activity on the part of the protesters.

The following day we flew to Melbourne, where more than half a million people jammed the streets to see the president. Several times along our motorcade route, situations developed that were untenable to the Secret Service but a delight to LBJ. The cars were completely halted, encased in people, solidly packed front and rear and all around. We had received intelligence that Communist factions in Melbourne and Sydney would attempt to disrupt the president's visit, and we were extremely uncomfortable until we could get the cars rolling again.

At one point along the route, after we had worked our way through the jam and were moving with relative ease along the street, a young man suddenly broke from the crowd along the curb and lobbed two objects at the president's armored limousine. They were bombs—paint bombs—one red, the other green. The green bag burst against the windshield, and the red on top of the car. President Johnson, Lady Bird, and Bob Taylor, who was inside the car with them, were untouched. But those of us outside—Lem Johns, Jerry Kivett, myself, a few other agents, and a number of bystanders—were covered with the stuff. While the Australian police hauled the paint bomber away, we continued to our destination.

The only place we could find enough solvent to clean ourselves up was a nearby hospital, where we presented a Christmasy sight all decked out in red and green. But as an intern gingerly wiped paint out of my eyes, I gave a little prayer for that particular demonstrator's having chosen paint rather than acid as a means of expressing his sentiments.

The limousine spent the night in a paint shop and was as good as new when we arrived in Sydney the next day. It was a repeat of Melbourne, insofar as the greeting of the president was concerned, except that in Sydney, being a larger city, the crowds were proportionately larger. Estimates ran as high as a million and a quarter, and standing in the command post in the *Queen Mary*, behind the president's car, and seeing people from horizon to horizon, I had no reason to doubt it.

There were no bombs, paint or otherwise, thrown in Sydney, but when we reached Brisbane later that evening, and another tremendous turnout, the demonstrators did throw something. They threw themselves, directly in the path of the president's limousine. People lying in the street pose a problem that is simply stated. You stop the car, or you keep rolling and crush the demonstrators beneath the wheels of a seven-thousand-pound Lincoln, or you remove the demonstrators. Obviously, the first two are unacceptable on practical as well as humane grounds.

Special Agents Ron Pontius and Bob Taylor were working the positions at the left and right front of the limousine for this motorcade, and when the first demonstrator stretched out in the street ahead of them, Ron grabbed his arms and Bob his feet, with the intention of lofting him back into the crowd, hopeful that those along the curb would part long enough to let him land.

The first one must have felt like he was on a medieval torture rack, because Bob and Ron were straining in opposite directions. Standing in the *Queen Mary*, I saw the problem, picked up the bullhorn, and yelled: "Throw him to the side of the senior agent!"

It went smoothly from then on, with demonstrators sailing from the front of the president's car like snow from a snowplow.

While he was attending the conference in Manila a few days later, the president made an unannounced, though not unexpected, side trip. Operating under secret conditions, with only short notice to a select few, *Air Force One* took off across the South China Sea and put down at Cam Ranh Bay, South Vietnam. This was the first time an incumbent American president had visited a battle zone since Franklin D. Roosevelt went to Casablanca in 1943. In many ways, it was like a stopover in any city in America, LBJ wading out into the crowds of GIs that surrounded him, signing autographs, "pressing the flesh," and talking with the men.

The flight to Vietnam, however, presented relatively little risk from the security standpoint. General Westmoreland had seen to the security of the military base, and although it was generally expected that while he was so close to Vietnam, LBJ would not miss the opportunity of going there, the time and place were not announced in advance. In fact, our security problems were much greater in countries far removed from the war zone.

The president stayed on the move as we went into 1967. The Vietnam War grew more frustrating and seemingly insoluble with each passing month, and in March, LBJ flew to Guam for conferences with the South Vietnamese leaders, Thieu and Ky. A month later, we were in Punta del Este, Uruguay, where LBJ met with the presidents of several South American countries, and soon after that, we flew to Germany for the funeral of former Chancellor Konrad Adenauer.

In Washington, there were some internal changes affecting the Secret Service. Jim Hendrick took over David Acheson's job as assistant to the secretary of the Treasury assigned to oversee the Secret Service, and at the White House, Ralph Stover retired as chief of the White House police and Glenard Lanier moved up to that important post.

In June, Luci, who had married Pat Nugent the previous August, had a son, Lyn, thereby making the president a grandfather and giving us another principal to protect. This little principal had a role, at least in part, in the success of the Glassboro Summit Conference held two days after his birth. On June 23, 1967, President Johnson and Soviet Premier Aleksei Kosygin met at Glassboro College in New Jersey. When Johnson told Kosygin of his newly born grandson, the two world leaders, both grandfathers, reaffirmed their desire to prevent a nuclear disaster in the interest of future generations.

December brought both happiness and tragedy. On December 9, one of the biggest social events of the year in Washington took place at the White House. Lynda Bird Johnson became the bride of Captain Chuck Robb (USMC).

On the eighteenth, news came from Australia that Prime Minister Harold Holt had disappeared while swimming in shark-infested waters near the coastal town of Portsea. LBJ had established a warm relationship with the affable Holt on his visit there in 1966 and during a visit by Holt to Washington the following spring. The president decided that he would personally attend the memorial services, and the following day, *Air Force One* was once more en route to Australia.

It turned out to be a more extensive trip than was originally intended. We were halfway around the world, and just before we started back, the president decided we might as well go the other way. The radios aboard *Air Force One* crackled out messages for preparation ahead to Thailand and Cam Ranh Bay, where the president visited the men fighting the Asian war, which seemed to have no end in sight.

The spontaneity of the trip once Australia and the war zone were behind us was such that even as the big jet streaked westward from Asia, the decision as to whether to put down at Rome or Paris had not been made. Rome got the nod, and racing the sun, the president set foot on Italian soil the same day he had talked with American GIs in Thailand and Vietnam.

The antiwar feeling directed toward the United States had spread to Europe, so no motorcades were planned for the short stopover in Rome. A helicopter took LBJ from the airport to Italian President Saragat's villa, where LBJ, Saragat, and Premier Moro conferred briefly, and then in a rain-drenched night, it lifted off again, taking the president to the Vatican and an audience with Pope Paul VI before heading home. This short flight caused as much apprehension as any other incident on this round-the-world trip. But the pilot, whose skill I was thankful for, brought the big chopper thundering down amidst the ancient buildings and into a rose garden, where it sank almost wheel deep into the rain-soaked soil.

It was Christmas Eve when we looked out the windows of *Air Force One* and saw the familiar runways of Andrews Air Force Base and the subdued skyline of Washington in the distance.

CHAPTER 13

Hubert Horatio Humphrey

As SAIC of the White House Detail, my contact with the new vice president had been minimal, restricted for the most part to functions involving both the president and the vice president. When I became an assistant director, the Vice Presidential Detail then came under my direction, and I included myself on some of Humphrey's travels.

LBJ had gotten used to having me around, so I still rode with him occasionally. I was with him one Monday in January 1966 when he attended a special service at the National Presbyterian Church. Humphrey was also in attendance, and when it was over, the two men paused outside and talked for several minutes. The president suddenly took Humphrey's arm.

"Come on, Hubert," he said, "ride back to the White House with me."

It is strictly taboo, from the security standpoint, for the president and the vice president to ride together in the same car, boat, plane, wagon, or anything else, but they were inside the car and had resumed their conversation before I could voice an objection. Since we were only a few blocks from the White House, I shrugged, climbed in, and told Norman Edwards to move out. I could not help thinking of the ivory-tower planners who view protective work simply as an immutable list of do's and don'ts, and of what their reaction to this might have been.

I did bring it to the president's attention later that day, however. "Well, you went and did it, didn't you?"

"Did what?" He gave me an innocent look.

"Rode in the same car with the vice president, that's what."

"Well, we had some business to talk over."

"Next time, sir, would you mind waiting till you get back here?"

"Okay, pardner," he said. "You're right. It won't happen again."

At eleven o'clock that night, I found out what they had been talking about. Glenn Weaver, SAIC of the Vice Presidential Detail, phoned me at home.

"Rufe," he said, "the vice president's going to Shastri's funeral."

I had read in the newspaper of the Indian prime minister's death. "When is he leaving?"

"Would you believe midnight? I could use some help on the arrangements."

"Okay." I thought about what was involved and added, "Why don't I just go with you? We'll do the advance on the way. I'll meet you at Andrews."

For the past five years my suitcases had never been fully unpacked. I threw in a few last-minute items suitable for the climate in India, kissed Peggy, and drove to Andrews. *Air Force Two* was well on its way across the Atlantic by the time Glenn and I finished talking to our embassies along the route and settled down for a few hours' sleep.

India, as I have mentioned before, is a country where a flat tire can draw enough people to fill the Astrodome. The funeral of a prime minister results in a flood of humanity that you don't even believe when you see it. New Delhi was not merely wall to wall with Indians; they were up the walls, up the utility poles, and up everything else that afforded a view of anything or anyone. I have never encountered an unfriendly crowd in that impoverished country and would hate to do so. Friendly crowds there, by their sheer size and enthusiasm, can pose a hazard, as Ike's visit to New Delhi in 1959 proved when he and Nehru were almost smothered by the affectionate mob.

Vice President Humphrey was just one of many foreign dignitaries attending Shastri's funeral, however, and he was not singled out by the crowd the way Ike was, so we came through this one with a minimum of bruises. The trip did give me an opportunity of seeing what sort of man we would be working with.

A month after we came back from India, President Johnson met with South Vietnam's leaders, Thieu and Ky, in Honolulu, and on the final day of the conferences, he decided to have Humphrey visit Vietnam and other Asian countries. As LBJ flew back to Washington, I sent agents ahead to do some of the advance work for HHH's tour, and I waited in Hawaii for his arrival.

In summation, all this sounds simple. But the logistics of a movement of this sort, on short notice, are staggering. There are shots to be taken, passports and visas to arrange, transportation to schedule, personnel to rearrange, housing, food, and so on, ad infinitum.

Chuck Bailey, one of the senior newsmen assigned to go along on this trip, told me that the press would be very interested in stories concerning Humphrey's security.

"Well, there'll be the usual methods," I told him, "and in critical areas, we'll have considerable assistance from the military, and if the going really gets rough, we won't hesitate to fall back on two of our secret weapons."

His ears perked up. "Secret weapons?"

I nodded. "Prayer's the first one. I don't have to tell you about how that works. The press is the other, and it's greatly underestimated."

"How's that?"

"Bodies. With all you guys standing around our man, you'll stop a lot of bullets before they get to him."

I never did see Chuck's story on the secret weapons of the Secret Service.

Humphrey carried out his mission like a real trouper in Vietnam, going out to visit the troops in the combat areas, and not restricting his activities to the comparative safety of Saigon.

I dropped off the tour in Bangkok and went back to Saigon where Bob Taylor and Bill Livingood were wrapping up the loose ends. I had asked them to try to locate my son-in-law, Lieutenant Darrell Rumpf, who was somewhere out in the boondocks, and get him to Saigon for a couple of days if it could be arranged without disrupting the war effort. They accomplished their mission, and I had good news to relay to my daughter Joy when I got back to the States.

As vice president, LBJ had not had to face some of the problems that befell HHH. Because of the rankling feeling about the Vietnam War that was constantly increasing in the United States, Humphrey was often beset by hecklers when he spoke. This can be one of the most frustrating experiences imaginable, and on one occasion, it reached a point where one of our agents did something agents are not supposed to do. Humphrey was scheduled to speak at a large university, and hecklers were lying in wait for him. The Secret Service had intelligence of this, but there was little that could be done about it. The hall erupted into a near melee only minutes after Humphrey started to speak and was drowned out by the hecklers, and when the dust began to settle, the agent (who shall forever remain nameless) phoned me in Washington.

"I put my foot in the bucket tonight, Rufe," he said. "I have to resign from the Service."

"What happened?"

"I belted one of those damn militant hecklers. You know how it's been with the vice president lately. You can't help but admire him for keeping his cool when they're giving him so much hell. One of 'em was standing right in front of me just below the podium, screaming up at the Man while he was trying to speak, calling him a bastard and a few other things. The next thing I knew, there was a lot of pushing and shoving and I had my fist down his throat." He gave a halfhearted laugh. "I think I broke my hand. But you know something? It really felt good! Anyhow, there was bedlam all over the hall by then, and we got the vice president out."

"Where are you now?" I asked him.

"At the airport, I heard some of the press saying one of the ringleaders was screaming that a Secret Service agent poked him, but he wasn't able to tell them which one."

"Okay," I said. "You tell the vice president what happened, have a doctor look at your hand, and get back here to Washington. Maybe you should take a little annual leave."

Humphrey did not condone what had happened—he couldn't. But he was understanding, and it went no farther than him. I had no choice but to reprimand the agent. But it was a rough year to be traveling with Hubert Humphrey, and no one knew that better than Humphrey himself.

The mood of the country being what it was, an overseas trip was often looked upon as a vacation compared to domestic movements. But not always. In July 1966, LBJ sent the vice president to the Dominican Republic to represent the United States at the Inauguration of the new president Joaquín Balaguer. That tumultuous island nation had not completely recovered from the conditions that had forced President Johnson to send in the Marines the previous year, and some of our intelligence reports prior to Humphrey's visit made it out to be a volcano, seething and about to blow. We requested—and got—the presidential armored parade limousine, and Glenn Weaver and I, along with other Secret Service personnel, flew down on the transport plane that carried the car to do some of the advance work.

We were briefed at the U.S. Embassy in Santo Domingo, then went over the various routes and visited all the places the vice president would be going, taking notes, mapping possible evacuation routes, and generally familiarizing ourselves with the entire itinerary.

A final meeting was held at the Embassy prior to Humphrey's arrival. In fact, *Air Force Two* was only an hour out of Santo Domingo when an Embassy aide burst into the meeting.

"We just got an unconfirmed report that there's machine-gun fire in the palace!" he announced.

The National Palace in the Dominican Republic is the equivalent of the White House in Washington, and machine-gun fire there was obviously an extremely serious matter. But one word had caught my ear.

The aide went on, looking at Glenn and me with a worried expression. "It's not too late to abort the vice president's plane to Puerto Rico!"

Glenn and I glanced at each other, obviously thinking the same thing. Glenn said, "We're not aborting on the basis of an unconfirmed report. Let's get it confirmed."

"But there's not time—" he started to explain.

"Then we'll make time," I put in.

If the vice president had shown up in San Juan, as it turned out, his arrival there would have been embarrassing to explain. The "unconfirmed report" had apparently been turned in by an informant who needed the five or ten dollars he got for reporting. The "machine-gun fire" had (1) not been at the National Palace, and (2) had not been machine-gun fire, but merely citizens shooting off firecrackers in celebration of the Inauguration of the new president.

With this out of the way, Glenn and I boarded an ancient Army helicopter that was to take us to the airport to meet HHH. The old bird clattered and shook its way up to about 1,500 feet, and following the coastline and the freeway paralleling it, we headed for the airport. From time to time, indentations in the shoreline would take us over the Caribbean, and at a particular moment when I happened to be gazing down at the azure waters and thinking of stories I had read about the man-eating sharks that abounded in the area, the roar of the engine suddenly ceased.

The pilot glanced around at us. "Tighten your belts, fellas, old Betsy's going down again." While he gave a vivid description of the ancestry of old Betsy's engine, we began to windmill downward, and I stared below to see if we were headed for the man-eating sharks or the freeway and the Dominican drivers, who all seemed to think they were riding the pole at the Indianapolis Speedway.

Our pilot had learned well from previous engine malfunctions, however, and he brought the old chopper down with bone-crunching precision on the median strip of the freeway. Even before my teeth stopped rattling, he was on the radio advising his base as to the location of his latest forced landing.

"It'll take at least fifteen minutes to get another chopper out here," he told us.

With the vice president due to arrive shortly, Glenn and I thanked him for the ride, climbed out, and flagged down the first thing that came along headed in our direction. It happened to be a pickup truck, and I shouted something about *aeropuerto* while the four guys packed into the seat grinned and said "*Si, si!*" Off we went, riding in the back between a chicken coop and a sack of fertilizer, to be on hand for the arrival of the Vice President of the United States.

Even though the machine-gun fire report had been a false alarm, we did not take lightly the intelligence reports warning of possible trouble, and we kept Humphrey under tight security until Balaguer was safely sworn in and *Air Force Two* was once more airborne and bound for Washington.

Just as LBJ had done as Kennedy's vice president, HHH drew many of the ceremonial foreign assignments. Whenever there was a state funeral or a new leader taking office, Humphrey generally attended to represent the United

States. In July of 1967, President Chung Hee Park of South Korea was sworn in for a second term, and I joined the Humphrey entourage for this. On the way back from Seoul, *Air Force Two* stopped off at Anchorage, Alaska. The vice president wanted this to be a sort of "winding down" stop, and the whole group checked into the Western Hotel.

Humphrey was scheduled to be principal speaker that evening at a rally in the ball park, and as we left the hotel to keep the engagement, we encountered some kids passing out handbills. Glenn Weaver took one, read it, glanced in my direction, and started laughing. He gave it to the vice president, and the reaction was the same.

"What's so funny?" I asked as one of the kids handed me one. It read:

COME ONE COME ALL!
GIANT RALLY AT THE BALL PARK!
SEE! HEAR!
Vice President Hubert H. Humphrey!
See! The Eskimo Blanket Toss!
See! Martin Agronsky! Famous Commentator!
See! Rufus Youngblood! Famous Secret Service Agent!

I could feel my face turning red. The vice president walked over to me and slapped me on the back.

"You know, Rufus, I always try to look on the bright side of things, and I suppose I can be thankful that I got top billing over Rufus Youngblood, Martin Agronsky, and the blanket toss!"

It was a long time before I heard the last of that.

HHH needed a sense of humor, and he had it. It often meant the difference between an awkward moment or a good laugh. During the campaign in 1964, he had visited the LBJ Ranch, and with newsmen and cameramen all around, he and the president were inspecting some of LBJ's Herefords. Humphrey momentarily failed to watch where he was stepping, and suddenly, his left shoe became the focus of attention.

Calmly scraping the shoe on a fence rail, he quipped, "Mr. President, I think I just stepped in the Republican platform!"

In October 1967, Humphrey went to Vietnam for the Inauguration of President Thieu, and I went along with Glenn Weaver and the Vice Presidential Detail. As we stopped over at the Air Force base in Guam for refueling, I recalled that I had been there with the vice president on a previous trip. Even a refueling stop calls for a brief courtesy inspection of the base, and I had been in the lead car with the air provost marshal as we began the tour.

"A good friend of mine used to be stationed out here," I had told him. "He was the pilot of a B-17 I flew on in World War II, Bill Crumm—"

"*General* Crumm?" he had exclaimed.

Just then Bob Burke's voice had come in over the radio from the vice president's car. "Say, Rufe, there's a friend of yours back here. General Crumm says he'd like to see you when we stop at the Officers' Club."

Bill Crumm, I had reflected, *a major general, and CO of the Third Air Division. A long way from flying* Jack the Ripper *over Germany more than twenty years ago.* I had a nostalgic visit with Bill and his lovely wife, Tenney, and then *Air Force Two* was ready to go and we were on our way again.

When we came through on our way to Saigon this time, he wasn't there. A month earlier, I had attended a memorial service in Washington for General William Crumm. He had been piloting a B-52 on what was to have been his last mission. Two of the big bombers had collided over the China Sea. Bill Crumm had not been among the survivors. He was the first U.S. general officer to lose his life in the Vietnam conflict.

We expected trouble in Saigon this trip. The Inauguration of Thieu was an event the Viet Cong could hardly be expected to ignore, and they didn't. The ceremony was held at noon, October 31, 1967. Thieu and Ky took their oaths, after which the speeches seemed to go on interminably. Humphrey, Ambassador Bunker, and representatives from many other countries sat stolidly in the tropic sun. It was almost as if we were waiting for something to happen. Each minute that passed without a gun firing or a mortar shell dropping in was another minute to be thankful for. If it came, and if the first round missed us, we were ready for instant evacuation with a hidden armored half-track nearby. Finally, the ceremony ended and the concentration of targets dispersed.

But they reconvened that evening at a palace reception. Vice President Humphrey mingled with the other honored guests, and we mingled right along with him, keeping close. He was standing near one of the open doors leading out onto the spacious palace grounds, talking with General Westmoreland. It was just at twilight. Suddenly, there was a flash of light outside and a loud explosion. The building shook beneath our feet. People scurried for cover. Weaver and I moved in closer to the vice president to cover him as two more explosions followed the first.

It was over as suddenly as it began. "Mortars," an aide reported to General Westmoreland.

Later that night, the firing site was found nearly three miles from Independence Palace, which attested to the accuracy of the Viet Cong. They had removed a portion of the roof of a shanty in the Chinese sector of Saigon, set up their mortar, and lobbed three rounds at the palace. An old man who happened to see them was murdered as they abandoned the mortar and fled.

I think a man has to be almost oblivious to fear when he seeks the office of the presidency or the vice presidency. The jobs in themselves are awesome enough to discourage anyone with even a tinge of faintheartedness, even without taking into consideration the personal dangers that are occupational hazards. I have seen this in Harry Truman when he would stroll blithely out into the streets of Washington, not really concerned whether the Secret Service went along or not, other than for the conversational value of a companion during his walk.

Ike's visit to the front in Korea showed the same trait, as did Richard Nixon's doggedly pushing his way through South America as vice president. I detected no fear in Lyndon Johnson's voice or actions as I sat on top of him while Lee Harvey Oswald rained bullets down on Dealey Plaza. And the only thing I saw in Hubert Humphrey's face that evening in Saigon as the palace shook under the mortar bombardment was the sparkle in his eyes that had come to be something of a trademark with him. He knew what our intelligence had warned us of on that trip, and he was aware that he was one of the prime targets, that the Viet Cong would have scored a real coup if the Vice President of the United States had been killed or injured at the Inauguration of Thieu and Ky.

I was looking out the window beside my seat aboard *Air Force Two* a few days later at the clear Pacific sky as we headed homeward, thinking about this. The vice president came down the aisle and paused beside me.

"Rufus, I think you stayed out in the sun too long without a hat. Your head's peeling. You know, I was a pharmacist before I got into politics. You ought to get a bottle of witch hazel when you go on this kind of trip; it'll really help that sunburn." He moved on down the aisle and into the aft stateroom.

The vice president's physician, Dr. Edgar Berman, had overheard the conversation. *"Witch hazel?* Doesn't he know witch hazel went out with witch doctors?"

I turned and saw Humphrey's stocky figure disappearing through the doorway. Witch hazel or not, I really admired the guy.

Sometime after this, when I had become deputy director of the Secret Service, Humphrey said to me, "You know, Rufus, you and I are sort of like the Avis ads. We're number two, so we try harder." This became a running gag between the two of us. But I honestly don't believe I ever knew anyone who tried harder than Hubert Humphrey.

CHAPTER 14

The LBJ Ranch

During his eight years as vice president and president, Lyndon Johnson's home in Texas was one of his greatest sources of mental and physical rejuvenation. It was the place he went when he felt the mainspring beginning to wind too tight, and if there is one man in the country who needs a place to unwind, it is the president. Franklin Roosevelt had his Warm Springs and Hyde Park, Harry Truman had Key West and Independence, with Ike it was Augusta National and Gettysburg, and Jack Kennedy had the family compounds at Hyannis Port and Palm Beach.

LBJ had his ranch. By Texas standards, it was a relatively small spread, the major portion of which was situated along a proportionately small river, the Pedernales. A couple of small towns were just across the river—Hye and Stonewall—and the nearest big town was Johnson City (pop. 854), just down the road in Blanco County.

At the risk of incurring the wrath of Texans, in my home state of Georgia, it would have been called the Johnson Place on Pedernales Creek. But this was Texas, where everything is big, including the thinking.

I got my first look at the LBJ Ranch in the spring of 1961, not long after Stu Knight and I were named to be the two-man Vice Presidential Detail. The occasion was a visit by West German Chancellor Konrad Adenauer, who came down to Texas after conferring in Washington with President Kennedy. Special Agent Clarence Knetsch of our San Antonio Field Office was a native of the Texas hill country as the area thereabouts is called, and even in those early days of on-again, off-again Secret Service involvement with the vice president, Clarence was our ranch hand. There were several nearby communities with people of German ancestry, and Clarence spoke the language fluently, which was a distinct help when the Adenauer group arrived.

I soon learned, as Clarence gave me an orientation tour of the place, that there was more to the ranch than the handsome old-wood-and-limestone Johnson house and the land along the Pedernales. It was a fluctuating thing, including other ranches, lake houses, and various pieces of land scattered over several counties. The entire area abounded in wild life—deer, wild turkeys, armadillos, skunks, rattlesnakes, and others. From the Secret Service point of view, the LBJ Ranch was an area with a radius of some fifty miles, the ranch house proper being the center, reaching as far as Austin to the east and San Antonio to the south.

The ranch had security problems that were peculiar to it alone. Seasonally, migrant workers came through the hill country cutting the scrub cedar for the ranchers, and these people would often carry firearms, as they lived, to a large degree, off the land.

Then we had deer season which annually brought out a veritable army of hunters toting high-powered rifles. The pickup truck driving along Ranch Road 1, within firing range of the ranch house just across the Pedernales, with a rifle lying handy in the rack behind the driver, might be taking good ole Simon Burg over to look at some of his peach orchards. It could just as easily be carrying another Lee Harvey Oswald.

These we had to watch, but the logistics of ranch duty was the part of the Secret Service's job that could be a nightmare having either that smooth mesh of men, material, and time that makes the job look easy, or the botch of nobody being where he should be when he should be. LBJ's way of relaxing was to indulge in something we called "ranching," which came very close to being in perpetual motion. There was very little sitting at the swimming pool in the front yard, sipping a tall cool one and wiggling his toes in the water. When he wanted to go to the Haywood place—forty miles away at the lake—the Secret Service would have to have men there to secure the area. On the way over in the chopper, he might decide to go to Austin first, or up to Round Mountain to drop in on his good friend Judge A. W. Moursund. Since the helicopter could not carry all the agents needed for a shift of location with the president, we would have to have men scattered around the countryside at strategic points.

Despite certain apocryphal stories to the effect that Secret Service agents whiled away endless hours in the kitchen nibbling away at Mary Davis's incomparable cooking and swatting an occasional fly to look busy, I never saw a man come back to the White House from the ranch weighing more than when he left.

The general atmosphere at the ranch, however, was much less formal than at the White House. But even in this less ceremonious air, the regular disappearance of Lady Bird after dinner on Saturday nights did not go unnoticed, and after a while, someone asked her about this.

"Oh," she said smiling, "I just can't miss watching *Gunsmoke*. You know, as long as Matt Dillon keeps being nice to Miss Kitty, everything will be all right."

In the wide-open spaces of Texas there is widespread use of radio for personal communication, and LBJ, just as many other ranchers, had his own personal radio network with the capability of communicating with the ranch house from his cars, boats, and airplane. There was never a lack of radio traffic when LBJ was at the ranch.

Lyndon Johnson had an amazing range of skills and interests, but there was one relatively minor electronic fact that eluded him, and that was that the raising and lowering of sound volume in radio communication is a function of the receiver, not the transmitter. More than once, he sent the signalmen of the White House Communications Agency into paroxysms of laughter with something like this:

LBJ: (*from his car somewhere on Ranch Road 1, to me at the ranch*): Rufus, tell Dale to meet me in half an hour at the Lewis place. There're a couple of things that need fixing.

YOUNGBLOOD: Mr. President, Dale has gone into Austin for some supplies. Can somebody else meet you?

LBJ: What was that? I can't hear you, son. Turn up your volume!

YOUNGBLOOD: Mr. President, I've got it turned all the way up. How do you read me now?

LBJ: Read you loud and clear, pardner! Now, what was that about Dale? You could hear them breaking up out in the communications shack.

This personal network of the president's, however, was not used by the Secret Service for our own purposes; our communications capability was provided by the White House Communications Agency, which I just mentioned, and which was better known by its acronym, WHCA (pronounced Whocka). Wherever the Secret Service went, WHCA went. Whenever agents went out to do advance work for a presidential trip, WHCA men went with them. Whether our assignment was in Washington, at the ranch or on a South Sea Island, WHCA's job was to see to the installation and operation of telephones, radios, teletypes, and highly classified cryptographic equipment, as the occasion demanded. If it became necessary for me to talk to an agent in Paris while we were aboard the president's cruiser on a lake in Texas, WHCA would establish a circuit through phone patches, switchboards, keying lines, and relays, and all I had to do was flick the switch on my DCN walkie-talkie and start talking. The communications capability was essential wherever we went, and this was particularly true at the LBJ Ranch.

One of LBJ's favorite people was his cousin Mrs. Oriole Bailey, who lived in a small house a few hundred yards downriver from the main ranch house. He enjoyed dropping in to visit Cousin Oriole, who was considerably older than he was, and he wasn't above a practical joke if an opportunity arose. He bought a little car that caught his fancy; it was amphibious, with a watertight chassis and two propellers just beneath the rear bumper that could be activated by a control that shifted the power from the wheels to the propellers. Late one summer afternoon, he dropped in on Cousin Oriole, and after a while, he casually suggested that she take a ride in his new car.

President Johnson got in behind the steering wheel, with Cousin Oriole alongside him, and I got into the rear seat. Just in front of the ranch house, a dam across the Pedernales backs the water up to form a pond below a handsome grove of trees. A ramp was being built so that the new car-boat could go in and out of the pond, and the two workmen constructing it had knocked off for the day after laying down a mat of reinforcing wire and a thin layer of gravel preparatory to pouring concrete the following morning.

LBJ turned down the road leading to the ramp.

"How do you like the car, Cousin Oriole?" he said.

"It's nice, Lyndon," she said. "But why are you going this way?"

"Just want to take a look at some work down here."

Then it dawned on me what he was up to. "Mr. President—" I started to say.

"You just hold on back there, Rufus, and be quiet."

"But sir, you don't understand—" I was going to tell him the ramp was unfinished.

"Lyndon!" Cousin Oriole shrilled, drowning out my warning. "Slow down! Stop! The water!"

He was laughing as we hit the ramp at about ten miles per hour. The front end splashed into the pond and he shifted the power to the propellers, which churned down through the gravel and began to scoop up the reinforcing wire, winding it hopelessly around the shafts with an ear-shattering squeal of metal on metal.

It was too late to do anything about it as the engine choked down and we drifted out onto the pond, trailing a mass of tangled wire, the only sounds being the gurgle of water and Cousin Oriole screaming, "Lyndon! You know I can't swim!"

The Secret Service setup at the ranch, of course, was altered drastically when LBJ became president. A permanent detachment of special officers, who served as security guards, was stationed there. Clarence Knetsch moved to Johnson City and became SAIC of that detail. Ernie and Teet Hobbs's motel became the unofficial Secret Service headquarters when the president came to the ranch with his usual contingent of White House agents.

The mode of local travel also underwent considerable change. As vice president, LBJ's access to helicopters had been limited. As president, Marine and Army choppers were in constant readiness, both at Bergstrom Air Force Base in Austin and at the airstrip at the ranch. Any movement more than fifteen or twenty miles distant usually brought out a chopper.

The weather was about the only veto to helicopter movement, and on a particularly hairy day one spring, LBJ was scheduled to speak at a function in Waco after making an appearance in Austin, some ninety miles as the crow flies. However, our pilot, Marine Colonel Walt Sienko, was not flying as the crow flies that day. Out of deference to the weather conditions, automobiles were also en route to Waco, so if the chopper could not proceed, it could put down alongside the highway and the president could transfer to a car and still make his destination. Thus, Sienko was following the highway, and LBJ was silently supervising the navigation from his window.

At one point, Sienko banked away from the highway to avoid a particularly nasty thunderhead. The president immediately took note of the course change and tapped me on the arm.

"Go up front and find out what he's doing. Looks like he's turning back."

I went up to the cockpit, Sienko pointed out the thunderhead, and I went back to relay the information. LBJ was not satisfied.

"Tell him to stay with the road."

I sighed and went forward again. Sienko patiently explained the danger of an aircraft being caught inside a thunderhead. I went back with this. LBJ sent still another set of instructions forward. This time Sienko had had enough. He reached out and poked me in the chest.

"Look, Rufe, you go back there and deliver a message for me! You tell him I'm flying this damn thing!"

I was grinning when I got back this time.

"Well," LBJ snapped, "what'd he say?"

"Mr. President, he said for me to tell you *he* was flying this damn thing. Sir."

He glowered at me for a moment, cut his eyes toward the cockpit, then nodded. "Good man. We need more like him."

There were times when the president seemed less concerned with his own safety than with what the newspapers might say about him. One July weekend, LBJ, Lady Bird, and a group of friends were relaxing on Granite Shoals Lake in the president's cabin cruiser. Like most lakes on summer weekends, Granite Shoals was crowded with boats, among which were several carrying members of the press who were covering the president. He had informed them that he wished to be "off the record" during this outing, and our two Secret Service patrol runabouts were busy keeping these and other boats out of the big cove where the president and his party were relaxing.

Sergeant Paul Glynn, LBJ's personal aide, suddenly noticed smoke seeping up around the engine hatch and quickly pointed it out to me. I flicked the switch on my walkie-talkie.

"*Guardian One* and *Guardian Two,* come alongside. There's a fire aboard and we're evacuating immediately."

The two Secret Service boats moved up beside the cruiser. Paul had opened the hatch by this time, and although we saw no flames, smoke billowed up from the opening. There was no panic as Paul, Jerry Kivett, and I quickly assisted the president and his guests over the side and into the small boats. Paul and Jim Bartlett, a Navy petty officer assigned to the Secret Service for the maintenance of our boats, stayed aboard the cruiser as we pulled away. I maintained contact by radio, but LBJ, looking around and seeing walkie-talkie antennas sprouting up from all the boats, turned to me. "Do you have to keep waving those damn things around, Rufus? Get your signs down! The press is gonna see 'em and they'll get curious about what the hell's happening, and it'll be all over the newspapers tomorrow!"

The two men aboard the cruiser, fortunately, located the trouble before it got out of control, and there were no injuries, minimal damage, and no headlines about the president's boat catching fire.

We tried to keep him content, especially at the ranch, if his contentedness did not conflict too sharply with the protective mission. One December, the Johnsons showed us they were aware of our efforts and the difficulties we faced in trying to protect him while still allowing him the freedom of movement he needed when he was "ranching." They invited several of us down to the ranch, along with our wives, not as working Secret Service agents, but as guests. The girls got the LBJ red-carpet treatment, from barbecues along the Pedernales to personally conducted tours by the president.

For almost eight years, the LBJ Ranch played host to a broad political and social spectrum, ranging from kings to camel drivers, and while the pseudosophisticates might look down on the ten-gallon hats, the folksy barbecues, and the bucolic atmosphere as being pure Texan corn, it played an important role in keeping the president in good health, and it created a lot of goodwill among the long and impressive list of visitors who passed that way.

CHAPTER 15

Dark Days: 1968

The structural reorganization of the Secret Service had been completed by the beginning of 1968. On Director Rowley's recommendation, I had been named the deputy director, the number-two job in the Service. The four assistant directorships were now staffed by Lem Johns (Protective Forces), Tom Kelley (Protective Intelligence), Burrill Peterson (Investigations), and Phil Jordan (Administration).

It could not have been completed at a better time because the year that lay ahead of us would be one the Secret Service would long remember. It was a year that began to deteriorate early and was fated to get a lot worse before it got better. In January, the problems were more of an international sort. In South Korea, a plot to assassinate President Chung Hee Park was uncovered just in time to prevent its being carried out. Shortly after this, on January 23, an American electronics intelligence ship, the USS *Pueblo*, was captured on the high seas by North Korean naval units and was forced into port along with the eighty-three Americans aboard her. It quickly became apparent that effecting their release was going to be no simple matter. In addition to this, the enemy's Tet offensive began in South Vietnam, which brought on deeper American involvement there.

On the evening of March 31, President Johnson faced television cameras in his White House office and told the nation of the steps he planned to take to limit the war in Vietnam. And as he neared the end of his speech, he made a startling announcement that immediately changed the focus of both domestic and international affairs.

"With America's sons in the fields far away, with America's future under challenge right here at home, with our hopes and the world's hopes for peace in the balance every day, I do not believe that I should devote an hour or a day of my time to any personal partisan causes or to any duties other than the awesome duties of this office—the Presidency of your country.

"Accordingly, I shall not seek, and I will not accept, the nomination of my party for another term as your President."

The first reaction to this, by many people, was disbelief. In the press conference that followed his television appearance, the first question was "How irrevocable is your decision?"

"It is just as irrevocable as the statement says," he replied, "completely irrevocable. There were no shalls, no woulds, no buts; I just made it 'will.'"

There was speculation that he felt he would lose the election if he ran because of the feelings generated by the Vietnam War. Whatever his reasons, nearly ten months from the end of his term, he was a self-proclaimed lame duck. Having been associated with him so closely for the past seven years, even though the association had been nonpolitical, I began to detect a slight change of attitude toward me on the part of quite a number of people. But the events of 1968 did not allow me time for reflecting.

What seemed to be a glimmer of hope regarding the war appeared on the horizon almost immediately after LBJ removed himself from the political arena; the North Vietnamese let it be known that they were ready to establish contact with the United States for the purpose of discussing peace. For several weeks, the president had been scheduled to meet in Hawaii with our top people from the war zone, and this announcement added urgency to that meeting.

Although my new job as deputy director was of an even more administrative nature than my previous post, I was to make this trip with him. *Air Force One* was scheduled to leave Washington on the night of April 4. I was at home, packing my bags before driving to the airport, when I got a phone call from my office.

"We just received a report from Memphis that Martin Luther King Jr. has been shot," I was told.

King died within the hour. The president could not possibly leave Washington so the Hawaii trip was scrapped. Martin Luther King Jr. had been one of the most vulnerable men in the nation, and there had never been any question in the minds of law enforcement people that his assassination could plunge the country into racial turmoil such as had never before been seen.

At nine o'clock that night, the president once more stared solemnly into the television cameras and made an appeal to all citizens to reject the violence that had struck down the civil rights leader. But rioting and burning had already begun even as the president spoke, and long before the sun rose the next morning, Friday, buildings were in flames all over the nation's capital.

Not knowing what direction the rioting might take, the Secret Service immediately canceled all leaves and put off-duty agents on stand-by alert. A command post was set up in the Executive Office Building. Helmets and gas masks were brought out to be instantly available, and the helicopter that was to have taken the president to Andrews for the flight to Hawaii was kept in readiness should it become necessary to evacuate the president.

Roy Wilkins, Bayard Rustin, Whitney Young Jr., and other black leaders were contacted by the president and asked to meet with him at the White House on Friday morning to seek solutions. The rioting had spread all across the country, and more than forty major cities were the scenes of burning and looting. I remained at the White House throughout the night on Friday and again on Saturday, as we felt that protective security was a more critical problem during the hours of darkness.

I shall never forget the feeling I experienced early Sunday morning as a group of agents and White House personnel stood at the base of the south portico with the president. Troop carriers moved along the streets beyond the White House gates, carrying steel-helmeted, combat-ready soldiers. It was one of the few times that troops had been needed to patrol the capital since the Civil War. A thick haze hung over the city, and the acrid smell of smoke filled the air. I had intermittently spent more than fifteen years in and around the

White House, and it seemed almost incomprehensible that this was really happening. I felt a lump in my throat as I gazed on the face of President Johnson.

The initial frustration and despair had pretty well vented itself over the weekend, and by Monday morning, the situation had improved. We were now faced with a decision about Martin Luther King Jr.'s funeral which was to be held in Atlanta. The president made it known that he felt he should attend. Marvin Watson relayed this to the Secret Service.

There was no question about our position. "Absolutely not," I told Marvin. "The Secret Service feels that this would place the president in a potentially dangerous situation."

We had reports that many militants, those who advocated violence, were urging black people to take up arms and go into the streets in retaliation for the murder of King. Thousands of sympathizers, black and white, were already moving toward Atlanta from all over the country. The city would be packed, and we felt that a spark could touch off a condition in the Georgia capital that would make the previous weekend look like a picnic by comparison. The FBI added its weight in recommending strongly that the president not attend the funeral.

The president reluctantly heeded our advice, and Vice President Humphrey agreed to go in his stead. Since I had been so vocal in opposing the president's going, I felt that I should go with Humphrey. On Tuesday, we flew to Atlanta for the services, which were held at the Ebenezer Baptist Church, where King and his father had been copastors. As Glenn Weaver and I sat there with the vice president and his party, I saw Stokely Carmichael in a pew a short distance away, and I recalled a letter that had come to headquarters recently from a congressman who demanded that Carmichael be arrested. *Who on earth,* I thought, *would try to arrest Stokely Carmichael in the Ebenezer Baptist Church at Martin Luther King Jr.'s funeral?*

There were predictions of possible trouble during the funeral procession, which was to pass the state capitol on its way to the burial site. The Atlanta City Hall had been closed, as well as many businesses, out of deference to Dr. King. But Georgia's governor, Lester Maddox, refused to close the capitol, and he was backing his decision by making an armed garrison of the capitol, with two hundred armed state patrolmen and other officers waiting inside.

But the thousands of people who had come to pay their respects to the slain civil rights leader did so in the spirit of nonviolence he had preached, and the fears about Atlanta never became reality. Much of the credit for the tranquility of the city goes to a longtime professional acquaintance of mine, Chief Herbert Jenkins, for the excellent work done by the Atlanta Police Department.

With Johnson now out of the presidential race, Senator Robert Kennedy was one of the top contenders for the nomination. Campaigns were well under way in early June. He was on the West Coast, running in the California primary.

At 4:00 on the morning of June 5, I was awakened by a phone call. It was Lem Johns. "Get a good grip on the phone, Rufe," he said. "Bobby Kennedy was just shot. The report is that he's still alive, but it doesn't look good."

I turned on the television to catch the news reports, then phoned Director Rowley. Although Bobby Kennedy, as a candidate, had not been provided Secret Service protection under the existing law, we knew that what had just happened in Los Angeles would end, once and for all, the years of procrastinating on this point. We set a meeting to begin at 7:30 that morning at headquarters. As expected, the president had already requested the Secret Service to assign men to the other candidates immediately.

At headquarters, Rowley, Johns, myself, and several other Secret Service personnel met with Jim Hendrick and Charles Humpstone of the Treasury Department and Assistant Director "Deke" DeLoach of the FBI. We began immediately pinpointing the locations of all candidates and listing the agents to be assigned to them.

The meeting was constantly interrupted by incoming phone calls, and after taking a call from the White House, Rowley came back into the conference room and motioned to me.

"That was the president. He wants you to come over right now and bring him everything relevant to candidate protection, what legislation will be needed, manpower and budget estimates, and all the rest."

I gathered up the papers from my office and strode quickly the block and a half from our G Street Headquarters to the Executive Office Building. DeVier

Pierson, a White House legal aide, met me there with copies of the latest legislative proposals on candidate protection, and together we hurried over to the White House and up to the president's bedroom where we held a most important conference.

During the day, reports from Los Angeles concerning Bobby Kennedy's condition held out less and less hope. The following day, June 6, just over twenty-four hours after he had been shot in the back of the head, Robert Kennedy died. On the same day, Public Law 90-331 was passed unanimously by both House and Senate, providing Secret Service protection for "major presidential and vice presidential candidates" unless the candidate "declined such protection."

The job of determining who was, and who was not, a major candidate was given to the Secretary of the Treasury, and in this determination, he was to consult with an advisory committee made up of the Speaker of the House, the House minority leader, both the majority and minority leaders of the Senate, and a fifth member to be selected by the other four. The advisory board had been made completely bipartisan so that the complaints of any candidate who might not be assigned Secret Service protection could be coped with more easily.

A tacit moratorium on campaigning took place after Bobby Kennedy's death, and this gave the Secret Service a chance to organize for the enlarged task that lay ahead. As assistant director of Protective Forces, the organization of the details and direct responsibility for candidate protection fell to Lem Johns.

In the meantime, there was Bobby Kennedy's funeral. Services were held in St. Patrick's Cathedral in New York City. There were no intelligence reports of the sort that had previously stopped the president from going to Atlanta, so he announced that he would attend. He sent word to me that he would feel more comfortable if I went along with him, which, of course, I did.

As the limousines moved slowly down Fifth Avenue toward St. Patrick's, I looked out at the somber faces lining the avenue, and it brought back that day in 1963 when we had followed the caisson bearing the body of John F. Kennedy through the streets of Washington. It was a different city, different people were packed along the route, but the feeling and the sounds were the same. There was a hush as the procession moved past, broken only by the sound of people sobbing.

The funeral train that took Bobby Kennedy back to Washington to be buried near his brother in Arlington National Cemetery left a horror of its own in its wake. Hundreds of thousands of people had lined the tracks almost the entire distance from New York to Washington. They stood close beside the rails, many of them placing coins on the track to be kept as mementos. As the funeral train went through Elizabeth, New Jersey, several people fell beneath the wheels of an express train going in the opposite direction and were killed.

The political machinery could not stand idle for long, and the campaigning soon resumed. Initially, five candidates—in addition to Hubert Humphrey, who already had Secret Service protection—were designated as "major." These were Nelson Rockefeller, Harold Stassen, Richard Nixon, Eugene McCarthy, and George Wallace. Secret Service agents had been assigned to these men almost immediately after the shooting of Bobby Kennedy.

One more GOP candidate was soon added, Governor Ronald Reagan of California, and soon after agents were assigned to him, they proved their worth. One night in July, the agent on duty at the Reagan residence in Sacramento saw two men moving stealthily up the driveway toward the house. He shouted for them to halt, and when they turned and ran, he fired a warning shot. The men escaped, but two Molotov cocktails were found smashed on the pavement.

On August 8 in Miami, the Republicans made their choice. We pulled in the agents assigned to Stassen, Rockefeller, and Reagan, beefed up the detail with Richard Nixon, and picked up a new charge in the person of Spiro T. Agnew, governor of Maryland, and now the GOP nominee for vice president.

The security at the Republican Convention had gone virtually without a hitch. Two weeks later in Chicago, however, it was a different story with the Democrats. Yippies, hippies, militants, and various other protesters and demonstrators were there by the thousands, seemingly intent on breaking up the convention entirely. When it finally ended in a cloud of dust, the Secret Service withdrew the units assigned to Eugene McCarthy and two others it had picked up just prior to the convention—Lester Maddox and George McGovern. Hubert Humphrey was now the presidential nominee, and we assigned a new detail to Edmund Muskie, his running mate.

Lem Johns and I attended both conventions, Johns as head of the protective forces and I as the senior Secret Service representative. The reason for my attendance was more than just participation in the actual security. Candidate protection was obviously something that could—and did—create situations that required instant decisions, and someone had to be on the scene to handle these. The law specified that protection by the Secret Service would be provided for "major" candidates, and any candidate naturally considers himself "major." When some potential candidate or his representative would tell me that he was going to be nominated that night on the convention floor and wanted us to have his Secret Service detail ready, I would politely explain the law and inform him that I would pass the information along to the advisory board and be guided by its decision. It was unnecessary and impractical to surround every "favorite son" with Secret Service agents. If a particular candidate was not provided protection, and he wanted to complain, then his complaint would be to the board, not to the Secret Service. This was the only way we could lawfully comply and, at the same time, not allow protection to become a status symbol.

A third convention was held that year, and another protective detail was formed when presidential candidate George Wallace, of the American Independent Party, named General Curtis LeMay as his running mate. During the campaign LeMay made a three-day tour of combat zones in South Vietnam. This was an extremely tense assignment for the agents who accompanied him, but LeMay was returned safely.

At the end of the Democratic Convention, Senator George McGovern narrowly missed injury or death as he was being driven to the airport. A car in another lane on the busy freeway went out of control and crashed into the Secret Service follow-up car, killing the driver of the runaway vehicle and injuring two agents. Witnesses to the accident stated that if the Secret Service car had not been there, McGovern's car would have taken the impact.

By the time Richard Nixon won the election—by a scant seven-tenths of 1 percent of the popular vote—the Secret Service had tallied up more than a quarter of a million man-hours to the protection of candidates.

With his successor named, we found ourselves dealing with a different LBJ after the November elections. I think "waxing mellow" best describes it. During an award ceremony late in November, he became almost maudlin, but we appreciated it.

"I have abused you," he said, "I have criticized you, I have been inconsiderate of you ... I have spent more of my time telling you what you did wrong than what you did right. But ... I remember in Australia when I just couldn't keep back the tears when I looked in the faces of Jerry Kivett, Dick Johnsen, Jerry McKinney, Lem Johns, and Bob Heyn, and the dearest of all, Rufus Youngblood, with that paint streaming down their faces, splattered all over them, but their chins up and their president safe ... I remember Bob Taylor standing there and letting the Cadillac run over his foot in order to protect his president from harm."

When the president says things like this about your outfit, you cannot help but feel proud. Still, I wondered months later if that qualification as "dearest of all" had not been something like the kiss of death for me.

If it had—what the hell, it was worth it.

In December, Roy Kellerman, one of the ablest Secret Service men I ever had the privilege of working with, retired. He had deferred retirement earlier in the year to help us through the crisis of candidate protection.

Lem Johns, who, as assistant director of Protective Forces, had the monumental job of candidate protection thrust on him after the assassination of Bobby Kennedy, received the Treasury Department's Meritorious Service Award for his outstanding performance under great pressure.

There was much of the personnel shifting that accompanies the end of an administration, especially when the other party is picking up the reins. There was more to come.

CHAPTER 16

The New Nixon

I did not realize it at the time, but when I rode down Pennsylvania Avenue on January 20, 1969, it was the last time I would be riding in the car with a president in office. And the president was still Lyndon Johnson. In the rear seat with him sat President-elect Richard M. Nixon, who within the hour would take the oath that would make him the thirty-seventh President of the United States.

It was the fifth time I had taken part in this traditional trip from the White House to the Capitol: twice with Ike, once each with Kennedy and Johnson, and now with Nixon.

Nixon had also taken part in those first two as Ike's vice president. In 1953 and in 1957 they had ridden without fear in open cars, waving to the cheering throngs and seldom seeing so much as a frown in the crowd.

The times had changed in America in that sixteen-year interval, and along with the times, Secret Service security had changed. On this frigid day in 1969, we moved down Pennsylvania Avenue not in an open car, but in an enclosed limousine that was as bombproof and bulletproof as technology could devise. Overhead, helicopters circled like spotters in a war zone, the Secret Service agents aboard them in constant radio contact with a combined security force on the ground as large as a combat division. There were fifteen thousand men on duty in the capital—Secret Service, police, detectives, men from various other federal law enforcement agencies, and the military. The principal advance agents of the White House Detail who had been working for months in preparation for this day—Dave Grant and Bill Lovingood—had it running smoothly.

Our intelligence reports had confirmed that all of the thousands of people lining the route had not come just to see the spectacle. Several hundred, at least, had come to make a concerted effort to disrupt the Inauguration. They were content with shouting obscenities and waving placards as we drove toward the Capitol.

The Inaugural stand on the steps of the Capitol was crowded with VIPs—congressional leaders, members of the diplomatic corps, Supreme Court justices, the Joint Chiefs of Staff, and many others, not the least of whom were the outgoing vice president and his wife. Muriel Humphrey was as dedicated a political trouper as I have ever met. She put everything she had into every campaign, and she knew how to bite the bullet in defeat as well as how to accept victory. This day was the final nail in the exhausting 1968 presidential campaign, and although she had been suffering from a nagging head cold for several days and was in almost constant need of her handkerchief, she doggedly refrained from dabbing at her eyes and nose during the ceremony for fear it might be misinterpreted as tears of defeat.

At noon, on the Capitol steps, Nixon took the oath that shifted the load to his shoulders from Lyndon Johnson's. The Inaugural Parade moved back down the avenue toward the White House with the new president. Bob Taylor, SAIC of the White House Detail, rode in the armored car with Nixon. I rode at the command position in one of our two open follow-up cars, Lem Johns in the other.

The demonstrators were waiting for us. Rocks, bottles, chunks of concrete, jagged pieces of metal, smoke grenades, and miscellaneous other items rained on the procession. Viet Cong flags were unfurled, and in the open cars, we could hear that they had not forgotten the vocabulary they had demonstrated in Chicago. Perhaps they saw the Inauguration as a sort of double feature where they could vilify one president going toward the Capitol and another coming back. Cars were dented, windshields were cracked, and several agents wound up with cuts and bruises from the debris that filled the air. In Washington in January, Richard Nixon got the baptism he had missed at Miami in August.

LBJ, now a former president, was the first to leave office since the Secret Service had been assigned the job of protecting former presidents. His departure from Washington was in sharp contrast to that day in 1953 when Bess and Harry Truman had boarded a train at Union Station and almost forlornly had waved farewell to two Secret Service agents as the train pulled out for Missouri.

Nixon had placed the presidential jet at Johnson's disposal for the trip home to Texas. There were bands playing at Andrews Air Force Base as the Johnsons, along with a platoon of staffers and Secret Service agents, got aboard the big 707 for the last time. LBJ's smile, as he stood at the top of the ramp with grandson Lyn Nugent in the crook of his left arm as he waved the right, reflected the unique brand of relief that only an ex-president can know.

The Secret Service began once more adjusting to the style of a new president and to a new White House staff. Nixon, of course, was not the stranger to us that his vice president, Spiro Agnew, was. During his eight years in the vice presidency, agents had been intermittently assigned to Nixon. But with the change in the times and in the mood of the country, there were some changes in Richard Nixon. He had made a dramatic political comeback in reaching his ultimate goal, and he no longer allowed himself to become as vulnerable as he once had. This carried over from the political to the physical as well, for he was no longer as disdainful of Secret Service protection as he once had been.

For the Secret Service, a change of administration is always a period of transition. There were new protective units to start up, others to reduce or close down. New units were set up to guard the president's home at Key Biscayne, Florida, and a few months later at a home he acquired in San Clemente, California. Installations in Texas were to be phased down. In Johnson City, Clarence Knetsch remained to supervise the detail assigned to the former president. Most of the agents formerly assigned to Lynda and Luci, who no longer received protective coverage, were reassigned to work with Knetsch. A former president did not require the elaborate communications equipment that had been essential while he was in office, and within ten days of the Inauguration, I went down to Texas to assist in making the changes.

It was a different place from the hectic days of the previous five years. When the work was done, LBJ asked me to "stay over and protect me a few more days."

It was like a visit of two old friends as we rode and relaxed around the ranch. He talked, but not the way he had the year before. He was a Texas rancher, not a United States president.

"Nixon's got the hardest job in the world, Rufus," he told me. "He and I belong to different political parties; still it's my patriotic duty to give him all the help I can because he's the only president we've got."

LBJ was one of four men alive who knew the loneliness of that pinnacle, and I had been close to enough presidents to agree with him.

Still, the abrupt change of being put out to pasture after all those years of climbing to the top in Washington seemed to leave him a little lonely at this end of the line. Before I flew back to the capital, he shook my hand. "Don't forget us, Rufus. Come down here and see us when you can, and don't ever hesitate to call on me if I can be of any help."

We had been through a lot together since we had met in Dakar almost eight years before, and I would have been a pretty cold fish if I had not been touched by his sentiments.

President Nixon was on the move within a month of taking office, flying to Europe in February to establish personal contact with various leaders. Director Rowley went along as headquarters representative, and as his deputy, I stayed in Washington to mind the store. It occurred to me, in looking back, that this was the first presidential trip to foreign lands I had not made in more than five years.

On March 28, only a few weeks after the president had returned from Europe, General Dwight Eisenhower died. Ike's death had not come unexpectedly; he had been hospitalized for some time, and the tenacity with which he clung to life amazed even his doctors. Still, it was an occasion of national mourning.

I went to Walter Reed Army Hospital as soon as I learned of his death to convey my condolences and those of the Secret Service to his widow. In days gone by, when I called on the Eisenhowers, Mamie would always remind me to "look after the General," and Ike, who always seemed to be on his way to the golf course, would pause long enough to say, "Take good care of Mamie, Mr. Youngblood."

As the widow of a former president, she continued to have protective coverage, and Herb Dixon and his agents continued to take excellent care of Mamie.

During the slightly more than two years that I remained in the Secret Service under the Nixon administration, my contact with the president and his staff was minimal. The only two occasions that I had worked with him during his two terms as vice president occurred when he campaigned unsuccessfully for the presidency against Kennedy in 1960—once when he visited Jackson, Mississippi, and again in Atlanta, where I was assigned as his driver for the motorcade. His wife was with him on the campaign trip, and she had been presented with a large bouquet of beautiful red roses, which she carried throughout the motorcade. When it was over and I delivered the Nixons to Atlanta Airport for the flight back to Washington, Pat Nixon smiled and handed the roses to me.

"Thank you very much for your help," she said. "I'd like you to take these home to your wife."

In my capacity as deputy director, I maintained headquarters contact with all our protective units, which called for periodic visits to New York, Independence, Austin, Gettysburg, and Augusta. The deputy director does not necessarily take an active part in protective missions, other than in the overall planning and policy stages, and I did not have the lengthy personal contact with this president that my assignment had required with his predecessor.

I did make several trips with President Nixon, however; the first in June 1969, which began with a western tour to South Dakota, Colorado, and California, and then took us on to Hawaii and Midway Island, where he conferred with South Vietnam's President Thieu.

There was continued shifting of assignments and other personnel changes within the Secret Service. Lem Johns transferred back to his hometown, Birmingham, Alabama, to head the field office there. Clint Hill moved from the

White House Detail to become SAIC of Vice President Agnew's detail. A rapport was quickly established with the new vice president, a rapport that, within a short time, prompted Agnew to express his personal feelings in a note to Clint and his men commending them on the fine job they were doing, and thanking them on behalf of himself and his family, for the fact that "security is provided unobtrusively, in good spirit and friendship, rather than coldly and impersonally, which makes our lives more enjoyable."

A sincere pat on the back by the boss is seldom a lost gesture.

At President Nixon's request, protection was extended to Hubert Humphrey for six months after the change of administration, and Glenn Weaver continued with that assignment. Glenard Lanier, the very able commanding officer of the White House police force, retired, and in the absence of Director Rowley, I officiated at his retirement ceremony.

The protective responsibilities of the Secret Service were further expanded in the early years of the Nixon administration. The White House police force was greatly increased in size, was renamed the Executive Protective Service, and in addition to the job of protecting the White House, took on the task of protecting all foreign missions in Washington. The Secret Service was also charged with the protection of visiting foreign heads of state, a job that had previously been handled by the State Department.

My last overseas trip with the president, in the fall of 1970, was something of a study in contrasts. In late September, the president left Washington to visit Italy, Yugoslavia, Spain, England, and Ireland, with a few side trips along the way. I went along as the headquarters representative. *Air Force One* left Andrews on Sunday morning, September 27, for our first stop, Rome. Nixon held meetings with President Saragat and Premier Colombo on the day after our arrival and had a late-afternoon audience with Pope Paul VI. The demonstrations we had expected in Rome were comparatively mild. As I recall, the only things thrown at the president's car were leaflets protesting Vietnam.

There was quite a bit of saber rattling going on in the Middle East at that time, and the president planned to visit the Southern European Headquarters of NATO after observing maneuvers of the Sixth Fleet in the Mediterranean off the coast of Italy. Impressive demonstrations of United States naval power were intended to underline our presence there, and the president choppered out to the carrier USS *Saratoga* to spend the night and watch the show on Tuesday morning. But as he retired to his quarters, a message was received aboard ship: Gamal Abdel Nasser, President of Egypt, had died suddenly.

You do not rattle your saber when a country is in mourning over the loss of its leader, and so the scheduled activities on Tuesday were toned down. After a chopper visit to the flagship USS *Springfield*, the president continued on to Naples for the NATO conferences, and then *Air Force One* roared over the Iron Curtain to Belgrade, Yugoslavia.

During the motorcade into Belgrade from the airport, Nixon and Marshal Tito rode in our new armored Lincoln although there were no militant demonstrations expected. One of society's ironies seems to be that the less freedom of action the people have, the more their leaders have. There may have been some anti-American sentiment in Yugoslavia, but it did not manifest itself during our stay there. Crowds in the city were huge, but there were no placards protesting anything, nothing thrown, and no demonstrators.

The same held true when we touched down at our next stop on Friday. If anything, the crowds lining the motorcade route from the airport into Madrid, Spain, were even larger than those in Belgrade, but the presence of General Francisco Franco, standing and waving in the back seat of an open car with President Nixon, was crowd control insurance at its best.

Places like Belgrade and Madrid are, as the old cliché goes, great places to visit—especially when you are on protective duty with the president—but you might find yourself a little restricted as a resident.

Ireland was another matter. After a stopover in London on Saturday and a short visit between Nixon and Prime Minister Edward Heath, *Air Force One* touched down amid intermittent rain at Ireland's Shannon Airport. Our motorcade set out for Limerick and the small town of Hospital beyond where the president was to spend the weekend at an estate, Kilfrush House, before going on to Dublin for official meetings on Monday. Along the way, the Irish crowds were generally friendly. Nixon even stopped the motorcade spontaneously at one point to get out and offer his congratulations to a bride and groom.

But there were other incidents. As we crossed a bridge over the River Shannon, a young man ran toward the car, yelling, "*Nixon, murderer!*" He was intercepted and hauled away by the local police. In Limerick, as the mayor was presenting the president with a ceremonial gift, a city councilman dashed forward with a placard reading "Stop the War in Vietnam." A few miscellaneous objects were lobbed at the motorcade as it moved on toward its destination, but the president insisted on keeping the sliding top of the armored car open and standing in the rain to acknowledge the reception of the people along the way.

Monday morning, the president choppered to the little town of Timahoe, where he had some ancestral ties, and from there, we took a circuitous route through numerous small communities dotting the Irish countryside and into Dublin.

We had no intelligence of hard-core demonstrators although we were not surprised to run into them. Our first significant stop was at the presidential residence, and from there through the heart of the city to Dublin Castle for the official luncheon. It was along this stretch that we encountered a well-planned egg-throwing demonstration. I rode in the follow-up car, and while Special Agent Andy Hutch drove and Bob Taylor handled the radio traffic, I took over the public-address microphone. I kept my eyes peeled for the lob shots that came with planned regularity as first one demonstrator and then another would step off the curb and toss an egg at the car as it passed, with the president steadfastly standing in the open top and waving.

I was tempted to yell, "One grade-A extra large, four o'clock high!" but I settled for "Watch it, Mr. President, on your right!" or "Duck, Mr. President!"

We managed to deliver the president to Dublin Castle without egg on his face, but the same could not be said for his limousine, which looked like an ill-conceived omelet. If Nixon's visit to Ireland did nothing else, it gave a boost to the egg business.

Of course, the Secret Service does not put any life-or-death importance on the throwing of eggs at the president, and the fact that none of the eggs fell into the open hatch of the armored car could be principally attributed to the poor aim of the throwers. The armored car with the sliding top offers a perfect example of the compromise the protective mission must make with the political mission.

My final trip out of the capital with President Nixon took us to Georgia in January 1971. The occasion was the death of Senator Richard B. Russell, and being a Georgian, I went along with President Nixon and his regular Secret Service detail to Atlanta, where Russell's body lay in state in the capitol.

In a sense, this was my coming full circle with the protective forces of the Secret Service. It had been almost twenty years ago that a green probationary agent stood nervously awaiting the arrival of Vice President Alben Barkley at Atlanta Airport. Now, I was back at the same airport aboard *Air Force One* accompanying the fifth president I had served.

Like many career men in the Secret Service, I had come almost unscathed through all the physical hazards built into the job of protecting the president. But when your work requires you to exist within the most political milieu in the nation—the White House—the fact that you are a nonpolitical professional does not guarantee you immunity to the political intrigue that is constantly going on there. There is the more subtle hazard of identification.

Although I had served five presidents, I was identified with one, and my career was not the first in Washington to reach a stopping point because of identification with a previous administration. If a change of identity could have been arranged by my denouncing anyone I had served, I would not buy that.

I had rounded out twenty years in the Secret Service and was now eligible for retirement. If I tried for twenty-one, I would only be overstaying my welcome.

But if I had it all to do over again, not having a crystal ball, I would do it all the same way.

Epilogue

Rufus W. Youngblood retired from the United States Secret Service in March of 1971. He published this memoir in 1973, almost a year after both former presidents Truman and Johnson had died--within a month of each other and within days of President Nixon's second inauguration. In 1975, he returned to his home state of Georgia with his family where he briefly resumed security work as head of Atlanta's security detail in Jimmy

Lady Bird Johnson hosted a reunion for the former Johnson administration and staff, "The Great Society Roundup," in 1990 at the LBJ Ranch. Rufus Youngblood stands to her left among former agents and friends. *RWY Collection*

Carter's 1976 presidential campaign. Afterward, he worked in real estate in Savannah, became a master gardener, and enjoyed spending time with his family, which grew to include eight grandchildren. He died in 1996 at the age of seventy-two from complications of lung cancer.

About the Presidents

Frank Gatteri/U.S. Army/
Truman Library

U.S. Navy/Eisenhower
Library

Abbie Rowe/NPS/JFK
Library

Yoichi Okamoto/WHPO/
LBJ Library

WHPO/Nixon Library

Harry S. Truman
33rd President (Democrat)
April 12, 1945–January 20, 1953
Vice President Alben W. Barkley
Born May 8, 1884, in Lamar, Missouri
First Lady Elizabeth Virginia "Bess" Wallace
Died December 26, 1972, near Independence, Missouri

Dwight David Eisenhower
34th President (Republican)
January 20, 1953–January 20, 1961
Vice President Richard M. Nixon
Born October 14, 1890, in Denison, Texas
First Lady Mamie Geneva Doud
Died March 28, 1969, in Washington, D.C.

John Fitzgerald Kennedy
35th President (Democrat)
January 20, 1961–November 22, 1963
Vice President Lyndon B. Johnson
Born May 29, 1917, in Brookline, Massachusetts
First Lady Jacqueline Lee Bouvier
Died November 22, 1963, in Dallas, Texas

Lyndon Baines Johnson
36th President (Democrat)
November 22, 1963–January 20, 1969
Vice President Hubert H. Humphrey (1965–1969)
Born August 27, 1908, near Johnson City, Texas
First Lady Claudia Alta "Lady Bird" Taylor
Died January 22, 1973, in Stonewall, Texas

Richard Milhous Nixon
37th President (Republican)
January 20, 1969–August 9, 1974
Vice President Spiro T. Agnew (January 1969–
October 1973);
Gerald R. Ford Jr. (December 1973–August 9, 1974)
Born January 9, 1913, in Yorba Linda, California
First Lady Thelma Catherine "Pat" Ryan
Died April 22, 1994, in New York City, New York

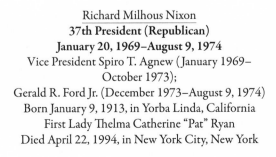

Acknowledgments

I would like to express my gratitude to Richard Hardwick for the many months spent assisting me in the writing of this book.

—Rufus W. Youngblood
(Original acknowledgement from first edition in 1973)

We have many people to thank for helping us republish this book. Numerous historians and archivists have aided with the research involved. We would especially like to thank the U.S. Secret Service and Archivists Mike Sampson and Jason Kendrick for their support, as well as Sarah Cunningham and Brian McNerny of the LBJ Library, Kathy Struss and Tim Rives of the Eisenhower Library, David Clark and Sam Rushay of the Truman Library, Maryrose Grossman and Laurie Austin of the JFK Library, Ryan Pettigrew of the Nixon Library, and Mark Davies and Stephen Fagin of the Sixth Floor Museum at Dealy Plaza. We also thank Kizmet Adams, Robert Baugniet, BookLogix consultants, Matthew Flanders, Megan Kennan, Diane Lasek, Sarah Medina, Trish Vaughn, Robert Smith of API Print Productions, and Robin Surface of Fideli Publishing for helping us "make it happen." We also appreciate Marlon Maloney for emphasizing that there is a younger generation who will appreciate this story.

We are ever grateful for the support of the Johnson family and the Association of Former Agents of the U.S. Secret Service. I am also grateful to the retired Secret Service agents Don Bendickson, Herbert Dixon, Clint Hill, Mike Howard, the late Lem Johns, the late Jerry Kivett, Jerry McKinney, and Paul Rundle; and Christi Bendickson, Sid Davis, Tom Johnson, Betty Jones, Nancy Rocheleau, and Mary Taylor, who shared their memories with me.

Lastly, in keeping with our father's convictions, we extend our appreciation to the men and women of our country who have devoted their lives to the protection of others.

—Rebecca Youngblood Vaughn,
on behalf of the Rufus and Peggy Youngblood family

Above: Rufus Wayne Youngblood (RWY) was born in Macon, Georgia, in 1924, then moved to Atlanta, Georgia, where he attended school. *RWY Collection*

Left: Days after the Pearl Harbor attack in December 1941, he enlisted in the U.S. Army Air Force when he was seventeen years old. He became a waist gunner on the B-17, *Jack the Ripper,* in the Eighth Air Force. *Bureau of Public Relations/U.S. War Dept.*

RWY's crew was chosen as the first experienced combat crew of his group to return to the U.S. to consult with the War Department, prepare a training manual, and participate in a public relations tour. **Standing:** S/Sgt. Andrew Markle, T/Sgt. Karl L. Masters, S/Sgt. Rufus W. Youngblood, T/Sgt. Peter F. Deboy, S/Sgt. James B. O'Donnell, Sgt. Glen C. Wilson. **First row:** 1st Lt. Mark H. Gilman, Capt. William J. Crumm, 1st Lt. William C. Leasure, 1st Lt. Robert L. Kleyla. March 1943. *Bureau of Public Relations/U.S. War Dept.*

In July 1943, RWY married his high school sweetheart, Peggy Elizabeth Denham, from Atlanta, Georgia, then completed U.S. Army Air Force Cadet Training as a 2nd Lt. Navigator. He was dual training as an engineer-navigator in B-29s when the war ended. The couple returned to Atlanta where he attended college on the GI Bill. *RWY Collection*

RWY graduated from Georgia Tech with an industrial engineering degree and briefly worked as a consulting engineer. He joined the U.S. Secret Service (USSS) in March 1951. (Four months earlier, an attempt had been made to assassinate President Harry S. Truman.) Initially, he worked in the Atlanta Field Office, then transferred to Washington, D.C., in 1952. *RWY Collection.*

"Best of Luck to Rufus Youngblood from Harry S. Truman 9-9-64." *Leo Stern/RWY Collection*

A hero's funeral procession: Secret Service White House Police Officer Leslie Coffelt was killed while protecting President Truman during an assassination attempt on November 1, 1950. *Washington, D.C., Abbie Rowe/National Park Service (NPS)/Harry S. Truman Library & Museum (Truman Library)*

President Truman's famous morning strolls: RWY was occasionally assigned to protective detail for President Truman during his walks around the city. USSS Chief Baughman voiced concern for the president's safety during these predictable outings, but the president remained an avid walker. *William E. Carnahan/Silver Spring, MD/Truman Library*

President Truman and his daughter, Margaret (on his left), attend the fifty-third annual Army-Navy football game, November 29, 1952. RWY is among the agents guarding the president during this event. *Abbie Rowe/NPS/Truman Library*

President Truman, a "whistle-stop man," used the railway as his preferred mode of travel. This photo shows Mrs. Truman, daughter, Margaret, and President Truman waving farewell to a crowd at Union Station, Washington, D.C. Later, after Dwight D. Eisenhower was sworn in as the new president on January 20, 1953, the Trumans returned to Independence, Missouri, by train without Secret Service protection. *Abbie Rowe/NPS/Truman Library*

DWIGHT D. EISENHOWER
34th President
1953–1961

U.S. Naval Photographic Agency (USN)/Dwight D. Eisenhower Presidential Library, Museum, and Boyhood Home (Eisenhower Library)

First Inauguration of Dwight D. Eisenhower: Chief Justice Fred Vinson administers the presidential Oath of Office to Dwight D. Eisenhower at the U.S. Capitol. Vice President Richard M. Nixon and former President Harry S. Truman look on. January 20, 1953. *NPS/Eisenhower Library*

Secret Service agents walk beside President and Mrs. Eisenhower's open convertible car during the Inaugural Parade. *Reni News/USSS Archives*

President Eisenhower arrives at Lowry Air Force Base, Colorado, the "Summer White House." The Eisenhowers frequented Denver, Colorado, visiting Mamie Eisenhower's mother. RWY (black suit) stands guard in the background. August 23, 1954. *NPS/Eisenhower Library*

President Eisenhower, an avid outdoorsman, enjoyed fishing in the Colorado mountains. *USN/Eisenhower Library*

Shown here, President Eisenhower grills out with former President Herbert Hoover in the mountains of Fraser, Colorado. RWY was among the agents on this trip. August 1954. *RWY Collection*

A golfing enthusiast, President Eisenhower is shown here at Cherry Hills Golf Course in Englewood, Colorado. RWY (in background right and pictured below) poses as his caddy. August 1953. *Colorado State Patrol/Eisenhower Library*

"Caddy" RWY. While the president golfed, his agents dressed in golfer's attire and carried golf bags with dummy club heads and a high-powered rifle or submachine gun. *Carl Iwasaki/The LIFE Images Collection/Getty images*

Maintaining the peace: Within the first year of his term, President Eisenhower negotiated the end of the Korean War. Ike, the former Supreme Commander of WWII strived to maintain peace during the Cold War. Seen here, President and First Lady Mamie Eisenhower bid farewell to one of their guests as RWY stands guard to their right. White House, Washington, D.C., May 27,1954. *NPS/RWY Collection*

Ten years after the end of WWII, the leaders of "The Big Four" powers met in Switzerland for the Geneva Summit. RWY was among the agents protecting the president on this trip. Shown here are Soviet Union Premier Nikolai A. Bulganin, U.S. President Eisenhower, French Premier Edgar Faure, and British Prime Minister Anthony Eden. Geneva, Switzerland, July 1955. *Ted Rohde/Stars and Stripes © 1955*

After experiencing the ease of travel on the German autobahns during World War II, Eisenhower championed the Interstate Highway System. He signed the Federal Aid Highway Act in 1956 to improve U.S. domestic travel, stimulate the economy, and fortify national defense via facilitation of evacuation and military maneuvers. *NPS / Eisenhower Library*

Inauguration Day fell on a Sunday in 1957. Thus, a private swearing-in ceremony was held at the White House that day. Shown here left to right are Barbara and John S.D. Eisenhower, First Lady and President Eisenhower, Vice President and Mrs. Nixon, Tricia and Julie Nixon, and Reverend Edward Elson after a pre-inaugural church service. January 20, 1957. *NPS/Eisenhower Library*

On the following day, the public ceremony was held at the Capitol followed by the Inaugural Parade. Shown here, the presidential party watches the parade from the viewing stand. RWY (with hat in hand) stands to the right of the stand. January 21, 1957. *NPS/Eisenhower Library*

Agents pose on the *USS Canberra* en route to the Bermuda Conference where President Eisenhower met with British Prime Minister Harold Macmillan, March 1957. **Left to right:** Front row — Agents George Weisheit, Dick Roth, RWY, Stu Knight, John Campion, Jim Rowley, Bill Shields, Floyd Boring, Arvid Dahlquist. Back row —Roy Kellerman, Harvey Henderson, Forrest Guthrie, Thomas Wooge, Deeter Flohr, Pat Boggs, Charlie Marris, James Jeffries, Jim McCown, and Herb Dixon. *USN/Eisenhower Library*

RWY requested and was transferred back to the Atlanta Field Office in 1958. However, he frequently worked on the presidential detail when the president traveled. Shown here, RWY is posted outside of "Mamie's Cabin" at the Augusta National Golf Course. Augusta, Georgia. *RWY Collection*

"For Rufus Youngblood. With regards and best wishes, John Kennedy." *Photo by Bachrach/RWY Collection*

Inauguration of John F. Kennedy: The newly sworn-in President John F. Kennedy delivers his Inaugural Address. Former President Eisenhower, Vice President Lyndon B. Johnson (LBJ), and former Vice President Richard M. Nixon look on. Washington, D.C., January 20, 1961. *Abbie Rowe/NPS/John F. Kennedy Presidential Library and Museum (JFK Library)*

Initially, vice presidential protection was assigned "at request" only. When President Kennedy assigned Vice President Johnson several international trips, Agents Stuart Knight and RWY became the intermittent "two-man detail." **Above:** RWY assesses the crowd as the vice president leaves Saigon, South Vietnam, where he met with President Ngo Dinh Diem. May 13, 1961. *Thomas O'Halloran/US News & World Report/ Library of Congress*

"You are leaving the American Sector" President Kennedy sent Vice President Johnson to Germany as U.S. troops were rolling into the city in response to the construction of the Berlin Wall. **Left to right:** RWY, General Lucius Clay, LBJ, Mayor Willie Brandt, and Ambassador Walter Dowling tour West Berlin. Afterward, Agents Knight and Youngblood toured the Communist-occupied sector with a small force of Army officials in the vice president's stead. August 20, 1961. *Cecil Stoughton/White House Photographic Office (WHPO)/LBJ Presidential Library (LBJ Library)*

Right: President and Mrs. Kennedy with their children, John Jr. and Caroline. Palm Beach, Florida, April 14, 1963. *Cecil Stoughton//White House Photographers (WHP)/JFK Library*

Left: President Kennedy championed NASA and the space program. Shown here, he views models of the Titan Rocket at Cape Canaveral Air Force Station, Florida. RWY stands guard behind him. September 11, 1962. *Robert Knudsen/WHP/JFK Library*

Right: The president views a mock-up Apollo spacecraft at the Manned Spacecraft Center in Houston, Texas. September 12, 1962. *Cecil Stoughton/WHP/ JFK Library*

On Friday morning, November 22, 1963, the president and vice president spoke at a rally in their hotel parking lot. Rain did not deter a large, enthusiastic crowd from attending. Fort Worth, Texas. *Cecil Stoughton/WHP/JFK Library*

They flew to Dallas, Texas, from Ft. Worth despite the short distance. **Above:** President and Mrs. Kennedy descend the stairs from *Air Force One*. **Left:** The Johnsons, whose plane arrived shortly before the Kennedy's, greet the first couple upon their arrival. RWY stands behind Mrs. Johnson. Love Field, Dallas, Texas, November 22, 1963. *Cecil Stoughton/WHP/JFK Library*

This photo, taken by Cecil Stoughton who was riding seven cars behind the presidential limousine, shows the motorcade traveling on Main Street. Secret Service agents riding in the presidential follow-up car are barely discernible towards the front. The vice presidential follow-up car (with the left rear door ajar) obscures visualization of the lead cars. *Cecil Stoughton/WHP/JFK Library*

The seven-passenger Lincoln Continental presidential limousine carrying President and Mrs. Kennedy and Governor and Mrs. Connally was followed by the Secret Service follow-up car, code named "Half-back." *Jim Walker Collection/The Sixth Floor Museum at Dealey Plaza*

The vice presidential Lincoln convertible, driven by Texas patrolman Hurchel Jacks, followed two cars behind the presidential limousine. Senator Ralph Yarborough sat on the left side of the rear seat, Mrs. Johnson in the middle, and Vice President Johnson on the right directly behind RWY (who was sitting in the front passenger seat). *Jim Walker Collection/The Sixth Floor Museum at Dealey Plaza*

The motorcade moments after the first shot is fired: Agents in Halfback turn towards the sound coming from the Texas School Book Depository. Agent Clint Hill (on the front left running board) sees the president slumping in his seat. Hill then immediately leaps onto the president's car in an attempt to protect the Kennedys. In the third car, Agent Youngblood also responds immediately by jumping from his position in the front seat to the back to shield Vice President Johnson with his body from further shots. Dallas, Texas. November 22, 1963. *Corbis Historical/Getty Images*

RWY, left, Vice President Johnson, center, and Rep. Homer Thornberry, right, leave Parkland Memorial Hospital after President Kennedy's death is pronounced. *Bettman/Getty Images*

Swearing in of Lyndon B. Johnson: Judge Sarah Hughes administers the presidential Oath of Office to Lyndon Johnson aboard Air Force One. Lady Bird and Mrs. Kennedy stand by his side. RWY, unseen in this iconic photo, was standing beside the photographer. Dallas, Texas, November 22, 1963. *Cecil Stoughton/WHPO/LBJ Library*

LYNDON B. JOHNSON
36th President
1963–1969

Upon arrival at Andrews Air Force Base in Maryland, President Johnson solemnly addresses the nation. RWY stands to his left as he speaks. November 22, 1963. *Cecil Stoughton/WHP/JFK Library*

President and Mrs. Johnson speak with RWY on the South Lawn of the White House after arrival from Andrews Air Force Base. Washington, D.C., November 22, 1963. *Robert Knudsen/WHP/JFK Library*

President Kennedy's State Funeral at the United States Capitol
Sunday, November 24,1963

The flag-draped casket bearing the body of President Kennedy was carried by a horsedrawn caisson from the White House to the Capitol. **Above:** Jacqueline Kennedy with Caroline and John Jr, and Attorney General Robert F. Kennedy wait at the foot of the Capitol steps. Behind them are pictured President and Mrs. Johnson, General Maxwell D. Taylor, RWY, Stephen Smith, Jean Kennedy Smith, Patricia Kennedy Lawford, and Agent Clint Hill. Washington, D.C. *AP Photo*

Military pallbearers carry the casket up the Capitol steps. It was taken to the Rotunda for the body to lie in state. Throughout the day and night, hundreds of thousands of people filed past the coffin to pay their respects. *Abbie Rowe/WHP/JFK Library*

**Funeral Procession to Cathedral of St. Matthew the Apostle
and Burial at Arlington National Cemetery,
Monday, November 25, 1963**

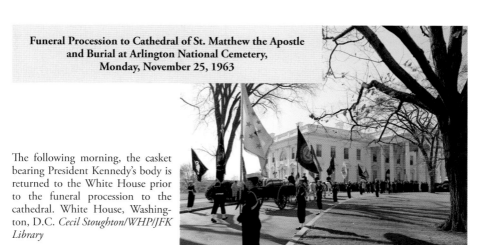

The following morning, the casket bearing President Kennedy's body is returned to the White House prior to the funeral procession to the cathedral. White House, Washington, D.C. *Cecil Stoughton/WHP/JFK Library*

Led by Mrs. Kennedy, the Kennedy family, Johnson family, and leaders of nations worldwide walk from the White House to the cathedral. Thousands of people line the streets to witness this somber event. **Left to right:** Attorney General Robert F. Kennedy, Jacqueline Kennedy, Senator Edward M. Kennedy, Jamie Auchincloss, Peace Corps Director R. Sargent Shriver, Steve Smith, President Lyndon B. Johnson, General Maxwell D. Taylor, First Lady Lady Bird Johnson, Lucy Baines Johnson, and Lynda Bird Johnson; flanked by Agents Clint Hill, Bill Livingood, Rufus Youngblood, Jack Ready, Floyd Boring, Jerry Behn, and Jerry Kivett. *AP Photo*

Former Presidents Truman and Eisenhower constrain their emotions outside St. Matthew's Cathedral. *Cecil Stoughton/WHP/JFK Library*

Hundreds of mourners attend the graveside service at Arlington National Cemetery. Agents Paul Rundle (on LBJ's right) and RWY (LBJ's left) are pictured among the agents guarding President Johnson. Arlington, Virginia. *Abbie Rowe/WHP/JFK Library*

In the White House Rose Garden, U.S. Treasury Secretary Douglas Dillon (to LBJ's left) presented RWY with the U.S. Treasury Department's Exceptional Service Award for shielding then-Vice President Johnson during the Kennedy assassination. The president then addresses the crowd as RWY and his family watch on. December 4, 1963. *WHPO/LBJ Library*

RWY with wife Peggy and children after the award ceremony. **Left to right:** Rebecca, Joy, Candy, and Mark. *WHPO/LBJ Library*

The Johnson family portrait. **Left to right:** Lynda Bird, Luci Baines, Lyndon Baines, and Lady Bird Johnson—all with initials, "LBJ". Washington, D.C., November 1963. *Yoichi Okamoto/WHPO/LBJ Library*

West German Chancellor Ludwig Erhard (with Lady Bird, LBJ, and RWY) waves to a welcoming crowd in Texas. The Johnsons hosted their first state dinner as a barbecue for the chancellor and his entourage in the Texas Hill Country, a region of rich German heritage. Fredericksburg, Texas, December 29, 1963. *WHPO/LBJ Library*

President Johnson seized any opportunity to drive when he was home in Texas. Here he drives General Maxwell Taylor and General Curtis LeMay (with RWY perched on the back) to the helicopter after their visit to the LBJ Ranch. Johnson City, Texas, December 29, 1963. *WHPO/LBJ Library*

President Johnson swiftly began launching programs to eliminate poverty and racial injustice to establish "the Great Society." This photo shows the president shaking a resident's hand in an undisclosed part of Appalachia during his war on poverty tour. May 7, 1964. *Cecil Stoughton/WHPO/LBJ Library*

RWY is acknowledged during President Johnson's address at a breakfast of the Georgia legislature in Atlanta, Georgia. The president remarked, "My life is in the hands of Georgia, and it is twenty-four hours a day under the direction of Rufus Youngblood." President Johnson had arranged for RWY's mother to be present at the affair. May 8, 1964. *WHPO/LBJ Library*

President Johnson signs the 1964 Civil Rights Act. Martin Luther King Jr. is among those standing behind him. July 2, 1964. *Cecil Stoughton/WHPO/LBJ Library*

Arthur Godfrey, Woody Taylor, and RWY are among the agents working to hold back an enthusiastic crowd from the President during a campaign visit in New England. September 28, 1964. *Cecil Stoughton/ WHPO/LBJ Library*

Perpetual Motion: The tireless president traveled from city to city during the 1964 campaign. Agents Ed Mougin, Lem Johns, RWY, Paul Burns, Bob Heyn, and Dick Johnsen encircle the president during a motorcade in Macon, Georgia, October 26, 1964. *Stanley Tretick/Look Magazine/Library of Congress*

President Johnson's motorcade in Pittsburgh, Pennsylvania, on the following day. Agents Lem Johns, RWY, John Chipps, and Dick Johnsen are identified. October 27, 1964. *WHPO/LBJ Library*

1965 Inauguration of Lyndon B. Johnson: Behind a barrier of newly installed bulletproof glass, Chief Justice Earl Warren re-administers the Oath of Office to President Johnson. Lady Bird and the newly sworn-in Vice President Hubert H. Humphrey look on. Behind them, RWY scans the crowd. Washington, D.C., January 20, 1965. *U.S. Army/USSS Archives*

Agents scramble to protect President Johnson during the 1965 Inaugural Parade when he spontaneously elects to walk a segment of the route. *U.S. Army/USSS Archives*

For the first time, the presidential party watches the Inaugural Parade from behind a bulletproof viewing stand. Shown here are Mrs. Humphrey, Vice President Humphrey, President, First Lady, Lynda and Luci Johnson. Agents Jerry Kivett and RWY are seen in the foreground. *WHPO/LBJ Library*

RWY and other agents dressed in tuxedos form a protective barrier for President and First Lady Johnson and Vice President and Mrs. Humphrey as they dance at an Inaugural Ball. *Cecil Stoughton/WHPO/LBJ Library*

RWY guards the president as he walks with officials and the press in Washington, D.C., May 26, 1965. *WHPO/LBJ Library*

Aboard the president's JetStar are Cdr. John V. Josephson, Jake Jacobson, Jack Valenti, Vicki McCammon, LBJ, RWY, Lem Johns. May 27, 1965. *WHPO/LBJ Library*

LBJ greets a crowd in Independence, Missouri, en route to the Truman Library. July 30, 1965. *Yoichi Okamoto/ WHPO/LBJ Library*

RWY watches as the Trumans greet the president and vice president outside of the Truman Library. Independence, Missouri. July 30, 1965. *WHPO/LBJ Library*

Former President Harry Truman becomes Medicare's first beneficiary as President Johnson signs the Medicare Bill at the Truman Library. Also pictured are Bess Truman and Vice President Humphrey with RWY standing guard in the background. July 30, 1965. *WHPO/LBJ Library*

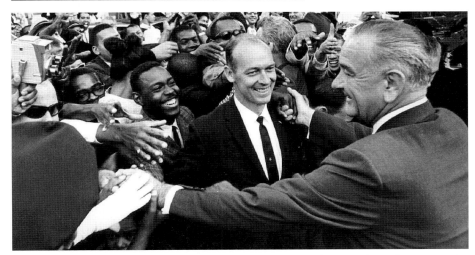

RWY stands between enthusiastic students at Howard University where President Johnson gives the Commencement Address "To Fulfill These Rights." Washington, D.C., June 4, 1965. *WHPO/LBJ Library*

RWY receives the "Johnson Treatment" as the president grabs his lapel. *WHPO/LBJ Library*

The presidential party arrives in New York where President Johnson signs the Immigration and Nationality Act at the foot of the Statue of Liberty. Liberty Island, New York City, New York, October 3, 1965. *WHPO/LBJ Library*

President Johnson meets with U Thant, Secretary-General of the United Nations, at the Waldorf-Astoria Hotel before a reception that evening. RWY, in a tuxedo, stands in the background. New York, N.Y. *WHPO/LBJ Library*

President Johnson escorts his daughter Luci Baines Johnson to her wedding. She married Patrick Nugent at the National Shrine of the Immaculate Conception. Washington, D.C., August 6, 1966. *Yoichi Okamoto/WHPO/LBJ Library*

In October 1966, President and Mrs. Johnson attended a seven-nation summit in the Philippines to discuss mounting concerns in Vietnam. While also visiting Australia, protestors to the Vietnam War threw paint bombs during an otherwise friendly motorcade through Melbourne. Shown here are Agents Lem Johns, RWY, Jerry Kivett, and Dick Johnsen splattered with paint as they walk beside the president's car. October 21, 1966. *Frank Wolfe/WHPO/LBJ Library*

In an unannounced side trip, President Johnson visits the troops at Cam Ranh Bay, South Vietnam. **Above:** Agents Lem Johns, RWY, and Bill Duncan are pictured near the president as he greets the crowd. **Right:** LBJ rides with Gen. Westmoreland and Agent Johns. RWY follows. October 26, 1966. *WHPO/ LBJ Library*

RWY, next to Prime Minister Thanom of Thailand, attempts to "blend in" while President Johnson addresses students at Chulalongkorn University. Bangkok, Thailand, Oct. 29, 1966 *(Yoichi Okamoto/WHPO/ LBJ Library)*

To express their appreciation to the agents who were constantly separated from their families, the Johnsons invited some of the agents and their wives to the LBJ ranch as guests. In this photo, the president addresses his guests. Identified at the table are Ann Kivett, RWY, Betty Godfrey, Woody Taylor, Beverly Olsson, Bob Taylor, Donna Duncan, Dick Johnsen, Clint Hill, and Peggy Youngblood. December 4, 1966. *Yoichi Okamoto/WHPO/LBJ Library*

Each couple posed for a photograph with the Johnsons. Here, Rufus and Peggy Youngblood, still in their ranch attire, pose with President and Mrs. Johnson. December 4, 1966. *Yoichi Okamoto/ WHPO/LBJ Library*

During the same weekend, the active President and Mrs. Johnson flew to Del Rio, Mexico, and met with President Díaz Ordaz. Shown here, USSS agents team with the Mexican security to hold back the crowds as their leaders ride in the motorcade in an open-top car. December 3, 1966. *Okamoto/WHPO/LBJ Library*

During a visit to Guam, President Johnson toured the Third Air Division (B-52 base) commanded by Maj. Gen. William J. Crumm. Also present: Sec. Dean Rusk, Sec. Robert McNamara, Amb. Ellsworth Bunker, Jake Jacobsen, and Gen. Westmoreland. March 21, 1967. *WHPO/LBJ Library*

Gen. Crumm and RWY briefly reminisce. Crumm was the esteemed B-17 pilot of their combat crew during WWII. Tragically, in July 1967, four months after the president's visit, Gen. Crumm was killed in a B-52 midair collision over the South China Sea. He was the first American general to be killed during the Vietnam War. *WHPO/RWY Collection*

The Glassboro Summit and Hope: President Johnson met with Soviet Premier Aleksei Kosygin **(Left)** at Glassboro State College in New Jersey. Luci had just given birth to LBJ's grandchild, Patrick Lyndon Nugent, in Austin, Texas **(Right).** The two world leaders, both grandfathers, acknowledged the importance of avoiding nuclear disaster for future generations. June 23, 1967. *WHPO/LBJ Library*

RWY was promoted to the position of Deputy Director in December 1967. Nancy Rocheleau, RWY's secretary, poses in front of their office in the USSS Headquarters Building. *USSS Archives/RWY Collection*

Lynda Bird Johnson married Capt. Charles Robb (USMC) at the White House. RWY and Peggy attended this spectacular wedding. December 9, 1967. *Mike Geissinger/WHPO/RWY Collection*

Agents RWY and Clint Hill accompany President Johnson to Australia to attend the memorial service for Prime Minister Harold Holt, who disappeared while swimming in Australian coastal waters. December 19, 1967. *Yoichi Okamoto/WHPO/LBJ Library*

"To Rufus Youngblood—a courageous, able, and dedicated officer to whom we are all indebted. With friendship and admiration—Hubert H. Humphrey."

RWY traveled with the vice presidential detail on many trips and strongly admired the hardworking Vice President Humphrey. *USSS Archives/RWY Collection*

Vice President Humphrey, General Westmoreland, and group are briefed aboard the USS *Benewah* before a visit to South Vietnam in October 1967. Agents Win Lawson (far right, standing) and RWY (sitting middle row) are pictured here. *Marty Nordstrom/Win Lawson/USSS Archives*

Dark Days

Vietnam War casualties and protests escalated. President Johnson announced he would not seek another term as president. In April 1968, civil rights leader Martin Luther King Jr. was assassinated. Riots ensued with destruction and burning of major cities across the nation. In June 1968, Robert F. Kennedy was assassinated while campaigning for the presidency.

Vice President Humphrey offers his condolences to Alberta Williams King, mother of Martin Luther King Jr. RWY accompanied the vice president to Dr. King's funeral in Atlanta, Georgia. Threats of violence precluded the president's attendance, but the thousands of mourners who came to honor the slain civil rights leader did so in the spirit of nonviolence he had preached. April 9, 1968. *HHH Collection/Minnesota Historical Society*

Mourners enter St. Patrick's Cathedral for Robert F. Kennedy's funeral. Agents John Paul Jones (far left with sunglasses), Clint Hill, and RWY are identified behind President and Mrs. Johnson. New York, New York, June 8, 1968. *Cecil Stoughton/WHP/JFK Library*

In the aftermath of Robert F. Kennedy's death, President Johnson promptly signed the Protective Candidate Law, providing Secret Service protection for "major presidential and vice presidential candidates." **Left to right:** Agents Bob Taylor, Art Godfrey, Lem Johns, Jim Rowley, Jack Parker, Chief of White House Police Glenard Lanier, Agents John Paul Jones, RWY, Clint Hill, and Emory Roberts stand behind him. Washington, D.C., July 6, 1968. *Mike Geissinger/WHPO/LBJ Library*

Lady Bird Johnson, LBJ's steadfast, political partner, traveled frequently with the president. Her early protective detail dubbed themselves "the KTBC group" (Kivett, Taylor, (Jerry) Bechtel, and Lady Bird's given name—Claudia) which were the call letters of the Johnson television station in Austin. Shown here, the First Lady poses with Agents Mike Varenholtd, Woody Taylor, Jerry McKinney, and Jerry Kivett in California, November 1968. *WHPO/LBJ Library.*

The President was greeted by enthusiastic crowds during his Central America tour, to include San Salvador, July 7, 1968. *WHPO/LBJ Library*

RWY and Peggy attend a diplomatic reception in the White House for Prime Minister and Mrs. Amir Abbas Hoveyda of Iran. White House, December 5, 1968. *Yoichi Okamoto/ WHPO/RWY Collection*

The president expressed his appreciation to the Secret Service agents during a presentation to Director Rowley. He later gave RWY this photograph, framed and signed, "To Rufus, My protector and always my friend, Lyndon B. Johnson" *Yoichi Okamoto/WHPO/RWY Collection*

To Rufus
My protector and always my friend,

RICHARD M. NIXON
37th President
1969–1974

WHPO/Richard Nixon Presidential Library and Museum (Nixon Library)

From an agent's perspective: RWY scans the movements within the large crowd during the Inaugural Ceremony. *Robert Knudsen/WHPO/Nixon Library*

First Inauguration of Richard M. Nixon: Chief Justice Earl Warren administers the presidential Oath of Office to Richard M. Nixon at the U.S. Capitol. Newly sworn-in Vice President Spiro Agnew, former President Johnson, and former Vice President Humphrey look on. (RWY is pictured two rows behind LBJ.) Washington, D.C., January 20, 1969. *WHPO/Nixon Library*

President and Mrs. Nixon, Mamie Eisenhower, Tricia Nixon, Julie Nixon Eisenhower and husband, David Eisenhower, Agent Vernon Copeland, and Barbara and John Eisenhower watch the 1969 Inauguration Day parade from behind a bulletproof encasing. *Jack Kightlinger/WHPO/Nixon Library*

RWY rode in the car with President Johnson and President-elect Nixon on the way to the Capitol, then rode aboard one of the follow-up limousines during the Inaugural Parade after President Nixon was sworn in. Also pictured here are Agents Art Godfrey (in car), Chuck Zboril, Chuck Rochner, Bob Newbrand, Lem Johns, and Dick Keiser *USSS Archives*

Nixon family portrait: David and Julie Eisenhower, President and Mrs. Nixon, and Tricia Nixon. With greater administrative duties, RWY had less personal contact with the first family than with their predecessors. However, RWY fondly cited an assignment when he had driven then-Vice President and Mrs. Nixon in Atlanta during the 1960 presidential campaign. Afterward, Pat Nixon had graciously given him the bouquet of roses she had carried during the motorcade encouraging him to "take these home to your wife." June 15, 1969, *Karl Schumacher/WHPO/Nixon Library*

As Deputy Director, RWY continued to interact with the Secret Service protective details and their protectees. Shown here, RWY visits with LBJ in his office in Austin, Texas, on February 3, 1969. *Frank Wolfe/WHPO/RWY Collection*

Eisenhower's State Funeral: The honor guard escorts the flag-draped casket of Former President Dwight D. Eisenhower during the state funeral procession from the Capitol to the Washington Cathedral. Thousands of people, including dignitaries from across the globe, paid homage to the former president. Washington, D.C., March 30, 1969. *Durrence/WHPO/Nixon Library*

Above: In June 1969, President Nixon traveled to several western U.S. states and Midway Island, where he conferred with South Vietnam's President Nguyen Van Thieu. RWY was among the Secret Service agents protecting the president on this trip. Midway Island, June 8, 1969. *WHPO/Nixon Library*

Right: RWY communicates with a young "gooney bird" during the president's visit. The Midway Atoll National Wildlife Refuge is home for the albatross and many other birds and marine life of the Hawaiian archipelago. *WHPO/RWY Collection*

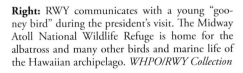

Nixon visited Italy, Yugoslavia, Spain, England, and Ireland in the fall of 1970. **Left:** President Richard Nixon and Spain's dictator, Generalissimo Francisco Franco, ride to Madrid. More than a million people lined the streets to view the motorcade. *Byron Schumaker/WHPO/Nixon Library* **Right:** President Nixon greets the crowd in Naples, Italy, before being choppered to the USS *Saratoga* in the Mediterranean. *Robert Knudsen/WHPO/Nixon Library*

Agents Art Godfrey, Robert Taylor, and RWY protectively encircle the president in Italy. These three agents had worked together since the early 1950's. September 30, 1970. *Robert Knudsen/WHPO/Nixon Library*

RWY provided consul for Actor David Janssen (above and right, standing with RWY) and producer Len Kaufman when they visited the Secret Service Headquarters in preparation for the television show *O'Hara, U.S. Treasury.* Washington, D.C., October 13, 1970. *WHPO/RWY Collection*

The Secret Service presents President Nixon with a gold Secret Service badge and medallion. Left to right: SAIC Robert Taylor, Assistant Secretary of the Treasury Eugene Rossides, President Nixon, Secret Service Director James J. Rowley, Deputy Director Youngblood, Assistant SAIC Robert J. Newbrand, and Assistant Director for Protective Forces Lilburn E. Boggs. Washington, D.C., October 6, 1969. *WHPO/ RWY Collection*

President Nixon traveled to Atlanta, Georgia, when Georgia Senator Richard B. Russell died. RWY accompanied the detail on this trip. Agents Robert Taylor, Dennis Shaw, and Gary Jenkins are identified with President Nixon in front of the Georgia capitol building where Senator Russell's body was lying in state. January 1971. *Jack Kightlinger/WHPO/Nixon Library*

Full Circle: This trip to Atlanta—the hometown and city where he had first been employed as an agent—marked RWY's last trip protecting the president. Two months later, in March 1971, RWY retired after working twenty years in the Secret Service.

Bibliography

Audio-visual Sources and Information

Dwight D. Eisenhower Presidential Library, Museum and Boyhood Home, Abilene, Kansas.

Gale Family Library, Minnesota Historical Society, St. Paul, Minnesota.

Harry S. Truman Presidential Library & Museum, Independence, Missouri.

John F. Kennedy Presidential Library and Museum, Boston, Massachusetts.

Library of Congress, Prints and Photographs Division, Washington, D.C.

LBJ Presidential Library, Austin, Texas.

Richard Nixon Presidential Library and Museum, Yorba Linda, California.

The Sixth Floor Museum at Dealy Plaza, Dallas, Texas.

United States Secret Service Archives, Washington, D.C.

Original sources: Public Documents

Public Papers of the Presidents of the United States: Lyndon B. Johnson, 1963-64. Washington, D.C.: U.S. Government Printing Office, 1965.

Public Papers of the Presidents of the United States: Lyndon B. Johnson, 1967. Washington, D.C.: U.S. Government Printing Office, 1968.

Report of the President's Commission on the Assassination of President John F. Kennedy. Washington, D.C.: U.S. Government Printing Office, 1964.

Original sources: Books

Associated Press. *The Torch is Passed.* Racine, WI: Western Printing & Lithograph, 1963.

Baughman, U. E., and Leonard Wallace Robinson, *Secret Service Chief.* New York: Harper and Row, 1962.

Bowen, Walter S., and Harry Edward Neal. *The United States Secret Service.* Philadelphia: Chilton Company-Book Division Publishers, 1960.

Donovan, Robert J. *The Assassins.* New York: Harper, 1955.

Dorman, Michael. *The Secret Service Story.* New York: Delacorte Press, 1967.

Reilly, Michael F., *Reilly of the White House.* New York: Simon and Schuster, 1947.

Smith, Merriman. *A President's Odyssey.* New York: Harper and Row, 1961.

Eisenhower, Dwight D.,*Waging Peace 1956–1961.* New York: Doubleday, 1965.

Johnson, Claudia T., *Lady Bird Johnson: A White House Diary.* New York: Holt, Rinehart & Winston, 1970.

Johnson, Lyndon Baines *The Vantage Point.* New York: Holt, Rinehart & Winston, 1971.

United Press International and American Heritage Magazine. *Four Days: The Historical Record of the Death of President Kennedy.* New York: American Heritage, 1964.

Index

To learn more about Rufus Youngblood, visit

www.RufusYoungblood.com

For media kit information,
book discussion questions, and to
request speaking engagements with
Rebecca Youngblood Vaughn,
go to www.rufusyoungblood.com